THE VANISHING TRADITION

THE VANISHING TRADITION

Perspectives on American Conservatism

Edited by Paul Gottfried

NORTHERN ILLINOIS UNIVERSITY PRESS

AN IMPRINT OF CORNELL UNIVERSITY PRESS   ITHACA AND LONDON

First published 2020 by Cornell University Press

Library of Congress Cataloging-in-Publication Data

Names: Gottfried, Paul, 1941– editor.
Title: The vanishing tradition : perspectives on American conservatism / edited by Paul Gottfried.
Description: Ithaca [New York] : Northern Illinois University Press, an imprint of Cornell University Press, 2020. | Includes bibliographical references and index.
Identifiers: LCCN 2019042244 (print) | LCCN 2019042245 (ebook) | ISBN 9781501749858 (paperback) | ISBN 9781501749872 (pdf) | ISBN 9781501749865 (epub)
Subjects: LCSH: Conservatism—United States. | Political culture—United States. | United States—Politics and government.
Classification: LCC JC573.2.U6 V36 2020 (print) | LCC JC573.2.U6 (ebook) | DDC 320.520973—dc23
LC record available at https://lccn.loc.gov/2019042244
LC ebook record available at https://lccn.loc.gov/2019042245

Contents

Acknowledgments

As editor I wish to acknowledge the assistance of those who made this work possible. First, I would like to thank the acquisitions editor, Amy Farranto, who actively encouraged our project. Amy also provided editorial comments that helped improve most of the contributions to this volume. We can only hope that the sales of this work will justify her faith in our collective endeavor. Jeff Taylor of Dordt College, Jesse Merriam of Loyola University of Maryland, and David Gordon of the Ludwig von Mises Institute also contributed useful feedback; and all of our essays benefited from their careful readings. I would like to acknowledge the boldness of those who wrote for this anthology, particularly those who submitted truly edgy criticisms. The spirited commentaries of the younger writers, who are still making their way up the academic ladder, are especially deserving of honor. I would also like to acknowledge the diligent efforts of my editorial assistant, Andrew Lundner, who patiently formatted each chapter in this volume. Without Andrew's help, this anthology would have arrived at the press in a far worse technical state.

Finally, an acknowledgment is owed to my wife, who kept telling me to "finish up fast." Mary believed (perhaps rightly) that my senior years should be devoted to more scholarly work than bashing media personalities. I responded by explaining in self-defense that as a political theorist and historian of political movements, I was dealing with something that lies within my wheelhouse. One can sometimes learn more about a subject from examining partisan popularizers than from investigating towering thinkers. Despite disagreement about this project, because of Mary's nagging and Amy's reminders, it was eventually finished.

THE VANISHING
TRADITION

Introduction

THE RIGHT IN CHANGING PERSPECTIVE

Paul Gottfried

The critical studies in this volume examine how the conservative movement presents its own history and how its interpretations depart from factual reality. Much of this self-interpretation has gone unchallenged because it satisfies conservatism's critics almost as much as its defenders. According to this received account, the conservative movement grew out of a once-isolated sect of anti-Communist activists; and as it moved beyond its parochial starting point, it gained in both sophistication and moderation. Established conservatism supposedly overcame its sectarian beginnings as it evolved into a vital part of the political conversation. Today at its best, it supposedly advocates for civility in American politics and for the application of "values" to our common life. Because conservatives oppose "extremism" while remaining dedicated to whatever they claim to believe, they insist that they are open to dialogue with others who share their reasoning.

Although the conservative movement, which has expanded as a media presence, admits to having changed over the years, it still offers a problematic self-portrait. Our investigations will address this self-representation by posing two questions. One, does the movement's present identity reveal ideological and programmatic continuity with what it was fifty or sixty years ago? Two, does the movement encourage an open, honest discussion of political differences, including with those who may be thought to be on its right? The following chapters demonstrate that the conservative movement has reconfigured itself with remarkable regularity and readily kicked out journalists and intellectuals who have balked at changing party lines.

Two developments are critical for understanding the direction in which the conservative movement has gone, particularly since the 1980s. One is the rise of the neoconservatives as the dominant force within the movement, a process that several of the contributors address in their chapters. A group of influential journalists and fund-raisers who combined strong anti-Soviet feelings with fervent Zionist sympathies, the neoconservatives have enjoyed commanding positions in conservative publications and foundations since the 1980s. One of their first acts in assuming leadership positions in the movement was removing uncooperative employees and activists who resisted their new party line. This consisted of a strongly pro-Israeli form of liberal internationalism in foreign policy with a willingness to move generally toward the left on most domestic issues. The neoconservative model of conservatism became permanent as their ideological and financial influence over the movement proved to be irreversible.

The other development that would shape the movement, and one related to the neoconservative ascendancy, has been a growing flexibility on social questions. There are few, if any, social positions taken by the Left, whether on immigration or LGBT (lesbian, gay, bisexual, and transgender) rights, that the conservative movement has not eventually incorporated. Conservative publicists have made these adjustments while promoting an activist foreign policy against countries depicted as human rights violators. A regular line of attack against Putin's Russia and Muslim opponents of Israel is their failure to recognize gay rights, or in the case of Russia, to permit gay pride parades. The Muslim mayor of London was designated in the neoconservative *New York Post* as a "conservative" hero because he has striven mightily to accommodate both Zionists and LGBT activists.[1] The fact that major conservative backers have been socially liberal Zionists may throw light on the positions taken by those whom they fund.

Over the years one encounters different forms of "American conservatism," some of which have vanished over time and others of which, particularly as we approach the present, have been stifled or weakened by better-funded groups claiming the conservative label. This volume deals principally with the second situation, in which those who previously represented conservative positions succumbed to successful rivals. Here we are not dealing with historically driven displacements—for example, when the exponents and defenders of archaic visions of order cease to have their ideas prevail under the force of social change or because cataclysms, like the American Civil War or World War I, resulted in social change. Rather, we are focusing on the systematic discrediting of certain ideas and sentiments associated with the Right that were thought to clash with the interests of an expanding business operation.

It is undoubtedly true that at least some of what the present conservative movement rejects is malicious and bigoted. There are indeed white nationalists and defenders of the Third Reich whom one can locate somewhere on the right, if we extend that side of the political spectrum far enough. But setting that group aside, the conservative establishment has unfairly degraded the rest of those on its right. We might note some of the offenses for which an older Right was read out of the movement by the 1990s. Such presumed enormities included opposing the First Gulf War, supporting Patrick Buchanan's presidential bid in 1992, and complaining about the influence of the American Israeli lobby.

Some of the same people had also been critical of the cultural effects of Third World immigration, the extensions of the Voting Rights Act that would increase the electoral strength of the Left and bring the electoral process almost totally under federal administrative control, and the elevation of Martin Luther King—a controversial figure of the Left in his own time—to iconic status with a national holiday. Although arguably this opposition may have been doomed from the outset, one could not fail but notice the disappearance from respected conservative publications of certain commentators who failed to make the desired turn The tolerance of dissent was in short supply here, as it was in other matters that those who were in commanding positions in the conservative movement decided for the rank and file. Moreover, the effects of landmark congressional legislation of the 1960s have been for the most part what its critics on the right predicted. These measures have contributed toward moving the country politically and in other ways toward the left. With regard to King, the Left has been perfectly justified in mocking the yearly ritual by Heritage, American Enterprise Institute, and various Republican websites and publications to claim the avowedly leftist civil rights hero as a "conservative." This transmogrification may exemplify the view of history as the tricks that the living play on the dead.

Throughout the 1980s, as Gary Dorrien documents in *The Neoconservative Mind: Politics, Culture and the War of Ideology*, Norman Podhoretz and other neoconservatives steadily denounced homosexuality and any public tolerance granted to this lifestyle.[2] This did not prevent the same activists from turning around and railing against the former presidential candidate Pat Buchanan for using the term "San Francisco Democrats" in an address before the GOP presidential convention in 1992. Buchanan was accused of having made a veiled attack on homosexual American citizens, although from the neoconservative perspective his real sin was to have mocked, rightly or wrongly, the "Israeli lobby in the US," before and while running for president. What Buchanan said at the Republican convention, however, never approached in intensity the antigay invective that had come from his neoconservative opponents.[3] Dorrien gives one obvious reason why even some on the left have been pleased with the direction of American conservatism: "Neoconservatives did not convert existing conservatism but rather created an alternative to it."[4]

The chapters that follow demonstrate how far and in what ways the conservative movement has misrepresented both its past and present character. A media phenomenon driven by ratings and its relation to its donor base, it demonstrably falls short of the ideals that it purports to be promoting. *National Review* senior editor Rich Lowry called for the removal of Robert E. Lee statues throughout the country in 2017,[5] at a time when Lowry had become a frequent guest on mainstream news programs. Leaders from Dwight Eisenhower to Winston Churchill to Bill Clinton, while still governor of Arkansas, lavishly extolled Lee's character and his dignity in defeat as a Confederate commander. And one of Lowry's colleagues at *National Review*, Kyle Smith, was allowed to ask the obvious question about the policy endorsed by his editor in chief: "Destroying symbols: where does it end?"[6]

This anthology examines the authorized conservative movement in a strikingly original way. All of the chapters present arguments that the reader will not likely find in the *New York Times* or in conservative house organs like *National Review* and the former *Weekly Standard*. According to the contributors, the conservative movement has insulated itself so well against examination by an independent Right that it no longer has to worry about inventing its past. It has become, with the docile compliance of the Center Left, the ultimate creator of its own account of how it got to where it is. What is suggested is that the voices of an older American Right operate on the media fringe and should be viewed as marginal to the conservative establishment. Most of the contributors to this collective work have some identification with the Right, but not with the lucrative business operation that goes by that name.

John Kerwick, a professor of philosophy who specializes in semantics, examines what he calls the "Big Con." He argues by means of copious examples that "conservative" media, including such mainstream conservative fixtures as Fox News and *National Review*, are neither consistently conservative nor a true alternative to the dominant or "mainstream" left-leaning media. Rather, the authorized conservative media are largely a system of Republican Party propaganda that has succeeded in making "conservatism" synonymous with the steady and changing interests of the GOP. Despite its occasionally misleading rhetoric, moreover, the GOP is almost as committed as its Democratic counterpart to expanding the size and scope of the central government. The GOP and its "conservative" front organizations are, moreover, no less committed than the Democratic Party to "political correctness," that is, to furthering a program of indoctrination and surveillance that has strengthened public administration at all levels. In fact, the conservative media, working in tandem with the GOP, have helped make big government and political correctness less and less objectionable to self-identified conservatives.

Keith Preston, author of, among many books, *The Tyranny of the Politically Correct* and editor of the website Attack the System, examines a major turning point in the expulsion of Southern traditionalists from the conservative movement. Preston looks at the precipitous downfall of Southern literary scholar M. E. Bradford, who in an explosive rebuke was refused the post of director of the National Endowment for the Humanities in 1981. Bradford's fall from grace in the Reagan administration was engineered by neoconservative journalists and foundation heads; and the attacks leveled against him in the press as a "Lincoln hater" and Southern reactionary continued long after he was kept from government service. Preston explores the likely reasons for these broadsides and how they targeted not only Bradford but, at least indirectly, other Southern regionalists, whom the neoconservatives in their ascent to power were interested in marginalizing. Contrary to a widespread misconception, the "Bradford affair" was more than a minor incident in the history of the conservative movement. It was fraught with significance in both demonstrating and consolidating neoconservative control of American conservatism.

Grant Havers, who chairs the philosophy department at Trinity Western University, elaborates on the distinctions between the Tory tradition and what now passes for American conservatism. In the post–World War II era, many prominent voices of the American conservative movement portrayed their cause as a noble continuation of the traditional English conservatism that such worthies as Edmund Burke and Benjamin Disraeli defended in an earlier era. Havers maintains that these claims are unfounded. By focusing on self-described Tory traditionalist writers such as George Grant, one can locate a wide gap between the neoconservative valorization of capitalist democracy and the inveterate conservative suspicion of what contemporary American conservatives are taught to venerate. Unlike traditional Tories, the advocates of "democratic capitalism," wherever they are present, represent globalization, not a conservative defense of particularity and organic social relations.

Joseph Cotto of the *San Francisco Review of Books* looks at one possibly overriding reason that conservative foundations have adopted certain favored positions. Cotto examines the funding sources of conservative policy organizations and the close connection between their policies and those who pay their tabs. Given the mass of material that exists on this subject, the author limits himself to only one aspect of the correlation between funding and advocacy. He examines the assistance that Republican think tanks in the Washington area receive from defense industries and from those who are pushing for a more activist foreign policy. Cotto's investigation leads to findings that conservative activists might find surprising, and among the more naive or idealistic, even disheartening.

Marjorie L. Jeffrey of Clemson University deals with the persistence of a neoconservative foreign policy in the conservative movement and why it has not been discarded despite its obvious limitations. Following the collapse of the Soviet Union and the end of the Cold War, the American Right faced an existential question: Would it support the continuation of a semi-imperial foreign policy, or would it seek to redirect political energies toward domestic policy? The 1992 Republican primary and the victory of the incumbent president, George H. W. Bush, against his challenger, Pat Buchanan, answered that question; and until the election of 2016, both major parties were in agreement on matters of foreign policy, except for working out the details. Jeffrey examines the philosophic claims of the interventionist, or "neoconservative," wing of the American conservative movement, against the foreign policy prescriptions of the American Founders, as well as those of such truly conservative modern critics as George Kennan and Buchanan.

Jesse Russell of Georgia Southwestern University discusses the rise and fall of perhaps the most unusual bloc within the neoconservative movement: the Catholic neocons. He traces how Michael Novak's best seller *The Spirit of Democratic Capitalism* caused Catholic neoconservatives to shift American Catholic discussion of economics to a defense of "democratic capitalism" as the purest distillation of Catholic social teaching. This argument was reinforced when another Catholic neoconservative, George Weigel, seized the public image of John Paul II for political purposes with the publication of Weigel's biography *Witness to Hope*. Once the neoconservatives were able to speak for conservative Catholicism in America, they rallied American Catholic celebrities to their positions on foreign interventionism, support for multinational corporations, and Jewish ultranationalism. Integral to this campaign was the success of Catholic neoconservatives in fashioning an American Catholic understanding of political philosophy, starting with the social teachings of St. Thomas Aquinas. In *The Hemisphere of Liberty*, Novak dwells on a statement made by the English Catholic classical liberal Lord Acton in order to present St. Thomas as the "First Whig." This was part of an arduous effort to reconcile medieval political philosophy with the neoconservative understanding of Anglo-American liberalism.

Nicholas W. Drummond, who teaches political theory at Black Hills State University, evaluates the neoconservative anti-Trumpers who view the Trump presidency as a betrayal of America's founding principles. These detractors have been especially critical of nationalist populism and its rejection of "globalist" policies like free trade, foreign interventionism, and immigration. According to Drummond, neoconservatives misunderstand our principles as a nation because they have relied heavily on certain sources, starting with the view of the American founding taught by the followers of Leo Strauss. This view overemphasizes Lockean natural rights and the merits of commercial acquisitiveness. Absent from this neoconservative analysis is an appreciation of three tenets of James Madison's political thinking, each of which accords with nationalist populism: civic republicanism, intergenerational duty to ancestors and posterity, and a warning that too much diversity will lead to a plutocratic oppression of society through a politics of divide and conquer. Although neoconservatives may have personal reasons to criticize the presidency of Donald Trump, their argument from the American founding is, according to Drummond, not particularly convincing.

Richard T. Marcy of the University of Victoria investigates the Alt Right and how it has developed as a response to the perceived inadequacies of the authorized conservative movement. Although Marcy does not ignore the Alt Right's antics and grandstanding, he focuses primarily on its psychological and cultural aspects. He cites examples of its tactics—for example, provocations leading to moral outrage from the Left and Republican establishment—and situates these acts within a broader cultural war. He stresses the efforts of a marginalized group to attract attention through outrageous gestures while at the same time aiming to join the political conversation. Marcy's chapter draws on relevant psychological and sociological literature and integrates historical scholarship dealing with earlier artistic-political avant-garde movements and their revolts against mainstream culture.

Boyd D. Cathey, a widely published authority on the political theory of Spanish counterrevolutionaries and the antebellum South, writes on the fate of Southern regionalists within a now-transformed American conservative movement. Cathey deals with the deliberate removal of the Southern traditionalists from this establishment, a process that was greatly accelerated once the neoconservatives became a force to be reckoned with. This displacement represented a major reorientation of the conservative movement, given that Southern Agrarians and, more generally, Southern traditionalists had been significant cultural and social critics in the post–World War II Right. The loss of a Southern conservative presence was so total that any memory of this influence has been shoved down a memory hole and/or bleached out of authorized histories of the conservative movement.

George Hawley, professor of political science at the University of Alabama, discusses what political science literature indicates about the degree of ideological consistency in the American electorate. Hawley explores the degree to which Republican voters meet the basic definition of what is popularly considered conservative. It is shown that those who fit the popular definition are not particularly numerous, even within GOP ranks. Complicating the matter, Republican voters may not be as desirous of maintaining conservative purity as many observers assume. Although most of these voters use the term "conservative" to describe themselves, it is often not clear what they mean by this designation. Quite possibly the conservative media are bestowing on their viewers and readers an inapplicable characterization.

My own contribution to this anthology, on conservative purges, deals with a topic that I have engaged before; and what is presented here is intended primarily for the benefit of those who are not acquainted with my earlier examinations of the postwar conservative movement. The purges herein treated have not received adequate attention, because the conservative movement and its apparent opponents have agreed on certain seemingly innocent misrepresentations, which need to be corrected. Purges have not been limited to removing undesirables from the masthead of conservative magazines nor to breaking social and professional relations. More typically, this shunning has been accompanied by campaigns of character assassination that have sometimes lasted years. What happened to Bradford was all too typical of this process of defamation. Conservative movement leaders have behaved in a way that one might have expected in an earlier age from the Communist Party USA. In all likelihood, however, American Communists would have been generally better read and more cerebral than those who draw their picture of reality from conservative media stars.

In organizing this anthology, I consciously gave preference to young scholars in their twenties and thirties. This seemed a better approach for this revisionist work than asking senior citizens to write about old grievances. The other reason for this decision is that most of the older scholars whom I approached were fearful of losing their standing within a movement that they still depend on financially. Understandably they turned me down when I asked them to contribute to this anthology. It is also fitting that a younger generation should be asked to expose what my generation failed to explain effectively. But it may not suffice for this endeavor that interpreters seek to reveal long-standing distortions and a continuing obscuring of facts. It is equally important that they examine the conditions that engendered this situation.

1

BIG CONSERVATISM AND AMERICAN EXCEPTIONALISM

Jack Kerwick

According to the conventional wisdom, America is home to a great partisan divide, a seemingly unbridgeable chasm between conservatives on the right and liberals or progressives on the left. The Republican Party is the party of conservatism, or the Right, while the Democratic Party is the party of progressivism. We may safely assume that most Americans, irrespective of their political sympathies, subscribe to this understanding of their country's political universe. Its popularity notwithstanding, however, the conventional wisdom on this matter is mistaken—and profoundly so.

In what follows, I show that "Big Conservatism," or "the Big Con"—that is, the contemporary conservative movement with which nationally recognized media personalities in talk radio, cable news, and especially well-established and generously funded print publications are associated—is not really of the Right. This movement is *neoconservative*. Neoconservatism, far from being a variant of conservatism, is in fact a species of the ideological politics against which conservatism has traditionally defined itself. Its cardinal doctrine of "American Exceptionalism," the creed that America is unique among the nations of the earth as the bodying forth of an "Idea" and may be the only country in all of history to have been founded on a *proposition*, is a patently Rationalist construct. It is precisely because "conservatism" is not merely a misnomer for this movement but a form of patently dishonest advertising that I refer to it here as "Big Conservatism," or simply, "the Big Con."

Some preliminary remarks regarding the structure and strategy of my argument are in order. I first identify the *epistemological* presuppositions that have distinguished conservatism as a political-philosophical tradition for the past two centuries. To this end, I allude to the thought of four thinkers—Edmund Burke and David Hume in the eighteenth century, and Russell Kirk and Michael Oakeshott in the twentieth—who are widely recognized representatives of classical or traditional conservatism. These references serve two purposes: they establish that conservative thought does indeed have an enduring identity and, at least as relevant, that the conservative conception of the nature of knowledge consistently leads its proponents to resist the abstract, ideological, and utopian political designs of their opponents. Next, I turn attention to Big Conservatism to show that it too depends on its own set of assumptions concerning the character of knowledge. These assumptions are identical to the philosophy of those radicals and revolutionaries against whom conservatives have railed in the past. And just as the epistemology of the conservative is inseparable from his politics, the politics of the Big Con also features an understanding of political knowledge that illustrates what Oakeshott characterized as "Rationalism."

Conservatism

It is impossible to come to terms with conservatism unless one understands it primarily as a response to Rationalism, a theory of knowledge distinguished on account of its neglect of—and not infrequently, disdain for—the constellation of culturally and historically specific contingencies that we call "tradition." Rationalists usually dismiss or relegate to insignificance experienced tradition as a source of knowledge. Genuine knowledge, from the perspective of the Rationalist, is essentially *propositional* in that it is believed to consist of principles and rules that can be learned or discovered by anyone, irrespective of one's circumstances. The twentieth- century philosopher Michael Oakeshott characterizes the Rationalist's view of knowledge as "a knowledge of technique" or "technical knowledge."[1] The latter can be learned from a book or picked up at a correspondence school. It can be memorized and mechanically applied. Because of its features, technical knowledge conveys the appearance of *certainty*. It is a self-contained technique, depending on nothing beyond itself.

Nearly two hundred years earlier, Edmund Burke called attention to this conception of knowledge among the apologists for the French Revolution. Burke remarked that Rationalists deny the individuating details of each situation by divesting them "of every relation" in favor of "all the nakedness and solitude of metaphysical abstraction." Although circumstances endow "every political principle [with] its distinguishing color and discriminating effect" and "render every civil and political scheme beneficial or noxious to mankind," for Rationalists they "pass for nothing."[2] Burke characterized Rationalists as "political-theologians" and "theological-politicians,"[3] "new doctors of the rights of men,"[4] "moral politicians,"[5] "men of theory,"[6] "levelers,"[7] peddlers of a "mechanic philosophy,"[8] of an "empire of light and reason."[9]

Oakeshott observes that the Rationalist's faith in a universal, transhistorical rationality renders him vulnerable to regarding the past as an "encumbrance,"[10] which in turn disposes him more toward "destruction and creation."[11] Burke compares Rationalists to "fools" who "rush in where angels fear to tread"[12] and says that "it is vain to talk to them of the practice of their ancestors, the fundamental laws of their country, the fixed form of a Constitution whose merits are confirmed by the solid test of long experience," for "they despise experience as the wisdom of unlettered men" and "have wrought a ground a mine that will blow up, at one grand explosion, all examples of antiquity, all precedents, charters, and acts of Parliament."[13] Hume too noted the destructive penchant of Rationalists for imposing "violent innovations" that produce more "ill than good."[14]

Rationalists also identify their political models as universal and conceive of politics in terms of ideals and principles—Freedom, Equality, the Rights of Man, Democracy, the Original Contract, the Will of the People, and so on. Their political principles are both abstract and seemingly universal in application. These political-philosophical fictions, which Burke colorfully described as "delusive plausibilities"[15] and "mazes of metaphysic sophistry,"[16] have been anathema to genuine conservatives.

With respect to the supposed Rights of Man declared during the French Revolution, Burke maintained that this dogma was no real alternative to historically based rights and that what it declared "admit[s] [of] no temperament and no compromise." Unfortunately no human government can hope to pass muster if it is to be assessed according to the abstract standard of the Rights of Man. "Against these rights of men let no government look for security in the length of its continuance, or in the justice and lenity of its administration."[17]

Against the idea that all just governments come into existence historically through the consent of citizens with equal rights, Hume famously responds that if Rationalists would "look abroad into the world, they would meet with nothing that, in the least, corresponds to their ideas, or can warrant so refined and philosophical a system." The truth is the contrary. Irrespective of time or place, "obedience or subjection becomes so familiar, that most men never make any enquiry about its origin or cause, more than about the principle of gravity, resistance, or the most universal laws of nature."[18]

From the conservative standpoint, society is not grounded in a contract. It is rooted in *tradition*, or *habit*. According to the Scottish Tory Hume, it is habit that "consolidates what other principles of human nature had imperfectly founded."

He explains that human beings "never think of departing from that path, in which they and their ancestors have constantly trod, and to which they are confined by so many urgent and visible motives."[19]

Burke makes this same point. It is not a priori principles of which knowledge, particularly political knowledge, consists but rather tradition: "general prejudices" constituting "the general bank and capital of nations and of ages."[20] The English, according to Burke, view their rights and liberties *not* as timeless, self-evident endowments. They are instead understood as "an *entailed inheritance* derived to us from our forefathers, and to be transmitted to our posterity—as an estate specially belonging to the people of this kingdom, without any reference whatever to any other more general or prior right."[21]

In Russell Kirk's treatment of Burke as the quintessential representative of "the conservative mind"[22] that Kirk sets out to defend, conservatism stands as the polar opposite of Rationalist, egalitarian politics. The conservative abjures abstract, universalist theorizing in favor of prejudice, "the half-intuitive knowledge that enables men to meet the problems of life without logic-chopping"; prescription, "the customary right which grows out of the conventions and compacts of many successive generations"; and presumption, the "inference" that is "in accordance with the common experience of mankind." The conservative, comments Kirk, regards as utopian folly "*a priori* designs for perfecting human nature and society,"[23] the "fanatical ideological dogmata"[24] of "metaphysical enthusiasts"[25] who are either unwilling to grasp or incapable of grasping that principles are "arrived at by convention and compromise" and "tested by long experience."[26] Kirk contrasts the conservative's "affection for the proliferating variety and mystery of human existence" with the "uniformity, egalitarianism, and utilitarianism of most radical systems,"[27] and his "faith in prescription" with the certitude of those rationalists "who would reconstruct society along abstract designs."[28] Prejudice, precedent, presumption—these are the ingredients of a tradition-centered conception of knowledge. Without them, man "is thrown back upon his own private stock of reason, with the consequences that attend shipwreck."[29]

Traditional knowledge is what Oakeshott refers to as "practical knowledge." Practical knowledge is not propositional. In fact, it "cannot be formulated in rules" and "exists only in use."[30] Propositional knowledge is actually the distillation of a tradition. As such, it necessarily omits the complex of nuances from which it is abstracted. Rationalists, however, do not appear to be aware of this and choose, instead, to believe that the knowledge of morality is "the same to every rational intelligent being," attained "by a chain of argument and induction," "metaphysical reasonings, and by deductions from the most abstract principles of the understanding."[31]

Conservatism, it should now be obvious, is ultimately as much an epistemological perspective as a political-philosophical one. As such, its tradition-centered conception of knowledge has made it the enemy of Rationalist or ideological politics. The latter inevitably presuppose an impoverished epistemology, one based exclusively on an abstract conception of rationality according to which universal *propositions* are the sole contents of the understanding. Although conservatives in different times and places have disagreed with one another over specific policy prescriptions, their shared epistemology has disposed them toward favoring institutional arrangements that accommodate and encourage social cohesion and continuity with their nation's past. They have also focused on preserving their own traditions rather than on saving the human race with what Burke contemptuously described as an "armed doctrine" in the form of human rights.

American Exceptionalism

The doctrine of American Exceptionalism (AE)—that America is an Idea with universal applicability—figures prominently within Big Conservatism. Indeed, AE is the center around which every other belief championed by the Big Con finds its place. Yet before proceeding to examine the contents of this particular idea, it is imperative that we consider the nature of an idea.

Ideas are abstract. They are mental and immaterial. An idea as such is universal in that a nonphysical or intangible entity cannot be limited to a specific time or place. Ideas are therefore *borderless*. They transcend particularities like race and ethnicity, which differentiate us as groups, since they belong to no one person or group of people. As to whether ideas ontologically precede the culturally and historically specific traditions to which they are related, or whether they are nothing more or less than the distillation of those traditions, it seems that Rationalists have always tended to assign ontological primacy to ideas in the context of their ideologies.

For the Big Con and advocates of AE, America is the paramount Idea. The reason for being of their country consists of its adherence to a Rationalist design that requires the constant striving toward making the entire world subject to an abstract plan. Through these conceptual lenses, it would appear that America is either the only country or the model for every other country "founded" on the Idea. This vision is based on certain unmistakable assumptions.

First, the epistemology of the Big Conservative is unambiguously Rationalist. Knowledge is, as Oakeshott characterized it, "technical." Political knowledge in particular is available with little difficulty, for it is simply a matter of committing to memory a small number of basic propositions (i.e., *self-evident* propositions, to which all human minds have equal and immediate access). Therefore, historically specific, religious, and other considerations are of secondary importance, if they have any relevance at all, for the acquisition of political knowledge or the study of the Supreme Idea. Tradition may help facilitate the realization of political knowledge, but it is not necessary for its attainment. The Rationalist epistemology underwriting AE, like all such epistemologies, is intrinsically equalitarian—as will soon be apparent.

Second, insofar as these propositions embody principles of "natural rights," they affirm egalitarian beliefs. Unlike Burke's opponents, the French revolutionaries, Big Conservatives point to the Declaration of Independence as proof that America is an Idea. They argue that their country was founded on the basis of natural right theory, which means it has now become sanctified by tradition. Nevertheless, if we insist that the cornerstone of American identity is a universal egalitarian ideal and that is *the Idea* that America embodies—then we are also saying that America is the Idea of Equality par excellence. That may be the case whether or not Thomas Jefferson had that concept in mind when he wrote about inalienable universal rights in the Declaration. It is also clear that what we are speaking about is not what Jefferson and those members of the Continental Congress who signed his document in 1776 had in mind about universal individual rights but rather how the Idea is now interpreted by those who claim to be American conservatives.

This second point leads us to a third: if equal natural rights, the proposition that "all men are created equal," is the proposition to which America is "dedicated," as Lincoln put it, then it would follow that only democratically constituted governments are morally justifiable. Note, democracy, from this perspective, is not merely a procedural basis for establishing authority. It "is the principle of equality which provides the moral justification for democratic rule,"[32] rendering democracy "uniquely valuable" inasmuch as "it embodies more fully than any alternative system the principle of fundamental moral equality of citizens."[33] To be clear, democracy is not morally neutral but, rather, a moral idea that precludes "the denial of equality" even when the majority votes to implement values in any given situation that conflict with the value of equality.[34] AE, which is the doctrine that America is ultimately an Idea or a Proposition, entails more than what is often explicitly stated. Not only does AE belong to the family of the same Rationalist constructions against which conservatives have always fought. It also combines them in what we are told is the only morally acceptable statement of American patriotism, even nationalism.

Neoconservatism: Big Conservatism, the Big Con

The Commitment to AE

Allan Bloom is a neoconservative academic whose book *The Closing of the American Mind* almost instantly became a classic within Big Conservatism. Bloom articulated what was in the 1980s a standard neoconservative conception of American identity. It belongs unmistakably to that Rationalist style of politics that conservatives had always vehemently opposed. Bloom's vision of America thoroughly informs the present version of what is viewed as conservative thought. Republican politicians and media personalities pay constant tribute to Bloom's picture of America as the embodiment of "the rational principles of natural right."[35] American patriots should be committed to this ideal in a way that disallows any consideration of race, class, gender, religion, or ethnicity.[36] America is the "liberal democracy" par excellence, "the regime of equality and liberty, of the rights of man," and indeed "the regime of reason."[37]

Bloom's account of America is the proverbial textbook illustration of Rationalist philosophy, an abstract metaphysic bound up with the imperative to universalize our practice of liberal democracy. America is seen as unique among the history of nations insofar as it is founded on, or expresses, a set of *propositions.* From this perspective, as Irving Kristol, a man widely regarded as the godfather of neoconservatism, puts it, America is "a creedal nation."[38] And because its creed affirms the principle of equal natural rights to which Jefferson gave expression in the Declaration of Independence, we should be steadily advancing our "universal" creed.[39] Indeed America is blessed with "a civilizing mission"[40] to promote its "values" around the planet.[41] We should proudly embrace our identity as an "ideological" nation.[42]

Thus we have statements from Bloom and Kristol, both leading lights of the Big Con, about AE. But they are far from the only conservative dignitaries who have held forth on this subject. William J. Bennett, who served in the Reagan and Bush I administrations and who, up until his retirement, was employed as a nationally syndicated talk radio host for Salem Broadcasting and as a contributor for Fox News, commends America's Founders for having done what, allegedly, no one else had ever achieved. They shaped "a new nation" on the basis of "a new self-evident truth that all men are created equal." America is grounded in this principle and in "the ideals of freedom and equality." America is unique among the nations of the world insofar as it is "a country tied together in loyalty to a principle."[43]

Bennett's Salem colleague, nationally syndicated talk radio host and Big Conservative columnist Dennis Prager, enthusiastically endorses AE. Belief in this concept, according to Prager, arises from the "Judeo-Christian" character of America's "values."[44] These "values" have "universal applicability," are "eminently exportable," and should be "applicable to virtually every society in the world."[45]

In the same vein, the late Charles Krauthammer, a Fox News celebrity and another nationally syndicated columnist, characterized America as "a nation uniquely built not on blood, race or consanguinity, but on *a proposition*" that all human beings are created equal and should possess equal rights.[46] Glenn Beck[47] and Dinesh D'Souza,[48] two well-recognized names within the world of Big Conservatism, were among those who expressed their enthusiasm over the declaration of musician Bono that America, in his words, is not just an idea—the idea that "you and me are created equal"—but "one of the greatest ideas in human history." America was the first to put this concept "on paper," but since this redemptive idea has now begun to spread everywhere, "the world has a bit of America in it." There is now no "copyright" on the idea of America.[49]

Jonah Goldberg, another *National Review* contributor and a Big Conservatism celebrity of the first order, argues *against* some of his *NR* colleagues who are not, by Goldberg's lights, sufficiently committed to AE. He refers to "that great and glorious cause, the American Idea," and elevates it above "the American nation." Goldberg even imagines a hypothetical scenario—one in which Kim Kardashian is elected by Americans to become their queen—that would justify fighting against what he conceives as "the American nation" in defense of "the American Idea." He castigates his colleagues for having failed to "defend the exceptional essence of American patriotism from the grubbiness of generic nationalism."[50] Also writing in *National Review*, David Adesnik, a fellow for the Big Conservative think tank American Enterprise Institute, sets "liberals" straight as to what AE signifies. What makes America exceptional, he remarks, "is the justification of our country's existence on the basis of universal rights, rather than religious creed, ethnic heritage, or some other narrow basis."[51]

Matthew J. Franck, lavishing praise on *National Review* editor Rich Lowry's book on Lincoln in the pages of *The Public Discourse*, writes that Americans routinely refer back to "their public figures of yesteryear—like Lincoln and the Founders (and Ronald Reagan and Franklin Delano Roosevelt)." After all, Americans "are 'people of the text,' formed into a nation and a people not by our having inhabited our land from time immemorial, not by having been all descended from the same ancestors, and not by all belonging to the same religious faith." Rather, we are held together "by the power of a shared commitment to certain ideas captured in words scratched out on parchment with quill pens in the last quarter of the eighteenth century." America is "constituted by its Constitution, which begins 'We the People,' and which in turn draws all its vitality from the Declaration of Independence, the *credo* or 'I believe' that states its principles with the words, 'We hold these truths to be self-evident.'"[52]

Francis Fukuyama, writing for the Big Conservative publication *Commentary*, expressly repudiates the position that America is a historically and culturally specific country in favor of AE: "In contrast to other Western European democracies, or Japan, the American national identity has never been directly linked to ethnicity or religion. Nationality has been based instead on *universal concepts* like freedom and equality that are in theory open to all people."[53]

It is worth quoting from a broad sample of representatives of Big Conservatism, lest there be any doubt in the reader's mind that the Big Con unequivocally affirms through AE that America is an Idea or Proposition. AE is every bit as Rationalist and planetary in its content as the alleged Rights of Man, against which conservatives in earlier times fought. Whatever other material considerations undoubtedly motivate the movers and shakers of the Big Con, it is critical for its friends and, especially, its enemies to recognize three things: (1) there *is* a philosophy lurking behind the policy prescriptions that the men and women of the Big Con embrace; (2) this philosophy is a variant of that Rationalism and its world-embracing claims against which conservatives have traditionally taken a stand; and (3) the metaphysical, epistemological, and political-moral postulates of the Big Con's Rationalist philosophy are to be found lodged in its doctrine of AE.

There is still another crucial point to be grasped: AE is a political religion, a set of political beliefs to which universal moral and spiritual significance has been assigned. The noblest ideals—Equality, Natural Rights, Democracy—supposedly became incarnate in this geographical region of the world within a specific people and during a specific time. The *Logos*, as it were, assumed flesh in this situation, but until now the world of time and space has precluded Americans from fully actualizing the Idea everywhere. Still, this sacred Idea is forever beckoning us to work more diligently on its behalf. Moreover, this vision of AE is quintessentially *progressivist*. It is a form of progressivism that presupposes a linear conception of time. In the end, if all goes well, we will see the full realization of the Idea that is America both here and everywhere else on the planet.

Neoconservative / Big Conservative Policy

The more honest or more consistent members of the Big Con do not hide certain facts from us, that they are of the Left and in their approach to international relations explicitly expansionist, in the traditions of the French and Bolshevik Revolutions. Douglas Murray, an unqualified apologist for the Big Con, informs us that his friends are interested in "erasing tyrannies and spreading democracy."

This lofty goal requires "interventionism, nation-building, and many of the other difficulties that had long concerned traditional conservatives."[54] And the well-known sociologist Nathan Glazer, editor of the late Big Conservative journal *Public Interest*, goes so far as to suggest that neocons (Big Conservatives) are essentially *socialists*: "It's very hard for us [neocons and socialists] to define what it is that divides us, in any centrally principled way." While *in some instances* there *may* be disagreement over "the details or the scope of health insurance plans," "the level of taxation that should be imposed upon corporations," or "how much should be going into social security," there does not appear to be any "principles that separate us."[55]

Irving Kristol confirms his ideology's progressivist orientation when he explicitly contrasts it with traditional conservatism by noting that it is "hopeful, not lugubrious," and "forward-looking, not nostalgic."[56] Big Conservatives, after all, embrace "the welfare state"—that is, "social security, unemployment insurance, some form of national health insurance, some kind of family assistance plan, etc."[57] As far as foreign policy is concerned, because of the United States' unique standing as "a creedal nation,"[58] it has a "civilizing mission"[59] to promote "American values"[60] throughout the world, to see to it "that other governments respect our conception of individual rights as the foundation of a just regime and a good society," in short, to "'make the world safe for democracy."[61] Charles Krauthammer expressed much the same idea under the name of his "value-driven foreign policy." He called for the implementation of "democratic globalism," a means by which we could facilitate "the spread of democracy" around the planet.[62] This kind of plan would entail providing those who are to be liberated with the necessary "technical knowledge" to follow our Idea. For example, those whom we would choose to instruct would have to be furnished with a constitutional document like ours, parties that are based on our system of government, and perhaps even directions on how to set up elections.

Ben Shapiro, who hosts among the most popular podcasts in the country, openly calls for an American *empire*. This policy, according to Shapiro, would serve America's national security interest while energetically "forwarding freedom." To be clear, Shapiro is *not* claiming that an American empire is merely a prudential step. He is not even claiming that it is *the most* virtuous course. Rather, he views it as a moral *imperative*, a "duty," for America. "If America is to survive and flourish, Americans must realize that empire isn't a choice."[63]

As a representative of Big Conservatism, which is fundamentally at odds with the classical, old Right conservatism of Patrick Buchanan, Shapiro accuses the latter of being an "arch-isolationist" who chooses to "ignore" America's need to become an empire. In pursuit of this geopolitical and ideological goal, America must be willing to act preemptively, as when it invaded Iraq. A similar step should be taken to spread democracy throughout the Islamic world. The United States should be ready to attack "Iran, Saudi Arabia, Syria, Egypt, Pakistan, and others" without warning, since preemption "is the chief weapon of a global empire." Empire may not be "easy," Shapiro says, "but it is right and good, both for Americans and for the world."[64]

The creed that America is an Idea implies that America, like any other idea, cannot be limited geographically. America, the "liberal democracy" par excellence, as Allan Bloom referred to it, should seek to bring democratic ideas to those benighted parts of the world that are still not blessed with this treasure. Moreover, since AE is based on an idea and technical knowledge about achieving its practice, anyone from anywhere should be able to become American with a bit of instruction.

Because America is an idea and ideas are borderless, to insist that becoming or being an American should in any way be limited by geographical borders is to be guilty of imposing limitations on that which is potentially limitless. It was reported that during a debate on immigration policy, President Trump referred to certain Third World countries, such as Haiti, as "shitholes."[65] In response, Republican senator Lindsey Graham rejoined that America is an idea, "not defined by its people but by its ideals."[66] It does not therefore matter from what place or culture a person hails, as long as that person embraces the Idea of America. Republican Paul Ryan enthusiastically endorsed the radical immigration agenda of Far Left Democrat Luis Gutierrez while referring to America as "an idea that people from all over the world aspire to achieve."[67]

Paul Greenberg, who has been regularly featured in Big Conservative publications for many decades, lavished praise on Barack Obama for paying "tribute to American Exceptionalism" by urging Congress to extend citizenship to illegal aliens. America is "exceptional," according to Greenberg, because it "is a nation bound together not like others, by blood or class or party, but by shared belief and hope—united . . . by . . . ideals," namely, the ideal that "all men are created equal, endowed by their Creator with certain unalienable Rights."[68]

In the symposium "Immigration and American Exceptionalism," hosted by the *Claremont Review of Books*, William Bennett noted that being an American is fundamentally about a commitment to "the nation and her ideals." Linda Chavez enthusiastically agreed, explaining that anything less than unadulterated enthusiasm over the massive influx of largely Third World immigrants into America betrays "fear of immigrants." Chavez admonished her fellow Big Conservatives to keep the "faith in the assimilative power of our exceptional nation" and do their "duty" to "help foster" the "assimilation" of immigrants." Angelo Codevilla, a senior fellow of the Big Conservative Claremont Institute, echoed the sentiment of his colleagues when he quoted Lincoln to the effect that all immigrants to America possess equally that "father of all moral principle," the Declaration of Independence. From this document we can learn the "self-evident" truth that "all men are created equal."[69]

David Brooks, the New York Times's resident "conservative," charges his fellow Republican and Big Conservative partisans with "destroying American exceptionalism" by way of what he depicts as their resistance to expansive immigration policies. In his column, Brooks contends that "the American Idea" precludes "look[ing] backward to an America that is being lost," an attitude embodying, as Brooks would have us think, a "desire to exclude." Rather, Big Conservatism (which Brooks calls "American conservatism") differs from other conservatisms that invoke "blood and soil." Big Conservatism is rooted in "a promise." Further, this promise is "the American idea." While all other nations have been defined "by their history," their past, the settlers, founders, and builders of America saw their country as "defined by its future, by the people who weren't yet here and by the greatness that hadn't yet been achieved."[70] Note that this notion of the American Idea as a "promise" is intrinsically progressivist, visionary, and future oriented. It may require us, according to its exponents, to absorb as much of the world as we can into our expanding country or else seek to convert the rest of the planet to our revolutionary Idea.

In this chapter, I have tried to prove that what is known as the conservative movement in America is not conservative in any traditional or historical sense. The present conservative movement is largely a creation of neoconservatism, which gained effective control of establishment conservative media in the 1980s. The Big Conservatism that emerged from this takeover is a recognizable form of the Rationalist, progressivist, imperialist Left, against which classical conservatives and later the interwar American Right were once furiously opposed. The movers and shakers of Big Conservatism, true to their ideological pedigree, anchor their political vision in a metaphysical abstraction, AE. From the perspective of AE, America is an Idea and perhaps the only nation in all of human history that is imagined to transcend history. It is on the basis of this equation of America with a concept—a borderless, immaterial, universal concept—that those in the Big Con seek to justify their policy prescriptions, particularly their linkage of idealistic military intervention abroad with unrelenting immigration at home.

A "conservatism" of this kind is in fact no conservatism at all. Even those who are not of a rightist disposition should view this leftist imperialism together with its media cheering gallery with the skepticism that it richly deserves.

2

THE SIGNIFICANCE OF THE M. E. BRADFORD AFFAIR

Keith Preston

The capture of the conservative movement by the neoconservatives is one of the great ironies of modern American political life. The fact that the neoconservatives, a group that was initially composed of former radical leftists, managed to effectively subjugate a conservative movement that was originally formed for the purpose of opposing the Left would seem a bit improbable. Part of the story of how this trajectory unfolded involves the significance of an event related to a relatively insignificant agency of the federal government, the National Endowment for the Humanities. The NEH was founded in 1965, and its creation constituted one of many efforts by the administration of President Lyndon B. Johnson to expand the role of the federal government in American life. The purpose of the NEH was, and continues to be, the promotion of research and education pertaining to the humanities. Yet a controversy involving the appointment of a conservative scholar by a Republican president to the leadership of a federal agency created by the Johnson administration proved to be a pivotal event in the ascendancy of the neoconservatives, and representative of the wider neoconservative conquest of the conservative movement.

When the conservative movement was originally formed in the 1950s under the leadership of William F. Buckley Jr. and *National Review* magazine, the stated purpose of the movement was support for anti-Communism within the context of Cold War geopolitics, and rolling back "big government" represented by domestic programs that were the legacy of the New Deal. Most participants in the conservative movement supported America's postwar military buildup and position of leadership of the "Free World" as a necessary effort to counter Soviet expansionism. Communism was regarded not only as a form of murderous totalitarianism but also as a threat to the survival of Western Christian civilization. The Soviet Union was a massive territory and nuclear armed power that fomented revolutions in the underdeveloped world. The Soviets also maintained a vast network of sympathizers throughout the Western democracies. Soviet-aligned Communist parties retained high levels of influence in major European nations such as France, Italy, and Greece. The postwar Soviet occupation of Eastern Europe and Communist conquests of China, North Korea, and Yugoslavia produced a world order where nearly half of the world's population lived under Communist regimes. Soviet-supported and/or Communist-led insurgencies were developing in Asia, Africa, and Latin America.

During the Cold War, most conservatives supported military intervention on anti-Communist grounds, including many who had taken an isolationist stance before America's entry into World War II. Those who dissented from *National Review*'s hard-line anti-Communism were purged from the movement at various points. Among these were the followers of the libertarian economist Murray Rothbard, the philosopher and novelist Ayn Rand, and the John Birch Society, which opposed the Vietnam War. Parallel to the purge of the noninterventionists was an embrace of former Communists and anti-Soviet leftists who expressed enthusiasm for the Cold War cause.[1] Some of these figures, such as Frank Meyer and James Burnham, became very influential in the conservative movement, and others became significant because of their efforts to build bridges between the conservative movement and anti-Communist tendencies on the left. Examples of the latter included the followers of Max Shachtman, a former associate of Leon Trotsky's who later embraced Cold War politics on anti-Stalinist grounds.[2] The Shachtmanites were associated with Social Democrats USA, a splinter tendency from the Socialist Party of America. Social Democrats USA was a fringe leftist party that took hawkish positions on foreign policy, including support for the Vietnam War, and were derided as "State Department socialists" by antiwar leftists.[3] It was within this context that the neoconservatives entered the conservative movement.

The development of the neoconservative movement began in the late 1960s and early 1970s in response to the rise of the New Left, the anti–Vietnam War and Black Power movements, and the counterculture. The early neoconservatives were left-wing anti-Communists and Cold War liberals who maintained their support for the New Deal and the civil rights movement. However, some neoconservative intellectuals expressed skepticism of the expansion of the welfare state through the Great Society programs of the Johnson administration, having been influenced by Daniel Patrick Moynihan's arguments that the welfare state would have the effect of expanding the African American underclass. Yet it was the pol-

itics of the New Left to which the neoconservatives expressed their greatest opposition. The neoconservatives objected to the New Left's largely pacifist stance
on the Cold War and frequent support for Third World Marxist regimes such as
Cuba and North Vietnam.[4]

The neoconservatives were staunch Zionists and regarded American power as
a critical protector of Israel. The New Left's growing anti-Zionism and support
for the Palestinians were particularly alarming to the neoconservatives. The perceived anti-Semitism of some figures in the Black Power movement offended the
neoconservatives as well. The neoconservatives also felt that the positions embraced by liberals in the 1960s and 1970s concerning social issues such as school
prayer, abortion, crime, and homosexual rights were alienating liberals from the
majority of American voters. The entry of the New Left into the Democratic Party
and the subsequent nomination of George McGovern as the party's presidential
candidate in 1972 had the effect of alienating the neoconservatives from the party.
During the 1970s, the neoconservatives began drifting toward the Republican
Party, embedding themselves in conservative think tanks such as the Heritage
Foundation and the American Enterprise Institute, and eventually offering support to the presidential campaign of Ronald Reagan in 1980.[5]

The Bradford affair occurred very early in the Reagan administration, and the
incident's primary significance is its foreshadowing of what was to come. During
the course of the next two decades, the neoconservatives would gradually become
the undisputed intellectual leadership of the "conservative movement" and, by extension, the Republican Party. The neoconservatives managed to achieve this
hegemony through a combination of utter ruthlessness, opportunism, and continuing to embed themselves into leadership positions in key conservative
foundations, think tanks, activist organizations, and media outlets. Similarly, the
neoconservatives came to dominate the Republican Party by embedding themselves in the staffs of key Republican politicians, the party apparatus itself, and
various federal bureaucracies during Republican presidential administrations.
Because of their hawkish foreign policy views, the neoconservatives were able to
gain the financial support of corporate interests connected to the armaments industry. And because of their support for economic policies favorable to the interests of the corporate class, the neoconservatives were able to gain influence
among corporate-sponsored political action committees. The steadfast Zionism
of the neoconservatives ensured them the support of the Israel lobby, and their
mutual support for Israel also allowed the mostly secular Jewish neoconservatives
to form an alliance with the Christian Zionists of the religious Right. The faux
social conservatism of the neoconservatives also helped cement their relationship
with the Christian Right generally. Perhaps the most enduring legacy of the neoconservatives has been their influence over the foreign policy of the George W. Bush

administration. As Senator Chuck Hagel noted, "So why did we invade Iraq? I believe it was the triumph of the so-called neo-conservative ideology, as well as Bush administration arrogance and incompetence that took America into this war of choice."[6]

One of the enduring consistencies of the neoconservatives throughout the course of their historical trajectory has been their unremitting hostility to what might broadly be called the "traditional Right." In particular, the neoconservatives have been zealous to exclude from the mainstream Right those whom they consider to be insufficiently cosmopolitan and egalitarian, or whom they suspect of being overly traditional, ethnocentric, parochial, or provincial. Like their supposed counterparts on the left, the neoconservatives have persistently raised cries of racism, anti-Semitism, and xenophobia when attacking their opponents on the right.

Foreign policy has always been the principal obsession of the neoconservatives, and the neoconservatives have consistently positioned themselves as the most aggressively interventionist element in American politics. Nothing raises the ire of the neoconservatives as much as those whom they suspect of having tendencies toward "isolationism." However, what the neoconservatives label as "isolationism" essentially amounts to the authentically conservative view that foreign policy should serve the best interests of the nation while being conducted in a way that is restrained, prudent, and realistic. Clearly, a recognition of the pitfalls of foreign policy adventurism conflicts with the zeal for "global democratic revolution" exhibited by the neoconservatives. A former assistant secretary of the Treasury during the Reagan administration, Paul Craig Roberts, has described the foreign policy views of the neoconservatives as emanating from the fanaticism that emerged during the French Revolution, observing "there is nothing conservative about neoconservatives. Neocons hide behind 'conservative' but they are in fact Jacobins. Jacobins were the 18th century French revolutionaries whose intention to remake Europe in revolutionary France's image launched the Napoleonic Wars."[7]

A similar critique of the neoconservatives has been offered by the conservative scholar Claes Ryn.[8] The ongoing project of the neoconservatives has been to purge from the American Right any tendency that is suspected of opposing aggressive military interventionism, the revolutionary spread of "democratic capitalism" on an international level, the geopolitical agenda of Israel's Likud Party, or the cultural values of urban cosmopolitanism. Meanwhile, the neoconservatives will make common cause with anyone on the left they deem aggressively militarist enough. This is demonstrated by the ease with which the neoconservatives will concede virtually any other issue that is normally associated with "the conservative movement" to the left-wing opposition such as immigration, gay marriage, abortion, fiscal policy, the welfare state, education, racial quotas, affirmative action, international aid, and countless other compromises. Indeed, a favorite tactic of the neoconservatives has been to adopt liberal and left-wing icons, ranging from Presidents Roosevelt, Truman, and Kennedy to civil rights leaders such as Rev. Martin Luther King Jr., as supposed exemplars of conservative values. A favorite tactic that has been adopted by the neoconservatives has been to attempt to appeal to racial minorities and liberal advocates of civil rights by claiming that "Democrats are the real racists." This claim is supposedly evidenced by the granting of emancipation by Lincoln, the first Republican president, and the support for segregation offered by New Deal Democrats in the South such as George Wallace.

When Ronald Reagan was elected to the presidency in 1980, his first choice for the leadership of the NEH was Melvin E. "Mel" Bradford, a literary critic and legal scholar who had held an academic post as a professor of literature at the University of Dallas since 1967. He was a personal acquaintance of Reagan's and had worked in Reagan's presidential campaign. In many ways, Bradford seemed to be an ideal choice for such a position. His work was admired by leading conservative intellectuals such as Russell Kirk, and political figures such as Senators John East and Jesse Helms. Professor Bradford was a native Texan, born in Fort Worth in 1934. After receiving undergraduate and graduate degrees in English from the University of Oklahoma, Bradford received his doctorate from Vanderbilt University under the tutelage of Professor Donald Davidson, a scholar well known for his contribution to the works of the Southern Agrarians and Fugitive Poets.

Bradford built his reputation as a student of William Faulkner. Bradford emphasized the importance of Southern culture and community to understanding Faulkner's work. As a legal scholar, Bradford was an advocate of a "strict constructionist" approach to interpreting the Constitution, his view of the American founding as a conservative revolution, and his defense of the South against what he considered to be the usurpations of state sovereignty by President Lincoln during the Civil War. Aside from his lengthy tenure at the University of Dallas, Professor Bradford also taught at the United States Naval Academy and Northwestern State University of Louisiana. He was also a highly prolific writer and contributed to such publications as *Modern Age*, *Chronicles*, and *Southern Partisan*. Before supporting Reagan's presidential campaigns in 1976 and 1980, Bradford had been a supporter of former Alabama governor George C. Wallace in 1968 and 1972.

It was his previous support for Wallace and his critical view of Lincoln that earned Bradford the ire of the neoconservatives. When Bradford was first selected by Reagan to head the NEH, his nomination was supported by a wide range of influential conservatives including Senators East and Helms, the newly elected senator John Tower from Texas, veteran senator Strom Thurmond of South Carolina, Utah senator Orrin Hatch, former prisoner of war and senator from Alabama Jeremiah Denton, newly elected senator from Indiana and future vice president Daniel Quayle, Idaho senator James A. McClure, and numerous other Republican political figures. Additionally, Bradford's nomination was supported by leading conservative intellectuals and writers such as Russell Kirk, William F. Buckley, Gerhart Niemeyer, M. Stanton Evans, Jeffrey Hart, Andrew Lytle, and Harry Jaffa. Indeed, Jaffa was a long-standing and strident critic of Bradford's views on Lincoln but admired his character and scholarship, and considered his nomination to be appropriate. Many other conservative voices supported Bradford as well.

However, Bradford's nomination was vociferously opposed by the neoconservatives who were then a rising force in the conservative movement and in Republican political circles generally. The neoconservatives had entered into the conservative movement in the 1970s after having previously been associated with the Far Left wing of the Democratic Party in the 1960s. The neoconservatives abandoned the Democrats after the entry of the New Left into the party during the era of George McGovern's campaign for the presidency in 1972. Among the prominent neoconservatives who expressed opposition to Bradford were Irving Kristol, a former Trotskyite and the coeditor of the *Public Interest*, who is credited with having coined the term "neoconservative." The neoconservative movement's other leading intellectual, Norman Podhoretz, another former leftist and the publisher of *Commentary* magazine, also expressed opposition to Bradford's nomination. Other critical voices included Irving Kristol's son William, a future Fox News commentator; former Treasury secretary William E. Simon, a leading business conservative; and the philanthropist Michael Joyce of the Bradley Foundation.

The neoconservative choice to head the NEH was William J. Bennett, a Democrat, who would later become prominent in Republican politics as secretary of education under Reagan and director of the Office of National Drug Control Policy under President George H. W. Bush. At the time he gained support from the neoconservatives to head the NEH, Bennett was the director of the National Humanities Center, a private research organization located in North Carolina. Bennett had not been a supporter of the Reagan campaign and had voted in the Democratic primaries in 1980. Indeed, Bennett would not change his party affiliation from the Democratic Party to the Republican Party until 1986, after he had become Reagan's secretary of education. Bennett was touted by the neoconservatives as an accomplished intellectual. However, a copy of his doctoral thesis obtained some years later by the conservative scholars Paul Gottfried and Samuel Francis revealed a work that was only barely over a hundred pages (drastically short for a PhD dissertation), with limited source citations and numerous grammatical errors.

A crucial event in the battle over M. E. Bradford's nomination to head the NEH, and the subsequent replacement of Bradford by Bennett, was a column by George Will that appeared in the *Washington Post* on November 29, 1981. It described Bradford as "the nostalgic Confederate remnant of the conservative movement," thereby implying that Bradford was a racist and a likely apologist for slavery. Bradford's friend Fr. James Lehrberger, a colleague on the faculty of the University of Dallas, recalls his discussion of the Will column with Bradford. Lehrberger noted, "We only spoke once about the NEH episode. On that occasion I asked him about George Will's November 29, 1981 column which virtually accused him of being an apologist for slavery." Lehrberger stated Bradford claimed "Will had quoted his words out of context in order to make him look as though he favored slavery. Mel, of course, hated slavery. However, he stated that too many had failed to recognize the southern states' dilemma." Lehrberger related that in Bradford's view the South was simply in an impossible situation, and that Bradford planned to offer a response to Will.[9]

Although George Will's column, titled "A Shrill Assault on Mr. Lincoln," appeared more than two weeks after Reagan had already replaced Bradford with Bennett for the NEH nomination, Will's characterization of Bradford was consistent with the neoconservative line. Will's column claimed, "The rare occasions when Republicans wrestle with intellectual matters make one wish the occasions were even rarer. Consider what occurred in the process of selecting a new head for the National Endowment for the Humanities." Expressing outrage over the Bradford nomination, Will stated, "Some Republicans promoted the candidacy of a professor who believes that the first Republican president was unbalanced, evil and a national disaster. This provoked those, like me, who revere Lincoln and still smolder with indignation about the Kansas-Nebraska Act of 1854." He lambasted Bradford as a figure who "supported George Wallace's 1972 presidential campaign and represents the Nostalgic Confederate remnant in the conservative movement." Claiming Bradford would be a political liability to the Republicans, Will stated, "The nomination of Bradford would be a Christmas present to the Democratic Party, and evidence of Republican philistinism—indifference toward the Republican past and today's culture." Will implied that Bradford was a slavery apologist by stating, "To the South then (and, I gather, Bradford today) the issue was whether the federal government could constitutionally legislate morality regarding conduct (such as slavery) that was, in Bradford's words, 'not covered by the original federal covenant,' the Constitution."[10]

Bradford penned a response to Will that was published in the *Washington Post* on December 12, 1981, which was titled "It's George Will Who's Being Shrill." In his response, Bradford offered a brief defense of his scholarly work pertaining to the North-South conflict and the legacy of Lincoln.

Bradford noted that his work had been influenced by the previous insights of reputable scholars such as "Edgar Lee Masters, Donald W. Riddle, Willmoore Kendall, Edmund Wilson, Gottfried Dietze and Will's one-time editor, the late Frank Meyer." He pointed out that the focus of his scholarship had been on Lincoln's rhetoric, militarism, corruption within his administration, and the repression of his political opponents in the North. He also criticized Lincoln for having a grandiose vision of himself as a manifestation of divine will, noting similar characteristics among figures such as Napoleon, Lenin, and Hitler, and for a seeming indifference to the unnecessary waste of lives during the course of the war effort.[11]

Bradford's response to Will likewise serves as evidence of Bradford's magnanimous character. Bradford began the piece by congratulating Bennett on his appointment to the NEH, and with a defense of his own colleagues and supporters, claiming that Will had "grounded his perfervid assault on my supporters in the charge that no proper Republican could possibly tolerate an appointment in the Reagan administration of a scholar with my view of the American past." He stated that it was not his intention "to complain of the unseemliness of the advantage he has taken of a private person no longer involved in any public question," but insisted that he was "obliged to make some answer to his post hoc fusillade."[12]

Indeed, the magnanimity that Bradford displayed during and after the course of this episode was consistent. His friend and colleague Thomas H. Landess related that "in 1981, a Washington supporter suggested that we do the same kind of hatchet job on Bennett—who, to our knowledge, had behaved well throughout the struggle and had never engaged in Bradford bashing. Mel vetoed the idea. In the end, he agreed with Will Rogers, who said, 'I'd rather be the man who bought the Brooklyn Bridge than the man who sold it.'"[13] In 1993, toward the end of his life and shortly before his death following emergency heart surgery, Bradford remarked to Landess during their final telephone conversation, "If I go out tomorrow, I'll go without any bitterness in my heart. I'm at peace with everybody."[14]

Indeed, perhaps one of the most telling aspects of this episode is the ruthlessness with which the neoconservatives attacked Bradford in their attempts to portray him as a cranky buffoon who was nostalgic for the retrograde past of the American South, and a moral reprobate who did not appreciate the evil of slavery. David Gordon, a veteran libertarian scholar and personal acquaintance of Bradford's, points to what the neoconservatives really found troubling about Bradford, and the lengths they would go to oppose his nomination in the process. In the view of Kristol, Podhoretz, and their cohorts, Bradford was a "Southerner who stressed localism," and such a perspective was unforgivable to the neoconservatives. Gordon points out how the neoconservatives "did not confine themselves to magnifying the paltry virtues of their favorite" choice for the nomination in the person of William Bennett, "but launched smears against the president's choice, dredging up Bradford's 1972 support for George Wallace and—the issue that they stressed interminably—his criticism of Abraham Lincoln. Their efforts to portray Bradford as some latter-day Theodore Bilbo, however unwarranted, proved effective."[15]

Thomas Landess has described the range of underhanded tactics utilized by the neoconservatives in their attacks on Bradford. Among these tactics were incidents such as calling the English Department at the University of Dallas on multiple occasions and asking the secretary for negative information or gossip about Bradford.[16] Of course, in the ensuing decades the neoconservatives have consistently denied that they ever pursued an orchestrated campaign against M. E. Bradford. An illustration of this denial is provided by David Frum, a Yale undergraduate at the time of the Bradford affair who would later become famous as a neoconservative polemicist, political speech writer, and author of books with such titles as *An End to Evil*. It was also Frum who wrote the anti-paleoconservative screed "Unpatriotic Conservatives" in the pages of *National Review* in 2003 upon the commencement of the Iraq War.[17] The piece was a polemic against those on the right who had voiced criticism of the war as unnecessary, or expressed skepticism as to whether the war would have a beneficent outcome. In his own discussion of the Bradford affair, Frum offered the neoconservative rendition of how these events transpired: "But as the paleos themselves tell the story, the quarrel that erupted . . . began as a squabble over jobs and perks in the Reagan Administration—from the perception that, as [Sam] Francis later put it, neoconservatives had arranged matters so that 'their team should get the rewards of office and of patronage and that the older team of the older Right receive virtually nothing.'"[18] Frum repeated the accusations that had been made against Bradford concerning his support for George Wallace in the 1972 election and his criticism of Lincoln in his scholarly work. Yet it is not unreasonable to assume that the neoconservatives' problem with Bradford was rooted in motivations other than his criticisms of Lincoln and his previous support for Wallace. After all, it was Norman Podhoretz who in 1963 penned an essay titled "My Negro Problem—and Ours," where he describes his general dislike for African Americans.[19] Indeed, one is left wondering why Podhoretz would even be upset by Bradford's taking Lincoln to task over constitutional questions given his comments elsewhere.[20] Podhoretz once remarked to Gore Vidal concerning Vidal's intention to write a play about the U.S. Civil War: "Why are you writing a play about, of all things, the Civil War?" Vidal went on to subsequently explain that the Civil War was "the great, single tragic event that gives resonance to our Republic." To Vidal's explanation

Podhoretz replied, "To me, the Civil War is as remote and irrelevant as the War of the Roses."[21] Certainly, this is not the kind of comment one would expect from a Lincoln admirer.

Certain insights concerning the neoconservatives' real motivation for their antipathy to Bradford were offered, albeit indirectly, by the Marxist historian Eric Foner in a February 13, 1982, article for the *New York Times* titled "Lincoln, Bradford, and the Conservatives." Foner described how competition for grants from the NEH was just as likely a motivation for the opposition to Bradford as his former support for Wallace, noting " their real complaint was his pledge to distribute more N.E.H. grants to Texas and Oklahoma and fewer to prestigious Northeastern universities, where many neo-conservatives hold sway."[22]

Further, Foner pointed out that Bradford's sympathy for local autonomy, states' rights, and constitutional federalism conflicted with the "big government" (and strongly interventionist on foreign policy) agenda of the neoconservatives and their allies among the corporate class, the military-industrial complex, and the then-nascent "religious right." As Foner recognized, "If Mr. Bradford exalts the Old South as an organic community untouched by the individualism and unfettered capitalism of the North, what of the celebration of free-market values among the aggressive Sun Belt entrepreneurs and supply-side ideologues who surround President Reagan?"[23]

In other words, Bradford's real sins in the eyes of the neoconservatives were his views on the relationship between the Constitution and states' rights, and his respect for America's unique and organic regional identities such as traditional Southern heritage. The neoconservatives' efforts to derail Bradford's nomination to the NEH were no doubt motivated in part by a combination of northeastern parochialism and mere greed for grants distributed by the agency, as Foner observed. However, the zeal and ruthlessness displayed by the neoconservatives in their attacks on Bradford are illustrative of a fundamental conflict of visions.

The M. E. Bradford affair was the first incident where the neoconservatives were able to establish a position for themselves in the conservative movement and Republican politics by aggressively attacking and slandering an accomplished scholar, and by promoting someone who was much less accomplished in his scholarship in his place. The Bradford incident foreshadowed the decades-long neoconservative practice of promoting ideological loyalists over actual scholars. Bennett would subsequently hold several high-level posts in Republican administrations, becoming a conservative movement celebrity in the process. Bennett cultivated a reputation for himself as a champion of the classical virtues and was once even considered potential presidential material.[24] However, a comparison of the published work of Bennett and Bradford reveals that Bradford was by far the more accomplished of the two potential choices to head the NEH. While

Bradford was a recognized scholar and the author of numerous scholarly books and had been published in multiple academic journals, Bennett's published writing has largely been limited to popular works intended for lay-level "conservative movement" audiences and columns in the movement's in-house publications. Such is the legacy of the neoconservatives' successful effort to derail the nomination of M. E. Bradford to head the NEH, an incident that provided a glimmer of things to come.

3

THE TORY RIGHT AND THE AMERICAN CONSERVATIVE MOVEMENT

Parallel Universes?

Grant Havers

Since the Cold War era, some prominent voices of the American conservative movement have portrayed their cause as a noble continuation of the traditional English conservatism that Edmund Burke or Benjamin Disraeli defended in an earlier era. In this chapter, I show that these claims are not tenable. My discussion of the Canadian Tory philosopher George Grant demonstrates that there is a wide gap between the post–World War II conservative valorization of capitalist democracy and the inveterate conservative suspicion of this late modern system. I also contend that, unlike traditional Tories, the advocates of "democratic capitalism" as the best system for every society stand for liberal globalization rather than a conservative defense of particularity and organic social relations. Most tellingly, post–World War II conservatives have often ignored how state capitalism, the alliance of big government and big business, has historically undermined the cause of conservatism.

George Grant and the Meaning of Conservatism in North America

When George Grant wrote his most famous book, *Lament for a Nation: The Defeat of Canadian Nationalism*, the future of conservatism was in doubt on both sides of the North American border. In the United States, the Republican Party was still reeling from its colossal defeat at the hands of Lyndon B. Johnson's Democrats in the 1964 election. In Canada, the Conservative government led by Prime

Minister John Diefenbaker had narrowly lost its grip on power in 1963 to the Liberal Party, which had received the support of the Kennedy administration. *Lament* was published in 1965, at a time when the liberal consensus in America was very solid. With a Democratic majority in Congress, LBJ was starting to push through comprehensive legislation in support of his Great Society social programs as well as plans to escalate America's involvement in the Vietnam conflict. Popular opposition to this twofold social engineering at home and abroad had not yet materialized. Most Republicans offered only tepid opposition to LBJ's social programs while they enthusiastically supported the bombing of North Vietnam. It seemed that liberalism had triumphed over conservatism in America.

Grant emphasized the meaning of this triumph closer to home. The weakness of conservatism and what it meant for the survival of his country was the central theme of *Lament*. As a Canadian with deep ancestral roots in the Loyalist opposition to the American Revolution, Grant eloquently articulated the precarious nature of conservatism in the modern age. "The impossibility of conservatism in our era is the impossibility of Canada. As Canadians we attempted a ridiculous task in trying to build a conservative nation in the age of progress, on a continent we share with the most dynamic nation on earth. The current of modern history was against us."[1] According to Grant, true conservatism had to oppose "progress." More specifically, conservatives were supposed to resist liberalism, the political philosophy most devoted to progressivist political aims. The mind-set of Grant, which had deep roots in the High Tory tradition of Richard Hooker, Jonathan Swift, and Samuel Coleridge, stressed the preservation of tradition, organic social relations, and historical particularity,[2] or what Grant liked to call "love of one's own."[3] In contrast, liberal progressivism demanded the universal dissemination of "freedom" and "equality" at the cost of traditional attachments to one's hearth and home. In practice, capitalism was the means for accomplishing this ambitious goal, which, as Karl Marx argued, demolishes all traditions that interfere with the relentless expansion of the market economy. As Grant noted throughout *Lament*, once Canada's corporate elites had embraced the new American empire of the twentieth century, after severing their ties to the obsolete English imperium, the fate of the country's traditions and autonomy was effectively sealed.

For all these reasons, Grant doubted that American conservatism was a bulwark against the antitraditional forces of progress. The defeat of Barry Goldwater's Republicans in the 1964 election had demonstrated to Grant that the conservatism south of the Canadian border was too modernist in origins and assumptions to mount an effective resistance against liberalism. In fact, American conservatism, unlike Anglo-Canadian Toryism, was simply the older version of liberalism.

The Americans who call themselves "Conservatives" have the right to the title only in a particular sense. They stand for the freedom of the individual to use his property as he wishes, and for a limited government which must keep out of the marketplace. Their concentration on freedom from governmental interference has more to do with nineteenth-century liberalism than with traditional conservatism, which asserts the right of the community to restrain freedom in the name of the common good. . . . The founders of the United States took their thoughts from the eighteenth-century Enlightenment. Their rallying cry was "freedom." There was no place in their cry for the organic conservatism that predated the age of progress. Indeed, the United States is the only society on earth that has no traditions from before the age of progress. Their "right-wing" and "left-wing" are just different species of liberalism. "Freedom" was the slogan of both Goldwater and President Johnson.[4]

The fact that the Republicans under Richard Nixon returned to power in the 1968 election due to widespread discontent over Johnson's mismanagement of the Vietnam War, race relations, and the Great Society programs did not convince Grant that conservatism was making a comeback in America. In a new preface to *Lament*, which he wrote in 1970, Grant observed that no true ideological shift had taken place among the elites who controlled the centers of power in America. Rather, the "dominant classes" had to "content themselves with the clearer, if grimmer, technocratic skill of Mr. Nixon, and even with the direct bourgeois self-defence of Mr. Agnew and Mr. Mitchell."[5] Meanwhile, in Canada, people were still "quite proud of our 'show-biz' technocrat, Pierre Trudeau, in Ottawa, when the U. S. can no longer afford that luxury."[6] Even so, liberal progressivism on both sides of the border was facing little threat from the conservative side of the spectrum.

Grant's surgical distinction between Anglo-Canadian Toryism and American conservatism has encouraged a great deal of debate. Some admiring readers have argued that Grant's political philosophy is evidence for what Louis Hartz called the "Tory touch." Hartz argued that the Loyalists' breakaway from America constituted a "fragment" of traditional conservatism that repudiated America's rugged individualism.[7] Gad Horowitz elaborated on Hartz's thesis by arguing that Grant's political philosophy was an articulate defense of this tradition.[8] However, Grant has also had his critics, some of whom contend that he failed to provide an accurate picture of conservatism on both sides of the border. In particular, Grant's claim that America lacks a true conservative tradition has provoked considerable disagreement. Barry Cooper contends that Grant did not sufficiently recognize the liberal or Whiggish roots of Canadian conservatism that it shares with its

American cousin.[9] In fairness, Grant often acknowledged in *Lament* that Canada eventually embraced a Whiggish tradition that transformed conservatism at the expense of its Tory roots. This version of English liberalism had already triumphed in Britain by the time that the older conservatism "was inherited by Canadians."[10] Yet this admission has not satisfied critics who insist that the conservative tradition in Canada has *never* been independent of classical liberalism.[11]

These criticisms of Grant's conservatism have merit. There has always been considerable debate over the extent to which the Loyalists who were forced to flee revolutionary America still adhered to Whiggish views on politics. Many of these refugees retained liberal views of self-government, albeit ones that were often tinged with the resentment of defeat and expulsion at the hands of the Yankee revolutionaries.[12] These Loyalists also used John Locke's liberalism to their own advantage. Thomas Hutchinson, the Loyalist governor of Massachusetts, noted in his famous "Dialogue between an American and a European Englishman" (1768) that both sides to the growing conflict in the American colonies cited Locke in defense of their opposing positions.[13] As Bernard Bailyn observed, "Both speakers cite Locke (accurately) to defend their positions."[14] The American's position on the right to disobey unjust laws and the European Englishman's position on the need to obey laws in order to preserve order were equally Lockean. In other words, precious little distinguished Canadian conservatism from its American cousin precisely because they both heralded from the same English tradition of liberalism.[15] Moreover, Canada's political system, despite its Anglo-French roots, was not intended to conserve this dual heritage. Rather, the intent of the Fathers of Confederation was to build a liberal regime that welcomed all peoples, regardless of tradition, identity, or heritage.[16] In short, Grant, according to Cooper, was not "engaging in political analysis." Rather, he was "evoking a political idea or myth" of a Loyalist Canada that never existed.[17]

In fairness to Grant, he never denied that there were some liberal elements within the Loyalist tradition. He even remarked, in *Technology and Empire*, that the most educated Loyalists were "straight Locke with a dash of Anglicanism."[18] Still, he quickly added that these men also had the "desire to build a political society with a clearer and firmer doctrine of the common good than that at the heart of the liberal democracy to the south."[19] In *Lament*, Grant admitted that these gentlemen lacked a concrete political philosophy. The "British conservatism," which was their source of inspiration, "is difficult to describe because it is less a clear view of existence than an appeal to an ill-defined past. The writings of Edmund Burke are evidence of this."[20] Nevertheless, he insisted that many Loyalists truly possessed "an inchoate desire to build, in these cold and forbidding regions, a society with a greater sense of order and restraint than freedom-loving republicanism would allow."[21] Grant posed the provocative question: "If Lockian liberalism is the conservatism of the English-speaking peoples, what was there in British conservatism that was not present in the bourgeois thought of Hamilton and Madison? If there was nothing, then the acts of the Loyalists are deprived of all moral significance."[22] More pointedly, he asked: "If there was nothing valuable in the founders of English-speaking Canada, what makes it valuable for Canadians to continue as a nation today?"[23]

It is unduly harsh to dismiss these sentiments as merely expressions of a mythical consciousness or the historical resentment of the defeated. As the American historian Claude H. Van Tyne ably documented in his study *The Loyalists in the American Revolution* (1902), many Tories or Loyalists were "honestly aghast" at the fact that their fellow Americans could embrace the abstract or self-evident truths of the Declaration of Independence over and against the weight of historical experience as well as the benefits of British rule.[24]

What, however, is this "doctrine of the common good" that, Grant insisted, lies at the heart of the Tory mind? For the remainder of this chapter, I argue that what truly distinguishes Grant's Toryism from the current understanding of conservatism in America today is his critique of democratic capitalism. This system, which has enjoyed broad support within the American conservative movement since the Cold War, never truly inspired the traditional conservative mind, as Grant understood it. Edmund Burke, in *Reflections on the Revolution in France* (1790), famously took aim at the "sophisters, oeconomists, and calculators" who replaced the "age of chivalry" with the age of self-interest and economic man.[25] Furthermore, he repudiated the bourgeois view of the state that reduced it to "nothing better than a partnership agreement in a trade of pepper and coffee, calico or tobacco, or some other such low concern, to be taken up for a little temporary interest, and to be dissolved by the fancy of the parties."[26]

These sentiments were not entirely mythical or romantic in substance. The class conflict between the landed aristocrats and the nascent bourgeoisie in nineteenth-century England sheds some light on the history of Anglo-Canadian conservative misgivings over capitalism. Even though the Tory landowners did not see the agricultural proletariat as their equals within the class hierarchy, they both made common cause against the bourgeoisie's campaign for free trade and the repeal of the Corn Laws that had benefited both the aristocracy and farm labor (although these laws also kept the price of food artificially high). One should be cautious about understating the self-interest that motivated this alliance. Still, Oswald Spengler was unduly dismissive of the differences between English conservatives and liberals when he regarded business "in the piratical sense" as "the sum and substance of this politics, no matter whether Tories or Whigs are the bosses at any given moment."[27] Russell Kirk in a similar vein erroneously claimed that "the domestic quarrel between Old Tory and Old Whig shrank into insignificance" with the end of the French Revolution and the Jacobite rebellion.[28] Neither Spengler nor Kirk devoted sufficient attention to historical evidence that pointed to the English Tory suspicion of the ascendant bourgeoisie. The Marxist historian E. P. Thompson argued, in his classic study *The Making of the English Working Class* (1963), that the English proletarian and petit-bourgeois belief in a Tory elite that would protect their interests from the rising moneyed classes was very real in the late eighteenth and early nineteenth centuries. Although Thompson admitted that the "paternalist" legislation that flowed out of this elite group was often "restrictive" and "punitive" in its effect on the working classes,

> there was within it the shadowy image of a benevolent corporate state, in which there were legislative as well as moral sanctions against the unscrupulous manufacturer or the unjust employer, and in which the journeymen were a recognized 'estate', however low, in the realm.... The function of industry was to provide a livelihood for those employed in it; and practices or inventions evidently destructive of the good of the 'Trade' were reprehensible. The journeyman took pride in his craft, not merely because it increased his value in the labour market, but because he was a craftsman. These ideals may never have been much more than ideals; by the end of the eighteenth century they may have been threadbare. But they had a powerful reality, none the less, in the notion of what *ought* to be, to which artisans, journeymen, and many small masters appealed.[29]

Even if protectionist measures (e.g., a minimum wage law, passed in 1773) were eventually swept away by the tide of industrialization in the early nineteenth century,[30] there was a lingering sense of noblesse oblige among some English Tories that the state should benevolently care for the laboring classes.[31]

It may seem odd to quote a Marxist historian in a chapter devoted to an exegesis of the Tory mind. However, it is noteworthy that Grant admired certain features of the Marxist approach to history and politics that provided insight into the hegemonic power of the capitalist system.[32] Grant and other Tories have drawn on a rich body of historical evidence that supports their vision of a "common good" conservatism. Most famously, Benjamin Disraeli's call for "One Nation Conservatism" and Randolph Churchill's dream of "Tory Democracy" built on the assumption that the English aristocracy and working class were natural allies, even if they were not natural equals. Grant particularly admired Disraeli, who belonged to a conservative tradition "that has decayed in Canada before the ravages of capitalist liberalism."[33] In the words of Ron Dart, the "literary and political conservatism of Disraeli, as Grant was obviously aware, was about a concern for the poor and marginalized, and the use of the state and society to minimize glaring social injustices."[34] To this day, "Red" Tories who are suspicious of capitalism dream of restoring Disraeli's alliance between their party and the English working class.[35]

As a twentieth-century Anglican Christian, Grant was far more egalitarian than these Tory luminaries from the previous century. It is hard to imagine even Disraeli uttering these words: "Equality should be the central principle of society since all persons, whatever their condition, must freely choose to live by what is right or wrong."[36] Perhaps for this reason, Grant never forcefully defended the notion of a class hierarchy per se, even if he sometimes admired how the English aristocracy had produced men of quality such as William Gladstone and Disraeli, whose "level of education and character" had no equivalent amid the "undiluted triumph of capitalist democracy" in the modern age.[37] In short, Grant retained a Tory skepticism toward the ascendant capitalist class. Once again, a society based on "order and restraint" rather than "freedom-loving republicanism" was the Loyalist dream.[38] Yet it is hard for this conservative vision to survive in the age of capitalist modernity. From Grant's jaded perspective, liberalism and capitalism fit like hand and glove in their shared hostility to tradition and national identity. "Liberalism is the fitting ideology for a society directed toward these ends. It denies unequivocally that there are any given restraints that might hinder pursuit of dynamic dominance."[39] Moreover, the corporate elites of Canada "lost nothing essential to the principle of their lives in losing their country. It is this very fact that has made capitalism the great solvent of all tradition in the modern era. When everything is made relative to profit-making, all traditions of virtue are dissolved, including that aspect of virtue known as love of country. That is why liberalism is the perfect ideology for capitalism."[40]

The 1964 presidential election in the United States had demonstrated to Grant that the liberal establishment and corporate power were joined at the hip. At least since the New Deal era, big business in America had accepted and even welcomed the new managerial state. This fact was lost on the Goldwater Republicans:

> The clobbering of Goldwater at the polls in November of 1964 shows how little the American people cared about the early liberalism of their Founders. Johnson's "Great Society" expressed the new American "freedom" far better than Goldwater's talk of limited government and free enterprise. The majority tradition in the United States backs Roosevelt, Kennedy, Johnson, whose liberalism is the most modern. The older liberalism of the Constitution had its swan song in the election of 1964. The classes that had once opposed Roosevelt were spent forces by 1964. The leaders of the new capitalism supported Johnson. Goldwater's cry for limited government seemed as antediluvian to the leaders of the

corporations as Diefenbaker's nationalism seemed to the same elements in Canada. . . . The Goldwater camp was outraged by the sustained attack of the television networks and newspaper chains. Were they not aware who had become the American establishment since 1932? Corporation capitalism and liberalism go together by the nature of things. The establishment knew how to defend itself when threatened by the outrageous challenge of outsiders from Arizona. The American election of 1964 is sufficient evidence that the United States is not a conservative society. It is a dynamic empire spearheading the age of progress.[41]

Although Grant thought that his observations on the 1964 election were "platitudinous,"[42] it is hard to find any equivalent ideas within the modern American conservative movement. While there have always been a few American conservatives who have had similar misgivings about capitalism, critiques of its "inner workings" from the American Right have yielded to critiques of big government from the New Deal era onward.[43] As I will show, the post–World War II conservative movement has generally embraced capitalism without any serious ideological difficulty. This adherence to capitalism goes hand in hand with the confident view that the "democratic" version of capitalism that America embodies is a necessary bulwark against the intrusions of the state. What is absent in this movement is adequate recognition of the fact that capitalism and the managerial state have become intertwined since the 1930s. Grant often employed the term "state capitalism" to press the point that big business since the Great Depression has desired and needed the support of the state. Under this system, the state itself is not "capitalist": it does not take on the role of controlling the means of production for profit.[44] Rather, the state leaves the private ownership of capital untouched for the most part while providing crucial support for the moneyed interests. This support includes the maintenance of social order in times of economic distress, subsidies for major industries, and the dissemination of propaganda that legitimizes the system.[45]

While Grant supported the old Tory idea of a benevolent state that protects the poor, he was dubious about the overall merits of state capitalism, whose defenders also profess compassion for the underprivileged. The progressivist rhetoric that they employed also aroused his suspicions. For all of these reasons, Grant wrote: "State capitalism and liberalism are much more advanced manifestations of the age of progress than the Russian system with its official Marxism."[46] In contrast, the preeminent defenders of American capitalism often make the same mistake as the Goldwater Republicans in assuming that capitalism is still independent of, and opposed to, big government.

To demonstrate the vast divide between Grant's Toryism and postwar American conservatism, I compare and contrast his ideas with those of five famous defenders of the American social order who have had extensive influence on intellectual conservatism in the United States since World War II: Russell Kirk, Frank Meyer, Irving Kristol, Michael Novak, and Allan Bloom.

Russell Kirk's Conflicted Defense of Capitalism

Philosophical defenses of democratic capitalism in America emerged long before the advent of the Reagan era in the 1980s. The antecedents for this worldview are apparent as early as the 1950s. In 1953, Russell Kirk published his classic best seller *The Conservative Mind: From Burke to Eliot*, a work that William F. Buckley praised as "an act of conscious apostleship to a social and historical and philosophical order which is best described as 'conservative.'"[47] In this book, Kirk synthesized the ideas of British and American political philosophers, whose common opposition to modern revolution after 1790 demonstrated, at least to Kirk, a common conservatism. "Only Britain and America, among the great nations, have escaped revolution since 1790, which seems attestation that their conservatism is a steady growth and that investigation of it may be rewarding."[48] Unsurprisingly, then, Kirk devoted extensive attention to the Anglo-Irish parliamentarian and philosopher Edmund Burke, whose sympathy with the American Revolutionaries was the lynchpin of Kirk's thesis that conservatism as a whole is intelligible and desirable to peoples beyond the Anglo-American orbit. "A universal constitution of civilized peoples" was implicit in Burke's thought, after all.[49]

How traditional was this conservatism? Kirk was too careful a reader of Burke to argue, as many neoconservatives later did, that conservatism must embrace ahistorical claims about the desire or ability of all human beings to contrive stable and decent constitutional regimes. He assiduously followed Burke's opposition to "abstraction," or "rather vainglorious generalization without respect for human frailty and the particular circumstance of an age and a nation."[50] For this reason, Kirk devoted several pages of *The Conservative Mind* to debunking the "natural rights" philosophy of Thomas Paine and others, a doctrine that falsely and dangerously downplayed the power of historical circumstances. He writes: "What may be a right on one occasion and for one man, may be unjust folly for another man at a different time."[51] No people had a "natural right" to bring a regime into place by force or violence if they were unready for government, as in the case of the French Jacobins. Even though Kirk's reference to an "eternal natural order which holds all things in their places"[52] conveyed the impression that his conservatism was universally applicable to all human beings, regardless of time or place, he never strayed far from his Burkean conviction that the preconditions for liberty, including religion, moderation, and experience, were far more important than the mere desire for liberty.

As Paul Gottfried has argued in *Conservatism in America: Making Sense of the American Right* (2007), Kirk's discussion of what he takes to be the common core of Anglo-American conservatism is oddly silent on the presence of a liberal tradition in the history of America, before and after the Revolution. Kirk never challenged Louis Hartz's famous thesis that America's primary political tradition was liberal, given the absence of a feudal heritage that characterized English and European climes.[53] I mention this fact because Grant in *Lament* endorsed Hartz's thesis (without actually citing Hartz) that American conservatism was just old-fashioned American liberalism, as we have seen. None of this implies that Grant would have disagreed with Kirk's thesis that the founding of America owes a great debt to English traditions. However, these traditions were liberal or Whiggish, hostile to the premodern traditionalism that, Grant believed, once defined true conservatism. Unlike Kirk, Grant did not attribute to Burke an elaborate political philosophy that clearly outlined what conservatism was. Nor did he conflate English liberalism with true "British conservatism," which was "already a spent force at the beginning of the nineteenth century when English-speaking Canadians were making a nation."[54] The conservatism that Kirk sought to defend was more liberal, in Grant's view, than what most American conservatives (Kirk included) recognized.

In his critique of Kirk, Gottfried exposes a more serious defect of his philosophy that also widens the divide between post–World War II American conservatism and Grant's Toryism. What Nietzsche called a "historical sense," or the need to understand the sheer temporal distance between one's own time and the past, is absent in Kirk's presentation of conservatism. The emphasis on "eternal" truths, a precursor to the universalistic rhetoric of neoconservatism, ignored the fact that the conservatism of the eighteenth century bore little resemblance to the post–World War II republic in which Kirk lived and wrote. The old conservative love of hierarchy, an established church, and ordered liberty seemed to have little place in the America of the 1950s. Gottfried writes: "What brought tears of pride to late eighteenth-century English eyes would not likely do the same for contemporary young urban professionals—or even for their parents who sold insurance, ran laundromats, or repaired TV's."[55] Although Kirk's star gradually waned on the right as the neoconservatives gained greater influence,[56] his optimistic attempt to bridge the historical gap between the colonial era and the America of the 1950s sounds uncannily similar to some neoconservative views that the oldest traditions of America were still viable in the twentieth-century republic. Gertrude Himmelfarb, spouse of the famous neoconservative journalist Irving

Kristol, could write in the early years of the third millennium that the liberal Enlightenment is alive and well, even a "source of inspiration today," in an America dominated by mass corporations and the Leviathan state.[57]

This lack of a historical sense explains the considerable difference between Kirk's and Grant's views on capitalism. This difference should not suggest that Kirk was always an unabashed defender of capitalism, in sharp contrast to Grant's withering critique. In *The Conservative Mind*, Kirk quotes Burke's famous attack on "sophisters, oeconomists, and calculators" who have succeeded the "age of chivalry,"[58] indicating his dislike for a cold-blooded capitalist mentality. He explicitly warned throughout the 1950s that conservatism and capitalism are not the same thing. In his words, "A conservative order is not the creation of the free entrepreneur."[59] Kirk also decried the corporate despoliation of the environment that his fellow conservatives often casually defended as the price of doing business.[60] These comments have led some interpreters to argue that Kirk was at times a serious opponent of capitalism, even though he did not harbor any practical desire to transform the system.[61] The famous left-wing activist Ralph Nader has praised Kirk as a stalwart defender of the environment against the depredations of capitalism.[62]

Nevertheless, these environmentalist concerns are absent in Kirk's later defense of capitalism in the early 1980s. In a published exchange with the American socialist author Michael Harrington in 1982, Kirk lined up with Irving Kristol to give "two cheers for capitalism."[63] Even though capitalism cannot guarantee "human happiness," which would have earned it a third cheer, Kirk emphasized that its twofold achievement of material prosperity for millions of Americans along with the freedom to enjoy unprecedented leisure time abundantly demonstrated that it was far superior to any socialist alternative.[64] Moreover, Kirk was utterly untroubled by the fact that it is up to capitalists to "control the use of capital, whether or not they personally *own* the capital."[65] This separation of ownership from control, which spelled the end of the bourgeois era, was of little importance. As the writings of James Burnham and Samuel T. Francis have made clear, however, this phenomenon explains why the managers of big firms have shown little opposition to the expansion of the managerial state since the New Deal era. If managers do not own their companies' assets, they have no vested interest in protecting them from statist intervention.[66] In short, "state capitalism" becomes an attractive option to big business in this climate.

Kirk, however, refused to believe that there was such a thing as state capitalism in modern America. In his exchange with Harrington, Kirk associated this sort of collusion with the kind of "state socialism" practiced in Sweden.[67] Unlike Grant, Kirk doubted that there was this sort of "unholy alliance of state capitalism and big business" in America.[68] There are two other significant differences between Grant and Kirk in their treatment of state capitalism. In "An Ethic of Community" (1961), Grant describes state capitalism as "more than a practical system for producing and distributing goods; it is also a system of ideas and ideals which determine the character of leadership and inculcates a dominating ethic in our democracy."[69] In contrast, Kirk denied that capitalism in general, whether free market or statist, is a "moral philosophy, or a body of moral habits."[70] Additionally, Grant worried far more than Kirk about the power that big business wielded over the political system and society as a whole. While Grant thought that "passive mediocrity" was a more likely outcome than a "just and creative society" under state capitalism,[71] Kirk was confident that the "free economy" of capitalism would continue to liberate "energies" and "enterprising talents."[72]

It would be unfair to accuse Kirk of completely ignoring just how much capitalism had changed in the twentieth century. He was just as aware as Grant that the "United States is no longer a society of small property owners, but of massive private and public corporations."[73] Kirk worried about the "strong tendency toward consolidation" that threatens "small firms, partnerships, and family enterprises."[74] Yet he refused to attribute this defect to the inner workings of capitalism itself. What he called "this very diminishing of competition" was due to ill-conceived public policies like inheritance taxes and government subsidies that harm small firms while enriching large ones. The reader is left with the impression that big business, in Kirk's view, is a mere bystander, not an agent, of this tendency toward greater statist intervention in the economy.[75]

While Kirk was arguably naive about the reality of state capitalism, he never abandoned his misgivings about the historical transformations that characterized American democracy in the Cold War era. Toward the end of his life, he penned a scorching essay on the likelihood that "Caesarism" would emerge out of American democracy. In particular, Kirk lambasted the dangerous tendency since LBJ toward an imperial presidency that centralizes power in the hands of the executive.[76] In this essay, he exhibited an admirable historical sense about the decay and decline of liberalism in American politics. According to Kirk, even an admirable politician such as Gene McCarthy used the term "liberal" only with the meaning that it had enjoyed since the time of FDR, not its classical version. On this point, Grant and Kirk agreed. In *Lament*, Grant sharply noted that liberalism, once the "voice of the outsider," is "now the voice of the establishment." Moreover, "Harvard liberalism was surely nobler when William James opposed the Spanish American war than when Arthur Schlesinger Jr., advised Kennedy on Cuban policy."[77] Kirk was also far from oblivious to the power of the Kennedys and the Rockefellers in the new liberal America.[78]

What I believe is consistently absent in Kirk's thought, however, is a "root and branch" critique of how political power and corporate power envelop each other in a state capitalist system.[79] As I have noted, Grant doubted that corporations have any reason to oppose the liberalism of the managerial state. Moreover, conservatives who fail to take this fact into account are doomed to irrelevance, in Grant's view. Although Kirk incisively exposed LBJ's Caesarist tendencies, he was silent on how many elements of the corporate establishment prefer a Caesar over a republican.[80] It is unsurprising, then, that Kirk offered no practical ways of reinventing capitalism. All that he could contemplate is the desirability of a "petit-bourgeois" economy that once characterized nineteenth-century America, without citing any measures that could effect this restoration.[81] Unlike Grant, Kirk seemed indifferent to the fact that this vision had no place in the age of state capitalism.[82]

Frank Meyer's Fusionist Conservatism

The post–World War II conservative synthesis of capitalism and traditionalism perhaps received its most ambitious defense in Frank Meyer's concept of "fusionism." According to Meyer, there is no fundamental conflict between freedom and tradition as long as the state does not impose a program of "virtue" or morality on its citizens. This limited form of government allows and protects the freedom of citizens to engage in virtuous activities such as the raising of a family. Any form of government that goes beyond the maintenance of law and order as well as the preservation of liberty and the administration of justice is not only ill suited to preserve virtue but will endanger it.[83] "Freedom, then, is a necessary political condition of a virtuous society, not only because the high likelihood is that the standards imposed by men with the power of the state would not in fact be virtuous standards, but also because, even if they were virtuous, to impose them upon individual persons would immensely reduce their ability to act virtuously at all and absolutely destroy their potentiality for active, creative, positive virtue."[84]

The night-watchman state that Meyer defended is the only hope for the preservation of that most conservative goal, a virtuous society. The "fusion" of freedom and tradition can succeed as long as the state sticks to its legitimate domain of protecting citizens from violence at home and abroad while citizens freely preserve the mores inherited from Christian civilization, including respect for the dignity of the person.[85] Meyer's belief that Americans are still interested in preserving traditional Christian morality would have struck Grant as naive. One of the recurrent themes in his writings is the importance of recognizing how Protestants in the twentieth century "accepted the liberalism of autonomous will" while failing to "provide their societies with the public sustenance of uncalculated justice which the contractual account of justice could not provide from itself."[86]

In Grant's view, the transition from bourgeois Calvinism to democratic liberalism (and hedonism) was a seamless one.[87]

There are important differences between Meyer's idea of fusionism and other versions of American conservatism in the Cold War era. Not all voices on the American Right have been enamored with Meyer's libertarian view of the state, which is prohibited from regulating sexual and social vices. Whatever the differences between Meyer and his critics (including Russell Kirk[88]), however, the lack of an adequate historical sense is just as apparent in the writings of Meyer as it is in those of Kirk. Meyer defended fusionism at a time when mass institutions, both public and private, were already employing their awesome powers of influence and surveillance to shape the consciousness of a democratic citizenry. It is hard to imagine why big business would even welcome this "fusionism" that severely imposed limits on the power of the state.

In fairness, it would be inaccurate to claim that Meyer was totally oblivious to the revolutionary changes that transformed American capitalism since the New Deal. He genuinely lamented the fact that "organization men," the bureaucratic class that had taken over the management of the corporation, had succeeded the old bourgeois elite. "They have no significant personal ownership of the industrial power they control, simply administering vast masses of capital in the name of stockholders, as government bureaucrats administer the state in the name of the 'people.'"[89] This new managerial elite was the product of the separation of management from control that had so fatefully redefined the large capitalist enterprise, as Burnham and Francis have argued. This class of corporate bureaucrats was interchangeable with the bureaucrats of big government who direct a "pliable mass public" to support whatever aims these managers saw as furthering their own interests.[90] Meyer also seemed to share Grant's pessimism when he admitted that a viable middle class that exhibited economic or intellectual independence was practically inconceivable in an age of mass private and public corporations that strove to "engineer the consent" of a "manipulable mass."[91]

Meyer never doubted, however, that his philosophy of fusionism could still push back against these collectivizing tendencies. For this reason, he trained his critical guns on the power of the state, not big business. Although Meyer was second to none in warning against the powers of the Leviathan state, he did not exhibit similar worries over the hegemony of big business, perhaps because he thought, as many postwar conservatives did (e.g., Kirk), that big business owed its hegemony to the expansion of the state since the New Deal era. Big government, in Meyer's view, was at fault for advancing the powers of corporations and trade unions. The "salaried manageriat" that characterized both business and labor was "almost entirely a creation of the years since 1932."[92] It did not occur to Meyer that large elements of the business class welcomed the New Deal or at least preferred it to a return to laissez-faire.

These developments on both sides of the border in North America preoccupied Grant. As he often noted in *Lament*, the last thing that the Canadian business elite wanted was limited government and free market economics. Since the end of World War II, the managerial liberalism of the New Deal, which Prime Minister Mackenzie King had adopted from his friend Franklin D. Roosevelt, was the favored ideology of Canadian big business. Corporations accepted the legitimate role of the state in "postwar reconstruction" as long as the government "never questioned the ultimate authority of business interests to run the economy."[93] The "confusion of populism, free enterprise, and nationalism" that Prime Minister Diefenbaker had offered was utterly unappealing to Canada's business elites.[94] It is hard not to arrive at a similar judgment of Meyer. Why would American big business in the 1960s, which stood to profit from the mass marketing of sexual libertinism in that decade, desire a fusionist society that blended traditionalism with libertarianism? Furthermore, why would corporations want the federal government to stay out of their business if this intervention was profitable to them?[95] As Grant argued, the technological state that capitalists favored encourages a version of freedom that has little time for traditional virtues. The only "pluralism" that liberals favored is the diversity of choices that express the freedom to be a thoughtless consumer of food, sex, and faith. The one proviso is that everyone could express these tastes as long as nobody seriously questions the system that provided this freedom.

> Tastes are different, and we should have a society that caters to the plurality of tastes. How much fairer this would be than the old societies in which standards of virtue were imposed on the masses by pertinacious priests and arrogant philosophers. But this is not what is happening in our state capitalism. In the private sphere, all kinds of tastes are allowed. Nobody minds very much if we prefer women or dogs or boys, as long as we cause no public inconvenience. But in the public sphere, such pluralism of taste is not permitted. The conquest of human and non-human nature becomes the only public value. . . . The vaunted freedom of the individual to choose becomes either the necessity of finding one's role in the public engineering or the necessity of retreating into the privacy of pleasure.[96]

Meyer's desire for a fusion of traditional virtues and capitalism would have likely struck Grant as antediluvian. By the early 1960s, when Meyer was defending this synthesis, big business and many consumers had already left this bourgeois ethos behind.[97]

Irving Kristol's and Michael Novak's Neoconservative Capitalism

The term "state capitalism" does not appear often in the modern American conservative lexicon, except as a phenomenon that is distinctly opposed to "democratic capitalism." As we shall see, defenders of democratic capitalism such as Irving Kristol and Michael Novak conceive of the modern corporation as an entity that is both distinct and separate from that of the state in American democracy. Yet the neoconservatives who support democratic capitalism are also opposed to Meyer's version of libertarian capitalism. As Novak argues in his *Spirit of Democratic Capitalism*, neoconservatives distinguish free market capitalism from democratic capitalism, since the latter is quite compatible with a "vision of social welfare" that requires a more interventionist state than the night-watchman state favored by laissez-faire capitalists.[98] Nevertheless, the state largely leaves the running of the economy to the private sector. Grant, however, believed that this conventional conservative understanding of the separation of big business and big government was as historically obsolete as laissez-faire. In his view, at least since World War II, it has become more difficult to separate the functions of business from the powers of the state, given the increasingly close relation or alliance between these two centers of power.

In his essay "An Ethic of Community," Grant noted how "the most dangerous result of state capitalism is that our society recruits its chief leadership from the executives who have been most successful in living out the capitalist ideal." Grant went on to observe that "the leaders of the great corporations are an overwhelming majority of the members of the governing boards of our universities." This domination of the university was, of course, an expression of great corporate power that had emerged since World War II.[99] "In 1945 the business elite in North America had in their hands the unquestioned leadership of the world." Yet Grant warned that this leadership is now passing "more and more into the hands of a tough communist elite." Part of the problem was the "restricted vision" of business leaders that "could only put up against it [Communism] the motives of corporate and personal greed and the impulses for personal publicity and prestige hunting." Grant concludes on a dark note: "It is, of course, not only the business community in North America which will pay for this failure of leadership, but all free men who care about the traditions of the West."[100]

At first glance, Grant's message looks identical to the neoconservatives' worry that businesspeople lack the imagination or verve to defend their system on the basis of high moral principle. Irving Kristol, in *Two Cheers for Capitalism* (1978), similarly argued that capitalists rely so heavily on the "acquisitive impulse," which has contributed to the prosperity of millions of people, that it is left "practically defenseless" against anticapitalists from the Left who dismiss this impulse as empty in the first place.[101] Unlike Grant, however, Kristol believed that big business is fighting, and losing, the ideological war against its very existence because of its *fundamental weakness* in the mass society that it created. According to Kristol, the "large corporation" is under great pressure to enter the political sphere against its will. He worries that it "is not going to be able to withstand those forces pulling and pushing it into the political sector unless it confronts the reality of its predicament and adapts itself to this reality in a self-preserving way."[102]

Kristol admits that the result of this process that undermines the "private character" of the big firm may well be "state capitalism," but not because corporations actively seek this integration with the state. Like Meyer, Kristol ultimately blames the state or forces external to the corporation. The corporations of the Cold War era faced an unprecedented level of hostility because of historical transformations affecting ownership and control as well as the direction of mass culture. Before the rise of corporate capitalism, the individual entrepreneur who had worked hard to create his wealth commanded the respect of most Americans.

> So long as business was an activity carried on by real individuals who "owned" the property they managed, the politicians, the courts and public opinion were all reasonably respectful of the capitalist proprieties. Not only was the businessman no threat to liberal democracy; he was, on the contrary, the very epitome of the bourgeois liberal-democratic ethos—the man who succeeded by diligence, enterprise, sobriety, and all those other virtues that Benjamin Franklin catalogued for us, and which we loosely call "the Protestant ethic."[103]

Yet the impersonal mass corporation of today exhibits none of these traditional bourgeois Protestant virtues. "Not only don't we know who the Chairman of General Motors is; we know so little about the kind of person who holds such a position that we haven't the faintest idea as to whether or not we want our children to grow up like him."[104] Both Grant and Kristol agree that the modern corporation has little interest or incentive in reviving the old Protestant ethic. Both men clearly doubted that the fusionist synthesis of traditionalism and capitalism, which Meyer most famously advanced, had much of a chance in the hedonist America of the post–World War II era. According to Kristol, the virtues famously embodied by the Horatio Alger myth had little place in modern America. "From having been a *capitalist, republican community,* with shared values and a quite unambiguous claim to the title of a just order, the United States became a *free, democratic society* where the will to success and privilege was severed from its moral moorings."[105] The upshot of this revolution is that "capitalism outgrew its bourgeois origins and became a system for the impersonal liberation and satisfaction of appetites—an engine for the creation of affluence."[106] In a similar vein, Grant re-marked: "In the age of high technology, the new capitalism can allow all passions to flourish along with greed. *Playboy* illustrates the fact that the young executive is not expected to be Horatio Alger."[107] In short, the moral status of the modern corporation is precarious, given its inability to stake out an ethical vision that goes beyond mere calculation.

Because the corporation fails to provide an ethical vision of its purpose, it is unwittingly dragged into the political system. As Kristol argues, the immense po-litical pressure to please different stakeholders and activists leads to an outcome whereby "the large corporation has ceased being a species of private property, and is now a 'quasi-public' institution."[108] This neoconservative critique of the mod-ern firm should not suggest that firms actively desire state capitalism per se, a sys-tem that "does constitute a huge potential threat to the individual liberties Americans have traditionally enjoyed." If state capitalism came into being, it would be due to the failure of the large corporation to "withstand those (politi-cal) forces pulling and pushing it into the political sector."[109] In fact, Kristol and other neoconservatives doubt that there is a special relation between business and the state, as Grant argued. Kristol even dismissed the idea that businesspeople have the power to influence the state. According to Kirk, "Most Americans are now quick to believe that 'big business' conspires secretly but most effectively to ma-nipulate the economic and political system—an enterprise which, in prosaic fact, corporate executives are too distracted and too unimaginative even to contem-plate."[110] Corporations, after all, have more interest in making money than bend-ing society or the state to their will. Meanwhile, none of this stops the business executive from being portrayed as "the natural and predestined villain" in the me-dia and culture at large.[111]

Kristol and other neoconservatives reject the label of "state capitalism," or the unholy collusion of business and the state, for another reason. In their view, the corporation, despised as it is, still constitutes an important check or restraint against the power of the state. The "concentration of power" that corporations enjoy should not blind us to the fact that "they contribute to a general diffusion of power, a diffusion which creates the 'space' in which individual liberty can sur-vive and prosper." Moreover, the "general principle of checks and balances, and of decentralized authority too, is as crucial to the social and economic structures of a liberal democracy as to its political structure."[112] Novak offers a similar ar-gument. "Without the large private corporation, there would be one fewer among the large private forces strong enough to check the growing ambitions of the ad-ministrative state. Were the state to acquire control over the large corporations, the political system would thoroughly dominate the economic system."[113] In his critique of Charles Lindblom's portrait of corporate power, Novak elaborates on the "checks and balances" theme to which Kristol alluded: "The contest between the leaders of the political system and the leaders of the economic system does not seem to be as one-sided as he (Lindblom) claims. Each side makes life more difficult for the other. The division between economic power and political power is deliberate, and so are the headaches involved. This separation can never be perfect, is always fluid, and is properly hotly contested."[114]

It is striking that neither Kristol nor Novak advocates a return to an older conservatism that manifests what Kristol calls "an acute yearning for order and stability," a vision that appears in the writings of Coleridge, Thomas Carlyle, John Henry Newman, and Michael Oakeshott. This conservatism, which was skeptical toward capitalism, had no place in America.[115] Rather, what corporations need to do, according to Kristol, is to "think politically," namely, to undertake a better presentation of their legitimacy through marketing and advertising that would stress their good citizenship over and above their mere focus on acquisition and profitability.[116] Otherwise, they will succumb to the pressures of their enemies who want to subordinate firms to the power of the mass state.

In contrast to Grant's analysis, then, neoconservatives argue that state capitalism is not something that corporations ordinarily seek. Instead, they prefer to protect their autonomy from the state. If they work with the state at all, it is due in part to pressure from a "New Class" of left-leaning bureaucrats and intellectuals who seek to drag the firm into the public sphere and render it powerless against political interventions.[117] "State capitalism," then, is a reality that these radical forces seek, not big business. Kristol writes: "There can be little doubt that if these new imperialistic impulses on the part of the 'public sector' (i.e., the political sector) are unrestrained, we shall move toward some version of state capitalism in which the citizen's individual liberty would be rendered ever more insecure. But it is important not to have any illusions about how much can be done to cope with this situation. The 'new class' is here, it is firmly established in its own societal sectors, and it is not going to go away."[118]

What is astounding about the neoconservative analysis of the history of capitalism here is the lack of attention to the vast body of evidence that big business has *always* desired a closer relationship with the state in order to secure and cultivate its power and influence.[119] Instead, Kristol's version of history suggests that big business has tried to maximize profit while avoiding as much as possible any steady connection to the political sphere, despite the revolutionary transformations that have taken place within the capitalist system. The "anonymous oligarchy" that runs the modern firm has little in common with the entrepreneurial business of the nineteenth century, in which an individual or family controlled and managed its capital.[120] This entrepreneur was a real person, not a "legal fiction."[121] By the late nineteenth century, large pools of capital as well as a "variety of technical expertise" were needed to "exploit the emerging technologies and create economies of scale."[122] Amid this revolutionary process, corporations have at times tried to evade the competitive laws of the free market, although not always with success.[123]

Although Kristol makes some valid points in his historical overview of American capitalism, Grant would likely consider this version of history incomplete. As we have seen, Grant argued that business exerts leadership in institutions (such as universities) that further the domination of corporate capitalism in our mass society. With a nod to leftist critiques of capitalism, Grant thought that the new corporate oligarchy had created "intractable inequalities" that arise from its distribution of wealth.[124] Moreover, "the powerful instruments of opinion have tried to identify in the minds of the general public the capitalist model of incentive with all possible systems of incentive."[125] Contra Kristol and Novak, big business has a vested interest in working with the state and other mass institutions to expand its ideological hegemony. It is an agent actively asserting its influence, not a passive bystander besieged by hostile forces.

What is also missing in the neoconservative version of history is the recognition that big business today has little interest in resisting the Left. Although Kristol portrays the modern firm as a victim of pressure tactics from an anticapitalist Left bent on destroying the corporation by subordinating it to statism and public opinion,[126] this interpretation ignores how the Left and big business often share common goals and work together in attaining those goals even though they often differ over the means. Grant doubted that the nineteenth-century distinction between "left" and "right" had much meaning today, because major political parties or ideologies "all live within a common horizon" that upholds technological progress under state capitalism.[127] As Grant put it, "The directors of General Motors and the followers of Professor Marcuse sail down the same river in different boats."[128]

For this reason, Grant took aim at the New Left in the 1960s for misunderstanding that the corporate and political elites share the goal of destroying historical particularity for the sake of achieving mass political equality. In his essay "A Critique of the New Left" (1966), Grant wrote:

> One immediate reason why I think the New Left is deluded about what is happening in North America is because it has misinterpreted the events which took place in the southern United States. It says today: look at our triumphs in the South; we will now carry these triumphs of citizen action into new fields of social revolution. What has been forgotten is that the powerful among the people and the institutions of North America were more than willing that the society of the white South should be

broken. The civil rights movement had behind it all the powerful forces of the American empire. It marched protected by federal troops, it had the blessing of the leading government figures. It was encouraged night after night by NBC and CBS. There was violence from the white South, but the white South is not an important part of the American power elite. It will be a different matter when the protests are against some position which is dear and close to the American establishment.[129]

As Grant had argued in *Lament*, the establishment's attack on the Goldwater Republicans in the 1964 election was motivated in part by a sense that his movement, largely supported in the South, was "the last-ditch stand of a dying culture."[130] Moreover, Grant would not have shared Kristol's fears about the power of the "New Class," since the powers that be are so effective in bureaucratizing or co-opting dissent. Dissent and protest "are taken into the system and trivialized. They are made to serve the interest of the system they are supposed to be attacking, by showing that free speech is allowed."[131]

Ultimately, Grant's Tory critique of capitalism has more in common with paleoconservatism than neoconservatism.[132] Both Grant and Samuel T. Francis, for example, fundamentally agree that the modern corporation's alliance with the state is not a relation that was undertaken with serious reluctance. As Francis argues in *Leviathan and Its Enemies* (2016), corporations need the mass state and media to disseminate advertising that controls demand for its products.[133] I have already noted that the gradual separation of management from ownership in the large corporation, a phenomenon that rendered the individual entrepreneurial owner obsolete, made it easier for corporations to work with the state. Whereas the old bourgeois elite, which owned its firms, had a vested interest in resisting the state, the new managerial elite, which often owns very little stock in the firms that it runs, has little incentive to protect the autonomy of the corporation. This "dematerialization of property" is the foundation of state capitalism in America.[134] Big business and the Left have also worked together in undermining the old bourgeois morality that put the brakes on instant gratification and sexual libertinism. While big business supported the sexual revolution for the sake of profits, the New Left celebrated it in order to advance a hedonism that would ostensibly lead to a healthier and freer society.[135] There was no tension between a libertine society and an imperialist determination to spread these values. As Grant wryly observed, the motto of North America may as well be "the orgasm at home and napalm abroad."[136]

This symbiotic relation between the Left and corporations should not suggest that they have identical aims at all times. As Gottfried observes, "Big business puts up with other members of its coalition (with leftist activists) just as store owners used to pay the mob to 'protect' them against disaster."[137] However, this alliance also reveals the willingness of the Left to give up the aim of abolishing capitalism while accepting its role as a representative of bureaucratized dissent that shares in the overall goal of destroying the remnants of bourgeois society.[138] Corporations that have enthusiastically supported affirmative action and transgenderism in recent years are advancing, however unwittingly, social engineering that destroys old traditions. In Marxian terms, the state performs the crucial task of "legitimization" by supporting measures, even those that are leftist in tone and content, that present capitalism as a system of freedom and equality. As Grant argued, there is no contradiction whatsoever between a state that intervenes in the economy and society, on the one hand, and a state that permits almost unlimited sexual freedom, on the other.

This last comment may seem unrelated to neoconservatives such as Kristol, Novak, and many other prominent voices on the American Right who have celebrated bourgeois values of self-restraint while they mourn their passing. Kristol never denies that the "cultural nihilism" of modern capitalism dissolves tradition, including the old bourgeois attachments to religion, individual responsibility, marriage, and family.[139] He would likely agree with Grant that the old Protestant or bourgeois version of capitalist individualism has morphed into the "demanded right to one's idiosyncratic wants taken as outside any obligation to the community which provides them."[140] Kristol even seemed to share at times Grant's doubts that capitalism would change for the better, although some neoconservatives have hoped that tax cuts for the rich may stimulate the old bourgeois ethic of hard work.[141] Despite these points of convergence, I suspect that Grant and Francis would also agree that the neoconservatives' acceptance of a limited welfare state and other inheritances from the New Deal belies any lip service to bourgeois ideals.[142] Oddly enough, this acceptance of statism does not translate into support for state capitalism, which, in Kristol's view, has been unfairly forced on big business. If Kristol is right, capitalism as a system does not merit the sort of root-and-branch critique that Grant offered, namely one that focuses on the sheer power that corporations enjoy within a state capitalist order. The much-victimized modern corporation still deserved two cheers for providing freedom and prosperity for millions of people. Absent in this neoconservative vision is the recognition that the corporation, for true conservatives, is part of the problem, not the solution.

Allan Bloom's Democratic Universalism

From the quasi-Marxian perspective to which Grant loosely adheres, every system needs to legitimize its existence through propaganda, rather than simply relying on brute force. The defenders of the state capitalist system, particularly its

American manifestation, present it as an order that is wedded to the universalization of liberty and equality. Francis writes: "Managerial capitalism must therefore articulate and sponsor an ideology of cosmopolitanism that asserts universal identities, values, and loyalties, challenges the differentiations of the bourgeois order, and rationalizes the process of homogenization."[143] Although the first generation of neoconservatives, Irving Kristol included, did not exhibit a strong desire to conflate America's values with the values of humanity, the second generation of this movement has dreamed of a Pax Americana that supports the spread of democracy around the globe.[144] Since the end of the Cold War, the new neoconservatives have insisted that it has always been the mission of America to disseminate its values, by force if necessary. This interpretation of America's history requires a radical reinterpretation of what counts as conservatism in the American tradition. James W. Ceaser insists that the spirit of liberal "internationalism" goes back to the Founders, who forged ideals for all peoples, not just Americans.[145] If Ceaser is correct, America is the only nation that can accomplish this imperial mission, given that it was founded on the basis of "nature," not myth or tradition. The American regime is based on the credo that the nature of humanity is to seek and enjoy the right of freedom, an ideal that calls for revolutionary action. "Americans were the first to bring nature down from the realm of philosophy and introduce it into the political world as a foundation of a full nation."[146] Since this foundation is based on nature, it must be accessible to all of humanity.

This enthusiasm for the promotion of democracy on a global scale was lost on Grant, who worried about the fragile survival of his own nation-state amid the conflict between America and Russia during the Cold War. He was not convinced that liberal democracy would be any more favorably disposed to national identities than Soviet Communism was. In *Lament*, Grant darkly warned that nationalism in an age of multinational capitalism would go the way of the dodo bird. "By its very nature the capitalist system makes of national boundaries only matters of political formality."[147] Moreover, "liberal nationalism" was an oxymoron. "The belief in Canada's continued existence has always appealed against universalism. It appealed to particularity against the wider loyalty to the continent. If universalism is the most 'valid modern trend,' then is it not right for Canadians to welcome our integration into the empire? Canadian nationalism is a more universal faith than French-Canadian nationalism. But if one is a universalist, why should one stop at that point of particularity?"[148]

Nothing sheds more light on the divide between Toryism and what passes for modern conservatism today than the disagreement between Grant and modern-day American conservatives on the "universalization" of values. This mission of spreading democratic values is often associated with the political philosophy of Leo Strauss and his numerous followers (including Ceaser). What complicates this comparison, however, is the fact that there is considerable debate on where Strauss himself stood on the desirability of this mission. Despite his famous portrayal of America as a regime based on the universal principles of natural right,[149] Strauss would have likely been more cautious or hesitant than many of his supporters in placing love of country above love of the good (or the divine). As he once soberly wrote, "No one claims that the faith in America and the hope for America is based on explicit divine premises."[150]

An additional complexity in this context is that Grant never tied Strauss to any imperial tradition of global democracy-promotion. In his view, Strauss was "a better philosopher than any practicing Christian I know on this continent."[151] The fact that Strauss was more sympathetic to the liberalism of the Cold War era than Grant was did not stop this Canadian Tory from portraying Strauss, however erroneously, as a conservative traditionalist.[152]

The differences between Grant and Straussians on what counts as universal and particular in politics should not obscure the fact that they have sometimes attacked the same target on the liberal left. In his *English-Speaking Justice*,[153] Grant presents certain criticisms of the famous liberal philosopher John Rawls that are identical to ones offered by the famous Straussian scholar Allan Bloom. Both men fault Rawls for presenting in his *Theory of Justice* an account of justice that is at once unoriginal and abstract. In Grant's view, Rawls's defense of liberty, equality, and statist protections for the disadvantaged adds nothing substantive to the policies of the Democratic Party since the New Deal era. "In practical terms, what he (Rawls) is saying is that the works of F. D. Roosevelt must be carried to their completion, probably by the Democratic party."[154] Moreover, his political philosophy "is so typical of current liberalism in both the intellectual and practical English-speaking worlds."[155] Yet Rawls's liberalism is oddly detached from the actual politics of this world. The abstract content of *A Theory of Justice* is "even more surprising when one remembers that the Vietnam War was justified in terms of liberal ideology, was largely planned by men from the liberal universities, the most influential of whom were from Rawls's own university."[156] Perhaps most tellingly, "Rawls' theory of justice is enormously weakened by his failure to relate it to the facts of imperialism or of domestic corporate power."[157]

In his review of *A Theory of Justice*, Bloom similarly points out the parochial and abstract flavor of Rawls's consciousness, "which is American, or at most, Anglo-Saxon."[158] Readers "will be given a platform that would appeal to the typical liberal in Anglo-Saxon countries: democracy plus the welfare state—leaving open whether capitalism or socialism is the most efficient economic form (so that one need not be a cold warrior)."[159] Bloom also joins Grant in attacking Rawls for ignoring the historicism of Marx, who (along with Nietzsche) posed the most serious challenges to liberal democracy and "made it questionable whether an undertaking such as Rawls's is possible at all."[160] Both Bloom and Grant sound as if they are singing from the same philosophical hymnbook when they decry Rawls's reliance on self-interest as the basis for justice in a liberal democracy, a foundation that is alarmingly oblivious to the classical preoccupation with understanding justice in terms of living a virtuous life that transcends mere calculations of pleasure and pain.[161] Rawls's "original position," in which individuals who are ignorant of their future social status (the "veil of ignorance") ultimately opt for a society of "fairness" (namely, a Rawlsian one) that will protect the disadvantaged, has nothing to do with the Hobbesian-Lockean state of nature that its participants leave for a social contract that guarantees self-preservation.[162] All of these convergence points probably convinced Grant that he and Bloom were offering similar critiques of Rawls, since he praised Bloom's review as "a brilliant and extended account of the difference between the state of nature and the original position."[163]

Despite these family resemblances, Grant and Bloom fundamentally differed on two major areas of discourse: the historical (or religious) origin of the belief in equality, and the universal nature of the American mission in the world of the late twentieth century. These differences shed light on the overall disagreement between Grant's conservatism and Bloom's liberalism, even if Grant was unaware of the magnitude of these differences. Grant notes with some displeasure Rawls's conventionally liberal view that justice requires no grounding in religion. "The human species (according to Rawls) depends for its progress not on God or nature but on its own freedom, and the direction of that progress is determined by the fact that we can rationally give ourselves our own moral laws."[164] As a result, it is legitimate to treat religion as a "matter of private pursuit" that has no role in politics.[165] Yet Grant suspects that Rawls has "inherited the noble belief in political equality, and the belief that the 'free and rational person' is 'valuable' in a way quite different from members of other species" from a tradition that he does not acknowledge.[166]

Is this tradition a religious one? Although Grant does not specifically accuse Rawls of ignoring the biblical origins of these liberal credos,[167] he is clear in other writings on the necessary connection between the Bible and the belief in human equality and intrinsic value. In his "Ethic of Community," Grant warns leftists and liberals that it is naive to think that the belief in equality could survive without its biblical basis because secular philosophy or liberalism has so far failed to provide an answer as to why all human beings should be treated as valuable in a noninstrumental sense.

> It must be insisted, however, that the idea of equality arose in the West within a particular set of religious and philosophical ideas. I cannot see

why men should go on believing in the principle without some sharing in those ideas. The religious tradition was the biblical, in which each individual was counted as of absolute significance before God. . . . To state this historical fact is not to deny that many men have believed in equality outside this religious tradition. The question is rather whether they have been thinking clearly when they have so believed. This religious basis for equality seems to me the only adequate one, because I cannot see why one should embark on the immensely difficult social practice of treating each person as important unless there is something intrinsically valuable about personality.[168]

Although Grant had serious misgivings about the complicity of Protestantism (especially American Calvinism) with modern liberalism and capitalism,[169] and even struggled with the conflict between Christian universalism and "love of one's own,"[170] he never denied the overall importance of the Bible in shaping the moral consciousness of the Western soul.

While Bloom is not oblivious to these defects and omissions in Rawlsian liberalism, he does not draw the same theological conclusion as Grant does. To be sure, he takes aim at Rawls for assuming "that we are all egalitarians," perhaps because this is a sentiment that "we happen to like today" in our liberal age.[171] He also chides Rawls for ignoring "the challenge to his teaching posed by the claims of (biblical) religion."[172] In accord with his teacher Strauss, Bloom recognizes the complexity of the historical relationship between the Bible (Jerusalem) and philosophy (Athens).[173] Yet Bloom does not believe, as Grant does, that secular liberalism requires a traditional religious basis. In fact, Bloom never claims to be a conservative at all. Although he admires conservatives for their "firmness of character" amid a hostile academic milieu, he himself does not "happen to be that animal." Rather, the "preservation of liberal society is of central concern" to Bloom.[174] In his best-selling work, *The Closing of the American Mind* (1987), Bloom almost sounds conventionally liberal or secular when he dismisses Christianity as mere dogma that has had its day: "The domesticated churches in America preserved the superstition of Christianity, overcoming of which was perhaps the key to liberating man."[175] Bloom follows Strauss's line on the necessity of separating revelation from politics and political philosophy, an attitude that Grant, who admired Strauss, would have rejected as imprudent.[176] Yet Bloom must insist, like most Straussians, on the secular character of America so that the appeal of its values to non-Christian peoples is successful. If America's values are tied to a particular religious tradition, this connection may undermine the legitimacy of America's mission to export its values to the world.[177]

The universality of America's values, as Rawls presents them, also inspires utterly different responses from Grant and Bloom, which further highlight the gap between their political philosophies. This difference is not surprising in light of the fact that Grant was a critic of American imperialism while Bloom was a booster of an expansionist foreign policy. In *The Closing of the American Mind*, Bloom praises the global influence of America in the twentieth century as the necessary means to spread its democratic values that belong to all of humanity. This "democratic universalism" has been beneficial, since it "has had liberalizing effects on many enslaved nations."[178] Bloom adds: "And when we Americans speak seriously about politics, we mean that our principles of freedom and equality and the rights based on them are rational and everywhere applicable. World War II was really an educational project undertaken to force those who did not accept these principles to do so."[179] Bloom, however, notes that this "educational project" is far from complete. He chides the Far Left and Right for importing into America antidemocratic (especially German) ideas that undermine faith in democracy. He also blames historicists from the Far Left and Right for denying the universal applicability of American democracy.[180]

Yet these radicals are not the only ones who, Bloom believes, undermine American democracy and its mission. In his critique of Rawls, Bloom suggests that the liberal philosopher does a poor job of defending American democracy as the universal regime. Instead, Rawls commits the historicist sin of assuming that an advanced degree of economic development is necessary for the successful development of democracy. Bloom faults Rawls for adding the "codicil that liberty may be abrogated in those places where the economic conditions do not permit of liberal democracy (thus saving the Third World nations from being called unjust)."[181] What strikes some defenders of Rawls as admirable realism on his part[182] offends Bloom on the grounds that Rawls fails to demonstrate the suitability of American democracy for all human beings around the world.

Readers who are familiar with Grant's writings already know that he was a vehement opponent of the Vietnam War, one of the most famous attempts to impose American will onto a nation with little positive experience of Western traditions. Grant saw this intervention as an example of an empire that "uses increasingly ferocious means to maintain its hegemony."[183] Moreover, it was not a fascist dictatorship that was devastating Vietnam. "What is being done in Vietnam is being done by the English-speaking empire and in the name of liberal democracy."[184] The liberal ideology of the Johnson administration provided the rationale for this war. "Above all, we cannot dissociate what is happening in Vietnam from the principles of the Great Society. That ferocious exercise in imperial violence must surely be part of our pointing. Mastery extends to every part of the globe."[185]

What is glaringly obvious in Grant's writings (and absent in Bloom's works) is the drawing of a clear connection between imperialism and liberalism's universal ideals. While Grant's pacifism may have played a role in shaping his opposition to American foreign policy from World War II on,[186] I suspect that his conservative notion of "loving one's own" is a more prevalent motivation here. Grant's opposition to American imperialism directly parallels his opposition to the English imperialism of his Whiggish ancestors who justified this expansionist policy in the name of progress.[187] The conservation of tradition could not long survive in this context. "As Plato saw with unflinching clarity, an imperialist power cannot have a conservative society as its home base."[188] In general, loyalty to one's own traditions, people, and culture was preferable, in Grant's view, to the universal global empires that were competing with each other during the Cold War. Indeed, these loyalties "rather than principles are the mark of the conservative."[189]

Grant also doubted that liberal imperialism would succeed in its objectives to disseminate its ideals around the world, in part because the universalism of these ideals turned out to be hollow rhetoric in practice. The debacle in Vietnam would only be the first in a long sequence of failures to transplant liberal democracy in illiberal climes.

> Abroad, the tides of American corporate technology have not washed up liberal regimes on the shores of their empire. Indeed, to put it mildly, the ferocious determination of the Americans to keep Indo-China within the orbit of their empire made it clear that the rights of life, liberty, and the pursuit of happiness might be politically important for members of the domestic heartland, but were not intended to be applicable to the tense outreaches of that empire. In the light of these facts, the argument is still presented by liberals that unfree regimes arise in colonial areas when they are first being modernized, but that in the long run they will develop into liberal democracies. By this argument the identity of technological advance and liberalism is preserved in thought. The strength of the argument is necessarily weakened, however, as fewer and fewer colonial regimes remain colonial democracies. The question is then whether the argument is an appeal to progressivist hope, or to facts; or whether progressivist faith is indeed fact.[190]

These doubts about the success of transplanting liberal values abroad may have led Grant to oppose the parallel policy of multiculturalism in Canada, a policy that also assumes that all peoples desire freedom and equality.[191] Despite the divisive nature of these policies,[192] he doubted that the "progressivist faith" that fueled them would dissipate anytime soon. Once again, Grant was well aware that a liberal state capitalist order, like any regime that seeks legitimization, has a vested interest in inculcating its values within the minds of the citizenry, especially the young. There was little doubt in Grant's mind that this state was teaching a new public religion that would replace the old Christian one. Although he admitted that this civic lesson in democracy "should be carried on" because it is always valuable to teach the young about their "heritage of legal government,"[193] he also recognized the ideological purpose behind this pedagogy: the replacement of Christianity with a religion of the state. "The fact that those liberals who most object to any teaching about the deity are generally most insistent that the virtues of democracy be taught, should make us aware that what is at issue is not religion in general, but the content of the religion to be taught."[194] For this reason, Grant vowed, as a parent and a Christian, to "keep careful watch on the inculcation of this democratic faith among my children in case they should confuse their loyalty to a particular ordering of this passing world with the absolute loyalty which they owe to that which is beyond the world."[195] Grant never abandoned his doubts about the outcome of this process. "When the state has become secularized, it will quickly free itself of its use of the church. The religion of humanity and progress will reign monolithically in the schools."[196] Unlike many of his contemporaries, Grant also entertained few hopes that the citizenry of a democracy would reject these measures. This was the same citizenry, as Grant often bitterly remarked in *Lament,* that no longer had the opportunity to "learn independent views" amid the hegemony of corporate media.[197]

In accord with Bloom's "democratic universalism," the logic of liberal democracy is to implement an "educational project" that presents these values as ones that owe nothing to a religious heritage so that they seem universal to all human beings. It would not surprise Grant that both sides of the political spectrum today present the same message. On the right, Bloom's fellow Straussian Walter Berns, in *Making Patriots* (2001), contends that America's leaders must present "Nature's God" as a deity that has no connection to the God of the Bible, whom the vast majority of Americans (mostly Protestants) worshipped during the Revolutionary Era.[198] In order to "make patriots," loyalty to this secular Supreme Being must be encouraged. On the left, Michael Ignatieff, who is Grant's nephew, assures his fellow liberals that the biblical "concept of the sacred" is no longer needed to buttress belief in human rights, even though secular education that promotes these values is as essential as ever.[199] Although it is a safe bet that Grant would have doubted the validity of these sentiments, it would not surprise him that prominent scholars in a liberal democratic order that coexists with state capitalism insist, in propagandistic ways, that this message of universal or human rights be publicly disseminated on a regular basis. This regime cannot leave to the church or any other private institution the primary role of teaching alternate values to the impressionable masses.[200]

Despite his distinction between loyalty and principle, Grant never truly separated the two in a surgical way. In his words, "love of one's own must ultimately be a means to love of the good."[201] Yet the "good" should not be identified with the epiphenomenal principles of liberal state capitalism, which discourages the preservation of tradition even as its defenders present it as the best regime for all of humanity. The love of one's own tradition also required an honest and thoughtful appraisal of how the modern corporation has weakened tradition. Grant was convinced that state capitalism, whatever its material benefits or democratic features, undermined loyalty to traditions and mores that constituted civilization as a whole. His tough-minded critique of this alliance between business and the state never led to any material reward for himself, while many post–World War II conservatives have benefited handsomely from their support of the moneyed interests aligned with the Leviathan state. True conservatives understand that principle and loyalty must inform each other, particularly if the love of one's tradition is a principled protest against the temptations of power and empire. To the end of his life, Grant fought the good fight for a conservatism that repudiated the dominant politics and economics of his time.

4

WHO FUNDS CONSERVATISM, INC.?

Joseph Cotto

By the metrics of conventional American politics, Donald Trump was not supposed to become president. This should be apparent to anyone who paid even
minimal attention to media reports about the 2016 election cycle. Exactly why
Trump was deemed unfit by the Washington, DC, establishment is something that
needs to be explored, and it is possible that there is no single right answer. A combination of factors may have rendered the Donald unpalatable to those with influence in America's political-media complex. His brash, unpolished nature may
have been even more repellent to establishment forces than his political stances.

What comes to mind when one speaks about the "establishment" is typically
left-leaning advocates and their causes. It is hard to imagine that anyone, outside
of the radical leftist fringe, considers the major American news media to be right-
wing in orientation. Nonetheless, it would be a serious mistake to overlook non-
mainstream news outlets, which are sometimes sympathetic to Republican positions and to those who hold them.

This would be even truer of think tanks, which represent for Republicans and
those who claim to be conservative a sort of alternative mass outlet. In these institutions one encounters advocates of tax cuts, those who support pro-business
economic policies (including tax credits for business enterprises), and opponents
of runaway government spending (unless expenditures are directed to military
use). These think tanks also feature social conservatives who preach traditional
values but who usually do not bring in as much funding as other groups represented in conservative think tanks.

In understanding the politics of think tanks, it is necessary to look at those responsible for lavishing wealth on them. Once it is made clear who funds the Center Right establishment—also known as Conservatism, Inc.—it should become obvious why some in establishment conservatism rallied against Trump's candidacy and continue to support public policy unpopular with most of the country.

There are certain common characteristics of these tanks, starting with where they happen to be located. Shortly after Donald Trump's election, *The Economist* revealed that in Washington, DC, alone "there are 397 think-tanks . . . each incubating ideas for new policies and frequently incubating the policymakers themselves during periods out of power." Trump seizing victory "was a shock for think-tank fellows because most are left-leaning." While "think-tanks are meant to be non-partisan to preserve their tax status," people who work at these organizations "live in a liberal town and their fellows usually have post graduate degrees," a demographic "that identifies Democratic 57% to 35%." Indeed, think tankers "are part of the American political establishment," and "the Republican primary as well as . . . the November general election" was a repudiation of it.[1]

It should be no surprise that "Donald Trump was unpopular even amongst right-leaning policy shops." Especially peeved by his success was "the Republican foreign policy establishment," whose luminaries include, among others, Colin Powell, Condoleezza Rice, Eliot Cohen, and David Gordon. Those last two wrote a letter alleging "that Mr. Trump was not qualified to be president and would put America's national security and well-being at risk." This letter was cosigned by forty-eight other "former Republican administration national security officials." According to these critics, Trump "felt no more respect for DC experts than they felt for him."[2]

Beyond those bonds uniting think tanks across the political spectrum, there are others peculiar to the Republican subspecies. Most relevant here are the strains shared by Center Right tanks that focus on foreign policy. These are the think tanks that provide the personnel for inciting and justifying military action. In a 2006 *New York Times* piece, commentator Thomas Frank explained that rather than dealing with fiscal issues exclusively, the American Enterprise Institute (AEI) "has long been the reliable source of corporate money" whose "deep thinkers . . . after moving into the Bush administration, dreamed up the war in Iraq." He added that the AEI boasts "a comprehensive directory of conservative Washington power" and that "there is no better-connected group of people outside the government itself."[3]

There are also certain corporate interests that have found a sponsor in "conservative" think tanks. In 2005, AEI chairman Christopher DeMuth refrained from delivering any specifics, but mentioned that one-third of his organization's yearly income came from corporations, another third from personal contributions, and the final third from other endowed organizations. AEI raised in total between $20 and $25 million each year. DeMuth also explained that his think tank relied on more than three hundred corporate contributors. How does the institute employ its largesse? Certainly, war is not a low priority. "Two of Washington's most successful think-tank hawks are Frederick and Kimberly Kagan," the former of whom is an AEI scholar, Salon reported nearly a decade after DeMuth's statements. The Kagans are a "husband-and-wife team who" authored "papers that advocate an aggressive U.S. military policy."[4]

This couple with think-tank roots "moved to Afghanistan in 2010 where they became 'de facto senior advisors' to General David Petraeus." While in Kabul, the Kagans "were given top-level security clearance." Both accessed "classified intelligence reports and participated in strategy sessions," utilizing "their positions to advocate substantive changes in the U.S. war plan." Unique about the Kagans was that they went "beyond traditional influence peddling" and had "the ear of the military man in charge of a real war." Perhaps even more notable is that they "were not paid by the U.S. government for their work, but their proximity to Petraeus provided valuable benefits."[5]

But AEI is not the only beneficiary of being associated with this power couple. "The Kagans' proximity to Petraeus, the country's most-famous living general," the Washington Post related, "provided an incentive for defense contractors to contribute to" the Institute for the Study of War, where Kimberly Kagan works. During a mid-2011 banquet commemorating Petraeus, she "thanked executives from two defense contractors who sit on her institute's corporate council, DynCorp International and CACI International." Petraeus's dinner "was sponsored by General Dynamics. All three firms have business interests in the Afghan war."[6]

Given the negative public impression of American military activities in Afghanistan and Iraq, it is understandable that various think tanks would decline to speak about receiving donations from defense contractors. Nonetheless, these donations continue to pour in and may well influence the positions taken by their recipients.

In December 2009, Foreign Policy bemoaned that the majority of DC think tanks portray "themselves as objective, quasi-scholarly institutions (indeed, they increasingly give researchers endowed chairs and other quasi-academic titles)." Yet, in reality, "unlike most universities, most think tanks remain heavily dependent on 'soft money,'" which makes them "bound to be especially sensitive to what potential donors might be thinking."[7] Around that same time, WIRED magazine explained how many tanks purportedly devoted to examining national security are really a veiled extension of the commercial defense sector: "Lockheed Martin, Raytheon, Boeing . . . contribute to many of the defense-oriented think tanks, although getting specific amounts is tricky" because the IRS's Form 990, which furnishes the public with data regarding nonprofit institutions, "does not break down individual donations."[8]

All hope is not lost, however, for deciphering donor identity. Some think tanks are more up front than others about who funds them. Take the Center for Strategic and International Studies (CSIS), which Fairness and Accuracy in Reporting (FAIR) deems "a ubiquitous voice on the topic of missile defense," with special attention paid to "the urgent threat of North Korea." CSIS champions American "deployment of the Terminal High Altitude Area Defense (THAAD) missile system . . . to South Korea."[9]

These words ran under the following headline: "Lockheed Martin-Funded Experts Agree: South Korea Needs More Lockheed Martin Missiles." The CSIS's top ten largest business contributors have their own special disclosure category of "$500,000 and up." Five of these corporations "are weapons manufacturers: Besides Lockheed Martin, this list includes General Dynamics, Boeing, Leonardo-Finmeccanica and Northrop Grumman."[10] Unlike AEI, the CSIS does not practice concealment about who floods them with funds.

Another generously endowed Republican think tank is the Heritage Foundation. Unlike other institutions of its type, Heritage has not allowed any daylight between itself and the administration of Donald Trump. According to *New Republic*, "No group is more responsible for helping to craft Trump's agenda than the Heritage Foundation." Ironically this tank initially blasted Trump because he had "no track record of allegiance to conservative causes." Despite this early riff, Heritage eventually had an impact "on virtually every policy Trump advocates, from his economic agenda to his Supreme Court nominees." This relationship "between Trump and the Heritage Foundation represents a return to prominence for an organization that was established in 1973 specifically as a Republican appendage.[11]

The foundation released a summation of its finances on the last day of 2016. Its budget for that year surpassed $85 million, with the previous one totaling over $91 million. In 2016, Heritage raised more than $58.6 million from donations alone, while 2015 brought it upward of $76 million. During the former year, Heritage reported net assets in excess of $240.6 million.[12]

How did Heritage acquire such staggering wealth? According to the Intercept: "The Pentagon decided in 2009 to cut funding for Lockheed Martin's F-22 Raptor fighter jet," described as "a weapons system with cost overruns in the billions of dollars" seldom utilized amid armed conflict. Nonetheless, "the Heritage Foundation fought tooth and nail to restore taxpayer money for the planes." Heritage insisted that the F-22 is a key instrument for promoting America's national interests. There was more than met the eye, however, at least insofar as the public went: "Lockheed Martin, a corporate donor to" the foundation, "met with [its] officials on nearly a monthly basis to discuss the F-22 and other defense industry priorities."[13]

Unauthorizedly released emails, which were eventually obtained by the Intercept, "show at least 15 meetings in 2008 and 2009 between officials at Heritage and Lockheed Martin, including one with Bill Inglee, who at the time served as a senior lobbyist" for the military aircraft manufacturer. The same emails "also suggest that Heritage continued courting Lockheed Martin for donations," placing "the company repeatedly in Excel spreadsheets used to collect pledges from past donors." As far as the contributions themselves go, "Lockheed Martin gave $40,000 to Heritage in 2008, bringing its total contribution to $341,000."[14]

The combined efforts of Heritage and Lockheed ultimately did not produce the desired outcome. Yet, before that became obvious, "Lockheed Martin directed its registered lobbyists to fight back against the cuts in Congress." The corporation also "took out full-page advertisements in D.C. publications." Meanwhile, "the Heritage Foundation produced a flurry of reports and media outreach efforts to encourage Congress to overturn the Pentagon's decision." The defense industry has "historically played an outsized role in shaping the national security debate through think tank funding." Moreover, "Lockheed Martin in particular funds an array of other policy institutes and think tanks." Beyond Lockheed, though, it is worth noting that "the nexus of defense contracting money and think tanks is poorly understood." The reason is that detailed disclosure of such information by think tanks has been voluntary.[15]

This report is not arguing anything as simplistic as the idea that AEI, Heritage, and other "conservative" and/or Republican think tanks advocate military entanglements because of their funding sources. The opposite could just as easily be the case. Military hawks and defense industries become associated with particular institutions because they know where they stand on foreign policy and grasp that their positions are compatible. But it is equally obvious that the dependence of certain think tanks on massive funding from certain sources strengthens their predisposition toward certain policies. It also renders it difficult for the funded institutions to change course if their interests will be compromised as a result of a policy shift. This dependence also steers the foundations under discussion away from embracing other issues and positions that are not financially profitable. For example, why should a conservative foundation put any moral capital into defending traditional social positions if it is being funded almost entirely for other reasons? Needless to say, Heritage and AEI were far more willing to jettison opposition to gay marriage than support for increased military spending and the policy of "standing up" to the supposed thug in the Kremlin.

It is even quite possible that if the Republican establishment fades and is replaced by Donald Trump loyalists, "conservative" think tanks will continue to showcase the same priorities. That, after all, is what they are being financed to do, even while they work to increase their leverage and presence in the White House. One might also note the hypocrisy when institutions that claim to be fighting "big government" are delighted to increase their size and cost, providing they are paid to advocate for that expansion. But these think tanks defend what they wish to increase as necessary costs and necessary expansion. That is supposedly because the "conservative policy community" stands behind these policies, and Fox News, which works hand in glove with that community, tells us repeatedly that everything its allies advocate is both "conservative" and good for the country.[16] That position will eventually turn into one that the leftist media will proclaim as the authorized conservative one.

Postscript: If most of the sources cited above came from Democratic and leftist publications, this should not surprise or disappoint the reader. Almost all journalists and activists associated with Conservatism, Inc., defend and, if possible, cover up the financial interests of their own think tanks. A detailed treatment of these funding sources at an earlier point in time can be found in Paul Gottfried's *The Conservative Movement*, revised edition (New York: Twayne Publishers, 1993). What stands out from comparing figures is how much less Heritage was taking in then (about $15 million a year in the early 1990s) relative to its present annual funding. At that time much more funding came from neoconservative-controlled educational foundations than from defense industry and military lobbyists.

5

IMAGINATION AND ITS FAILURES

The Struggle of a Conservative
American Foreign Policy

Marjorie L. Jeffrey

The rise of the American empire during the Cold War has been covered time and again, by better historians and analysts; and yet America still finds itself consumed by the debates of bygone ages. While it is undoubtedly true that, to paraphrase Winston Churchill, in history lies all the secrets of statecraft, since the fall of the Berlin Wall we have found American foreign policy trapped by recent history, largely because of the tremendous influence of leaders who came of age during what James Burnham called "The Struggle for the World." But the cage of our foreign policy consensus, rattled by the Donald Trump campaign of 2016, has burst open. What follows is a historical reflection on what led up to that campaign and what its consequences have been.

We begin with George F. Kennan's prophetic critique of America's emphasis on military power and spending during the Cold War, and then turn to the struggle for the American regime's political direction, best seen in the battle between Pat Buchanan and George H. W. Bush in the Republican primary of the 1992 presidential election campaign. From there, we can trace the continued rise of what is now called "neoconservative" foreign policy in the Clinton and Bush years, pausing to reflect on the difference between George W. Bush's campaign promises and his administration post-9/11. With some exploration of neoconservative power during the Iraq War years, we then consider objections to that consensus, including primarily what I call "the libertarian moment." This begins with Ron Paul's campaign of 2008 and is carried forward by Rand Paul's attempts to create a new libertarian-conservative fusionist wing of the Republican Party. Finally, we consider the Trump era, and how it tried to combine noninterventionism with bows in the direction of Buchananist cultural conservatism.

While this study contains some discussion of important political thinkers, with particular emphasis on George Kennan, its aim is to trace the trajectory of foreign policy on the American Right since the end of the Cold War. Of necessity, we cannot include a lengthy discussion of American foreign policy throughout most of its history, though of course this would enrich our understanding of our own position. It must be conceded that there is no going backward; we cannot return to a blissful, perhaps mythic time in American history when we followed perfectly the counsel of Washington's "Farewell Address" to abjure repeated and endless hostilities with foreign nations, or the fervent prayer of John Quincy Adams that his country "go not abroad in search of monsters to destroy" but defend only "her own" interests. Yet it is only by knowing how we arrived at the present moment that we can possibly hope to guess whither we are going.

The Rise of American Empire

In "Communism: The Struggle for the World," James Burnham notes that throughout most of America's history, the focus of political life has been directed toward internal issues. But writing in 1947, he says that "we have entered a period in history in which world politics take precedence over national and internal politics. . . . Everything else is secondary, absolute."[1] Burnham, formerly a dedicated Marxist who became a conservative, was referring to the struggle for global dominance between the Soviet Union and the United States. Burnham today is considered to be the intellectual godfather of several prominent paleoconservatives, but it must be recalled that he was also a founder of *National Review*. Once upon a time, in the early days of the conservative movement, all were united by a common cause, the struggle for the world; and the recognition of the importance of this struggle is what led many who would later be called "neoconservatives" into the ranks of the conservative movement.

It is easy to understand the Cold War as the formal cause of the buildup and expansion of America's military presence. The policy of containment, developed by George F. Kennan as a prudential response to a particular situation, necessitated this growth into what eventually became a soft military empire. It is ironic, or perhaps fitting, that it was Kennan himself who became the most prominent conservative critic of this empire, and especially of the "military-industrial complex," a term that Kennan helped popularize but did not originate.[2] In his 1984 essay "American Democracy and Foreign Policy,"[3] Kennan surveys the state of

American foreign policy, and the history of it since the end of World War II. What is perhaps most striking about the essay as a whole is how much it could apply to our current situation; though, if Kennan's criticism is valid, then the state we are in is much, much worse. His statements about our accomplishments are brief, since he focuses mostly on our mistakes. But he expects us to learn from this educational judgment: "Just as it does the human individual more good to reflect upon his failings than upon his virtues, I think the national society, too, has more to learn from its failures than from its successes."[4]

Kennan seems to hold no reservations about our position as a great world power. He accepts that role and does not advise us to try to change it. His concern is that, as a great power, we operate in the international realm prudently. Part of the difficulty he sees with American foreign policy in the early twentieth century is that it was childish, and likens it to "the relatively innocent erraticism of the relatively young adolescent who is becoming aware of his own strength and would like to use it, but lacks the maturity to know how best to do so."[5] But our real trouble began, as he sees it, with certain mistakes we made in our policy toward the Soviet Union. These mistakes "involved attributing to the Soviet leadership aims and intentions it did not really have,"[6] by turning them into a kind of large-scale caricature of the Nazi regime, and by assuming they could be defeated in the same way as Germany had been. Whatever their intentions were, we made a mistake in jumping to conclusions. Our national confidence was high, and we had little experience of anything but success. Furthermore, Wilsonianism—a willingness to spend American blood and might for the freedoms of peoples around the world—contributed to our overreach. Another mistake involved "embracing the nuclear weapon as the mainstay of our military posture."[7] Here, Kennan makes a distinctly moral as well as prudential argument. "We made the primitive error of supposing that the effectiveness of a weapon was directly proportionate to its destructiveness—destructiveness not just against an enemy's armed forces but against its population and its civilian economy as well. We forgot that the aim of war is, or should be, to gain one's points with the minimum, not the maximum, of general destruction, and that a proper weapon must be not only destructive but discriminating."[8] It could be argued that any nation in the modern era would have made this mistake, in the wake of the two great European civil wars of the twentieth century. But it may also be a fact of American history, given our limited experience with premodern warfare, that the first great mass democracy was fated to conduct war based on numerical and weapon superiority. Arguably the first truly modern war with massive civilian casualties, a strategy of breaking the spirit of the civilian population, and a penchant for the dehumanization of the enemy was the American Civil War. Moreover, both world wars "ended in unconditional surrender, encouraging us in the mistaken view that the purpose of war was not to bring about a mutually advantageous compromise with an external adversary (now seen as totally evil and inhuman), but to destroy completely the power and the will of that adversary."[9] Kennan's tone seems to be reminiscent of the argument of the German legal philosopher Carl Schmitt, who believed that modern warfare is characterized by the absolute demonization of the foe.

From these mistaken attitudes, says Kennan, issued our vast military-industrial complex. Kennan attributes this overreliance on massiveness to our lack of a serious diplomatic tradition. Curiously he does not discuss the size of the American bureaucracy or the struggle for power between Congress and the president. He takes issue with American democracy itself. He maintains that American leaders have a tendency "to be more concerned for the domestic-political effects of what he is saying or doing than about their actual effects on our relations with other countries."[10] Policies are often judged by how popular they are at home, regardless of whether they will work outside the country. This "degenerate" foreign policy follows from Alexis de Tocqueville's observations about the nature of the conduct of foreign affairs in democratic regimes. We have a huge national constituency, which now operates in the form of multiple lobbies and special interest groups that have a corrosive effect on the policymaking process.

What is to be done in this circumstance? Kennan asks. He thinks it would be naive to suppose that the structure of our regime will change to fit the demands of great power diplomacy. Like James Madison, he admires whatever in our system of government protects civil liberties. But the lack of coherence in our international affairs stems, at least in part, according to Kennan, from the dialectic that is implicit in the Constitution, in which ambition counteracts ambition. And if this system is the only feasible one to govern such a heterogeneous mass of people as exists in America, Kennan will accept this situation for want of a better alternative. All he asks for is a modicum of prudence and the acceptance of limits to what we can reasonably hope to change: "Let us recognize that there are problems in this world that we will not be able to solve." "It will not be useful or effective for us to plunge into dilemmas in other regions of the globe that will have to find their solution without our involvement."[11] This is a plea that has largely fallen on deaf ears.

Kennan was (and still is) seen by many Cold Warriors as an early example of what David Frum would attack as an "Unpatriotic Conservative."[12] But his prediction about the resilience of what he called the military-industrial complex would prove to be true. Not everyone shared his concern. In a critical review of Kennan's latest book in 1977, Edward N. Luttwak wrote in *Commentary* that Kennan went too far in calling for a reduction of military spending to an "indispensable minimum." Kennan expressed disapproval that the Pentagon's spending had reached 6 percent of GDP. According to Luttwak: "One would have imagined that Mr. Kennan the historian would remember that historically the United States has grossly underspent on defense."[13] Luttwak further contends that Kennan's objections to tremendous military power and his "refusal to give military power its due reflects only an emotional revulsion."

Let us note that Kennan wrote prophetically in 1984:

> The habit of spending from two to three hundred billions of dollars annually on preparations for an imagined war with Russia—a habit reaching deeply into the lives and interests of millions of our citizens both in and out of the armed services, including industrial workers, labor-union officials, politicians, legislators, and middlemen: This habit has risen to the status of a vast addiction of American society, an addiction whose overcoming would encounter the most intense resistance and take years to accomplish even if the Soviet Union had in the meantime miraculously disappeared from the earth.[14]

He further observed: "Were the Soviet Union to sink tomorrow under the waters of the ocean, the American military-industrial establishment would have to go on, substantially unchanged, until some other adversary could be invented. Any thing else would be an unacceptable shock to the American economy."[15] Kennan's predictions may have been prophetic. After the wall fell, America was faced with a choice as to which way it would go. Would it continue its mission of world peacekeeper and leader and principal funder of operations for the North Atlantic Treaty Organization (NATO)? Or, would it find a way to pare back its military obligations and focus on internal rather than external affairs?

The Buchanan Years: New World Order versus America First

The first great skirmish for the soul of the Republican Party (and by extension, of the conservative movement) after the Cold War was in the 1992 Republican presidential primary. In that confrontation the political choice was between Pat Buchanan (a former adviser to Richard Nixon and Ronald Reagan, newspaper columnist, and panelist on *Crossfire*) and President George H. W. Bush. The 1992 election was unusual because of the number of "outsider" candidates (a relatively new phenomenon in American politics) and because an incumbent Republican president lost to the relatively unknown Democratic governor of Arkansas. But much of this strangeness could be attributed to a new development in American politics, the disappearance of the Cold War as a central issue. In the Republican primary, Patrick J. Buchanan ran against what George H. W. Bush had called the "New World Order," a phrase that meant to Buchanan the disappearance of national sovereignty. Bush's "Toward a New World Order" speech, given before a joint session of Congress on September 11, 1990, framed the new world order as an American objective in the Gulf War. The role of the United States would be to enforce the rule of international law, in cooperation with the rest of the international community.

An article in *National Review* written by Richard Brookhiser in early 1992 throws light on the Buchanan campaign.[16] In "Waiting for Righty," Brookhiser stresses certain aspects of Buchanan's campaign that seem to anticipate Trump's, down to Buchanan's quips about ejecting ACT-UP demonstrators who interrupted his speeches.[17] At his campaign announcement in Concord, New Hampshire, Buchanan compared the American situation to the bureaucratic takeover of European nations: "We Americans must not let that happen here. We must not trade in our sovereignty for a cushioned seat at the head table of anyone's New World Order."[18] From foreign affairs, he turned to economic problems, beginning with America's outsized financial commitment to the protection of other countries and calling for the reform of international organizations. Finally, Buchanan spoke of the cultural crisis that had been placed on the back burner during the Cold War. The candidate closed with what later would become a Trumpian sentiment: George H. W. Bush "is yesterday and we are tomorrow. He is a globalist and we are nationalists. He believes in some Pax Universalis; we believe in the Old Republic. He would put Americans wealth and power at the service of some vague New World Order; we will put America first."[19]

Brookhiser's criticisms of Buchanan (protectionism, lack of experience, and supposed hints of anti-Semitism) were relatively mild. Moreover, *National Review* praised the candidate during this election, particularly in its cover story "The Case for Buchanan" in early March.[20] This was tame compared with the attacks on Buchanan that came from the neoconservative establishment during his later presidential campaigns. Buchanan's high water mark in the 1992 campaign was receiving 38 percent of the vote in the New Hampshire primary, but that year he also won the straw poll at Conservative Political Action Committee (CPAC) with over half the vote. John O'Sullivan, the editor of *National Review*, wrote that he would support Buchanan until a "millisecond" before he dropped out. Then he would back Bush with reluctance because "no conservative in his heart wants to endorse a President who has raised taxes and extended racial and sexual quotas."[21] Buchanan eventually did drop out, and O'Sullivan then endorsed the president, who in the interest of party unity allowed his former opponent to give a primetime speech at the National Convention. This led to Buchanan's delivery of the famous "Culture Wars" speech, which was the last time that Buchanan was allowed to speak at a Republican National Convention.

Although Buchanan lost that year, so did George H. W. Bush. He ran again in 1996 but did worse than he had four years earlier. In his 1992 presidential campaign, Buchanan had no chance of going anywhere, but his followers liked seeing him push Bush further to the right, especially on taxes and regulations. In 1996, Buchanan was seen by the party as a mere nuisance. James W. Ceaser and Andrew E. Busch observed that "setting aside all the statements and the mathematics, there was one major political story of 1996 and that was Pat Buchanan. Brief as his moment of national exposure was, its intensity was extraordinary."[22] Buchanan's appeal to the white lower and middle classes was summed up in one of his campaign slogans: "The peasants are coming with pitchforks." Buchanan often showed up at rallies with a pitchfork, becoming "Pitchfork Pat" to his supporters, who began buying the same object for their front porches.

In a profile of a likely Buchanan entrance into the election in 1995, Robert Novak wrote that the "second worst nightmare" for "Republican establishmentarians" would be for Buchanan to make strong showings in New Hampshire and South Carolina, and thus to be a genuine "conservative alternative" to Robert Dole.[23] (Their very worst nightmare, he wrote, would be an independent candidacy of Buchanan in the general election.) Buchanan won the Louisiana Caucus in a surprise showing and went on to another surprise victory in New Hampshire, a primary that Dole was supposed to win. After that unexpected victory, William F. Buckley criticized Buchanan's "isolationist" positions on foreign policy and his commitment to repeal the North American Free Trade Agreement (NAFTA), but praised his positions on cultural issues: his crusade against abortion, his "call for a national common culture . . . against Bilingual America," and his "earnest suspicion of predatory government."[24]

Though the conservative intelligentsia remained troubled by Buchanan's isolationism and protectionism, it is clear that his positions on immigration, racial quotas, and the plight of the working-class man and woman were genuinely appealing to many on the right. The editors of National Review wrote after the New Hampshire primary that Buchanan's appeal to cultural and moral issues was familiar territory for a GOP candidate, but "his appeal to blue-collar voters anxious about their economic future takes him furthest from Republican—and conservative—orthodoxy."[25] The Weekly Standard, an explicitly neoconservative publication, was less subtle in attacking Buchanan's campaign and published a heated assault on the unconventional candidate by Norman Podhoretz. This critic charged Buchanan with anti-Semitism, calling his positions on foreign policy and the economy "wrong and indeed dangerous."[26] An article in the same edition of the magazine, trying to make sense of Buchanan's victory in New Hampshire, called his "style and substance . . . more than a little unpleasant and spooky."[27] The author, David Tell, goes on to explain that there really was no sector of the

American population with whom Buchanan's core issues resonated, especially not, heaven forbid, "economic populism." In the end, Tell argues that Buchanan is simply a more talented campaigner than Dole, and his success will harm the Republican Party in the long run. All this provides some sense of the mood among neoconservative elites during the ascendancy of "Pitchfork Pat."

Norman Ornstein, writing for the *Weekly Standard* in March 1996, concluded that the issues driving Buchanan's campaign were not going anywhere, but that was true only for the present. "Pat Buchanan will be back in 2000," he wrote, "with more credibility, a broader base, and even more momentum—and a second Buchanan in the White House, with a Congress more sympathetic to this one's isolationist and protectionist siren song, will no longer be a farfetched joke."[28] This proved to be only partially true in 2000, but truer in the much longer term. Buchanan's issues remained, even after the candidate withdrew from the race, after running as the Reform Party nominee and finishing fourth in the general election. In a twist of historical drama, Donald J. Trump also launched an exploratory committee in 1999 to consider a possible bid for the Reform Party nomination. At that time he excoriated Buchanan as "Attila the Hun" and "a Hitler-lover."[29] Trump eventually dropped out of the race and refused to support Buchanan as the Reform Party nominee.[30]

Pat Buchanan's prolific writing resulted in several popular books, and in 1999 he published *A Republic, Not an Empire*, a book peppered with references to George Kennan. In it, he scorned members of the GOP who sought to dismiss his policy recommendations as "isolationism" and "protectionism," arguing that his positions on economics and foreign policy were born of the long traditions of American political history. In what may now be considered a prophetic paragraph, Buchanan wrote,

> I believe deeply that the foreign policy I advocate for the twenty-first century is not only right for America, but will also be seen to be right, and will one day be embraced by the entire nation, for a fundamental reason: Present U.S. foreign policy, which commits America to go to war for scores of nations in regions where we have never fought before, is unsustainable. As we pile commitment upon commitment in Eastern Europe, the Balkans, the Middle East, and the Persian Gulf, American power continues to contract—a sure formula for foreign policy disaster.[31]

The publication of this book marked Buchanan's ideological break with the Republican Party, and both events spurred the *National Review* to produce a Buchanan-themed edition of the magazine, with the cover story by Ramesh Ponnuru, "A Conservative No More: The Tribal Politics of Pat Buchanan." Ponnuru concluded his article by stating, "Letting Buchanan continue to describe himself as a conservative would be not just irritating but destructive. He is in no important sense a conservative anymore. Let his failure be his alone."[32] In the same edition, Andrew Bacevich published a review of *A Republic, Not an Empire*, with the deprecatory title "Nativist Son." According to Bacevich, Buchanan's critique of "post-Wilsonian internationalism" was not accompanied by plausible alternatives.[33] Bacevich's primary charges against Buchanan were moral and cultural. He objected to Buchanan's negative attitude toward immigrants coming to America from the Third World. Buchanan, he wrote, wrongly imagined that these people "don't readily assimilate" or "provide suitable material for making real Americans."[34] According to Bacevich, both Buchanan's rejection of empire and his call for "enlightened nationalism" are equally ill advised.

George W. Bush won the 2000 presidential election on a slogan originally coined by Pat Buchanan: "compassionate conservatism." According to the political theorist Daniel J. Mahoney, "It must be remembered that neoconservative advocates of a militarily assertive neo-Wilsonian foreign policy were initially wary of George W. Bush and tended to support the internationalist John McCain in the 2000 Republican primaries."[35] In his presidential debates, the younger Bush seemed skeptical of the humanitarian interventions of the Clinton years and promised to pursue a "more humble foreign policy." Some of this appealed to establishment Republicans because of their congressional opposition to President Clinton's intervention in Kosovo. A little less than a year into Bush's administration came the September 11 attacks.

The Neoconservative Zenith and the Libertarian Moment

The events of 9/11 accelerated neoconservative dominance over American foreign policy, but while the attacks increased this trend, its organizational infrastructure had been building for years. The Project for the New American Century (PNAC), a think tank launched in 1997 by William Kristol and Robert Kagan, was founded to "promote American global leadership," and sought to put together a political coalition to support what Kagan and Kristol called "a Reaganite policy of military strength and moral clarity."[36] Of the twenty-five signatories of the PNAC Statement of Principles (which included Norman Podhoretz and Francis Fukuyama), ten went on to serve in the George W. Bush administration, including Dick Cheney, Paul Wolfowitz, Donald Rumsfeld, and, notably, John Bolton, now a member of the Trump administration. It seems undeniable that many of the people within the PNAC circle had an enormous amount of influence on the

Bush administration after September 11. Following on the success of PNAC, one of its project directors and a Washington lobbyist, Randy Scheunemann, founded the bipartisan Committee for the Liberation of Iraq in 2002. The advisory board included John McCain and Joe Lieberman. Both of these lobbying groups disbanded a few years after the invasion of Iraq, when the former executive director of PNAC proudly noted that "our view has been adopted."[37]

What was "their view"? In what may be considered one of the founding documents of what became Bush-era neoconservatism, Kristol and Kagan wrote in "Toward a Neo-Reaganite Foreign Policy" that instead of either Clinton's "Wilsonian multi-lateralism" or Buchanan's "neo-isolationism," America should seek a policy of "benevolent global hegemony."[38] Shortly thereafter, in 1998, the same authors announced in the *New York Times* that "Saddam Hussein must go."[39] While the original aim was to put pressure on the Clinton administration, real success for PNAC came only with a crisis. On September 20, 2001, an open letter presumably written by William Kristol and signed by forty neoconservative policy advocates called for large increases in military spending, military action in Afghanistan and Iraq, and the removal of Saddam Hussein. The same letter demanded a war against terrorism in general (but specifically against the Taliban and Hezbollah) and added pressure on the Palestinian Authority to counteract anti-Israel activity. According to the letter, these steps were "the minimum necessary if this war is to be fought effectively and brought to a successful conclusion."[40] Most of these demands eventually received the approval of the Bush administration, together with resounding endorsement from neoconservative journals such as *Commentary* and the *Weekly Standard*.

Over time, an increased pushback against these policies took place, both from the Left and from the libertarian and paleoconservative Right. In 2002, the journal *American Conservative* was founded by Scott McConnell, Pat Buchanan, and Taki Theodoracopulos in order to oppose the Iraq War from the Right. Other fusionist antiwar publications then came along, like Justin Raimondo's Antiwar .com. Against these efforts, David Frum penned his famous "Unpatriotic Conservatives" essay in the pages of *National Review*, charging antiwar conservatives and libertarians with being anti-American: "They have made common cause with the left-wing and Islamist antiwar movements in this country and in Europe. They deny and excuse terror. They espouse a potentially self-fulfilling defeatism. They publicize wild conspiracy theories. And some of them explicitly yearn for the victory of their nation's enemies."[41] In a wide-ranging attack mostly on the hated paleoconservatives, Frum describes those he targets as self-absorbed cranks. In addressing their opposition to Bill Clinton's war in Kosovo, Frum states that instead of expressing American patriotism, these eccentrics flaunted their "Serbian nationalism." Finally, on the basis of quotations from Kevin McDonald, Joseph

Sobran, Samuel Francis, and Pat Buchanan, Frum levels the charge of "racism" before ending with this searing condemnation:

> They began by hating the neoconservatives. They came to hate their party and this president. They have finished by hating their country.
>   War is a great clarifier. It forces people to take sides. The paleoconservatives have chosen—and the rest of us must choose too. In a time of danger, they have turned their backs on their country. Now we turn our backs on them.[42]

Though the American conservative movement had been cracking up for more than a decade, this essay and its publication in *National Review* marked the end of any pretense of civility between the Neoconservative Right and the Old Right. It says much about the confidence of conservatives who supported the Iraq War that they felt comfortable excommunicating so many influential former members of the conservative movement. Ironically, a year later the founder of *National Review*, William F. Buckley, confessed that he too was an unpatriotic conservative, stating in the *New York Times*, "If I knew then what I know now about what kind of situation we would be in, I would have opposed the war."[43]

Jerome Tuccille wrote a popular history of the libertarian movement—the provocatively titled *It Usually Begins with Ayn Rand*—that has bearing on this study. Today that book might well be called *It Usually Begins with Ron Paul*. Much of the generation that came of age during the Iraq War era and that tended toward the Right were skeptical about military intervention. The coalition that provided support for Ron Paul's campaign in 2008 and 2012 included many young people, as well as older paleoconservatives, American nationalists, and military veterans who opposed George W. Bush's wars. Longtime congressman Ron Paul was steeped in the libertarian movement from the 1970s onward, but managed to rise above the movement's internal squabbles and become a symbol of liberty for a younger generation.

Paul's 2008 campaign was marked by a youthful earnestness, staffed by young people who met through local meetings and were bound mostly by their opposition to what they perceived as American wars of imperialism. There was a folksy charm to this campaign but also an obvious contrast between the aged and cantankerous candidate and his young, exuberant supporters. In what is now perhaps the best remembered moment of that first Paul campaign, a heated exchange about foreign policy took place between Paul and Rudy Giuliani. At the South Carolina primary debate, Paul reminded his audience that the "conservative wing" of the Republican Party "always advocated a non-interventionist foreign policy" and that George Bush had won his first election by campaigning on a "humble foreign policy." Moreover, "there's a strong tradition of being anti-war in the Republican Party." This message had almost disappeared from the GOP during the Bush years, but now it was presented by the only Republican primary candidate who opposed the Iraq War. Giuliani, seizing on Paul's use of "blowback" as an explanation for the events of 9/11, won the applause of the crowd with an emotional appeal to his record as mayor of New York City during the attacks.[44] While Ron Paul clearly did not represent the majority of Republican voters in 2008, in 2016, at another debate in South Carolina, Donald Trump viciously attacked Bush's record on Iraq—and won the South Carolina primary.

Ron Paul's campaigns failed to win electoral victories, but they built a real movement at the grassroots level. New groups such as Students for Liberty and Young Americans for Liberty began recruiting the kinds of students who were once drawn to establishment conservative organizations like the Intercollegiate Studies Institute and Young Americans for Freedom. In the meantime, the Obama years fueled middle-American resentment against intrusive administration, which gave rise to the Tea Party movement in 2010. The Tea Party was a relatively short-lived phenomenon compared with the institutions built by the Paul movement, but some Tea Party positions (e.g., lower taxes and a strict interpretation of the Constitution) came to the fore in Ron Paul's presidential run in 2008. While Tea Party groups did not raise foreign policy as a major issue, the midterm elections of 2010 brought an influx of Tea Party candidates into Congress, including Thomas Massie, Justin Amash, and Ron Paul's son Rand Paul. In 2011, the House Liberty Caucus was founded under the chairmanship of Justin Amash. This caucus includes in its Statement of Principles a strict constitutional understanding of presidential war powers, and expresses opposition to "the exercise of executive War Powers in the absence of a Declaration [of War], except in the face of an immediate and direct threat to the United States."[45]

Ron Paul's campaign in 2012 was a different animal from his earlier run. It was a far more professional outfit, with more serious political operative; and at least for a short time, he had prospects of winning the Iowa caucuses. It may also be worth noting that while Ron Paul fiercely opposed illegal immigration in 2008—and throughout his career—in 2012 he softened his tone and voiced opposition to building a wall on the southern border. Coming in third in New Hampshire, he stayed in the race after everyone else had dropped out. In some ways, this was like the Bernie Sanders campaign of 2016, with last-ditch efforts to use party convention rules at the Republican National Convention to change a predictable outcome. Paul was offered a speaking slot at the convention if he would endorse Mitt Romney, which he declined to do.[46] Thereafter Ron Paul would act as a godfather to the libertarian movement, while his son Rand would take a different approach, by endorsing Romney in exchange for a speaking slot at the convention. This illustrates the stylistic difference between Ron and Rand:

one is totally uncompromising and ran two mostly educational presidential campaigns leading to a lasting movement, while the other has attempted to work within the establishment. The difference between Ron and Rand can be illustrated by how they approach the issue of the Federal Reserve: one hopes to "end the Fed," while the other wants merely to "audit the Fed."

In 2011, Rand kept one of his campaign promises by cosponsoring an amendment to end birthright citizenship. He also stood out as a hard-liner in a sea of Republican senators anxious to support amnesty. Early in his Senate career, however, Rand tried to be a voice of moderation on foreign policy. Rand Paul delivered two memorable foreign policy speeches as a U.S. senator: one in February 2013 and another in October 2014. In both he questions what he calls "bipartisan consensus" on foreign policy and military intervention.

But he also showed a willingness to compromise that his father never demonstrated. In his 2013 speech, Rand Paul repositioned himself between neoconservatism and the isolationism of his father, calling himself a conservative "realist."[47] His speech "Containment and Radical Islam" relies heavily on the ideas of George Kennan as a basis for American foreign policy. Paul cleverly acknowledges the enormity of the problem posed by radical Islam—a problem that may require military action—but then asks why there is no substantive debate about what to do about it, or what to do about Iran's nuclear program. Even in Israel, he argues, there is pushback against a simple military solution to the problem of Iran. Paul states, "Let me be clear. I don't want Iran to develop nuclear weapons but I also don't want to decide with certainty that war is the only option. Containment, though, should be discussed as an option with regard to the more generalized threat from radical Islam." As an alternative model to what he criticizes, he proposes Kennan's policy of containment developed against the threat posed by worldwide Communism during the Cold War. This containment requires not the military occupation of foreign lands but the working out of less costly intervention. Paul went on to condemn not only the Obama administration but also its predecessor for engaging in nation building. Clearly Rand was going after establishment Republicans and their neoconservative advisers.

In 2014, Rand Paul delivered another foreign policy speech, this time to the annual awards dinner for the Center for the National Interest, entitled "The Case for Conservative Realism."[48] The speech is consciously less intellectual than his earlier one and reads like an appeal by a presidential candidate. Here Paul seems to go easy on radical Islam, stating that rather than having an "Islam problem," the world may have a "dignity problem." While Paul insists that wars should be declared by Congress, and that the United States should not "engage in nation-building," he also supports existing European Union and NATO sanctions against Russia and does not object to defense spending. Kennan is no longer the model for an American foreign policy; instead, Paul ends his speech with a call for increased trade and economic prosperity as preconditions for national security.

Rand Paul's near-constant rhetorical repositioning—even while he maintained his basic positions on free trade, liberty, individual rights, and a more restrained foreign policy—arguably weakened him as a candidate for president. In trying to be too clever by half, he abandoned the single-minded, fiery, no-holds-barred attacks on the establishment that distinguished his father's campaigns. But even in the best of circumstances, Rand Paul would not have been a match for the force of nature that Donald Trump was in 2015 and 2016. The question of course remains open whether Trump any more than Rand Paul can claim the legacy of either George Kennan or Pat Buchanan as an architect of foreign policy.

Blowback: Donald J. Trump

Trump famously began his campaign on June 16, 2015, with the issue of immigration, and it cannot be denied that that issue was more critical for his electoral success than his positions on foreign policy. Trump had been attacking President Obama's actions in Syria with his Twitter account for a few years, but in the South Carolina primary debate in 2016, which took place in the presence of Jeb Bush and Jeb's mother, Barbara, Trump unloaded on George W. Bush's war in Iraq. He did not hold back from asserting that "George Bush made a mistake. . . . We should have never been in Iraq. We have destabilized the Middle East." He then piled on his prey: "I wanna tell you, they lied. They said there were weapons of mass destruction, there were none, and they knew there were none. There were no weapons of mass destruction." The crowd (filled mostly with South Carolina GOP officials, operatives, and donors) booed Trump and cheered wildly when Jeb Bush stood up for his brother and his family.[49]

But a few days later, Trump won the South Carolina primary with 32 percent of the vote in a field of seven candidates. Significantly, Jeb Bush received less than 8 percent of the vote. One cannot overstate the significance of this primary victory, after a direct attack on the Bush dynasty and on neoconservatism, in a state that reelected George W. Bush in 2004, with nearly 60 percent of the vote. Not only did Trump's repudiation of neoconservatism not hurt him, but it may have even helped him recruit voters who had not been engaged in politics since the days of the Buchanan Brigades. Trump was reintroducing into the Republican Party what the neoconservatives and the party bosses had condemned as "isolationism."

In April 2016, after his nomination was all but secure, Trump decided to roll out a series of policy speeches. In the first of these speeches he spoke not about immigration or trade but about foreign policy. Trump scoffed at nation building and other forms of intervention undertaken without a clear American interest and called for both the containment of radical Islam and stronger diplomatic relations with Russia: "The world must know that we do not go abroad in search of enemies, that we are always happy when old enemies become friends and when old friends become allies, that's what we want. We want them to be our allies."[50] While Trump lacked the principled constitutionalism of Ron Paul, he appealed to voters who were tired of endless war under both Republican and Democratic administrations. In accents that could have come from Pat Buchanan, he called for an America First foreign policy. He tied the question of intervention to trade and immigration with this statement: "Under a Trump administration, no American citizen will ever again feel that their needs come second to the citizens of a foreign country." The rhetorical centerpiece of the speech once again recalled the campaign issues of Buchanan: "No country has ever prospered that failed to put its own interests first. Both our friends and our enemies put their countries above ours and we, while being fair to them, must start doing the same. We will no longer surrender this country or its people to the false song of globalism. The nation-state remains the true foundation for happiness and harmony. I am skeptical of international unions that tie us up and bring America down and will never enter."[51] In an influential essay of the 2016 election cycle, "The Flight 93 Election," the anonymous author Publius Decius Mus (later identified as former George W. Bush administration appointee Michael Anton, who would go on to briefly serve in the Trump administration) likened Trump to Pat Buchanan for bringing back the triad of key issues that appealed to the middle-American voter: trade, immigration, and foreign policy. Whereas Ron Paul was right about war, he wrote, Paul did not put that issue into a winnable campaign strategy. Trump, for all his failures, was the only candidate since Buchanan who had.[52]

Trump campaigned like a Patrick Buchanan without the sharp religious and social edge. He was admittedly a cultural conservative on immigration and toed the party line on abortion. And yet, in the aftermath of Supreme Court decisions, the Religious Right understood that the culture wars were over and that they had lost. They saw Trump as their best chance for at least minimal protection against the onslaught of the social Left. Buchanan graciously stated in an interview with *Politico* after the election that Trump had won with issues that he had raised: "The ideas made it, but I didn't."[53] But for Buchanan, the damage was already done. America had gone too far toward the social Left to be brought back. Although Trump also struck some gloomy notes in his 2016 Republican National Convention speech, he nonetheless promised that he would bring America back from the brink: in short, he would make America great again. Moreover, Trump took over some of Ron Paul's warnings about interventionism without seeming to be an extreme noninterventionist. Perhaps he came closest to positioning himself in the manner of Rand Paul as a "conservative realist."

Trump might have become a second George W. Bush under different circumstances, but this has not yet occurred. While his anti-interventionist base was outraged when he sanctioned strikes on Syria in April 2017, the strikes carried out were rather limited. Trump has not (yet) been pushed into war with Syria or Iran and has engaged in the kind of diplomacy with North Korea that has not been seen since Nixon's opening to China. Due to the swirling Russian collusion narrative, the president has been held back from undertaking ambitious negotiations with Russia.[54] And though he has placed pressure on its allies to contribute more money to NATO, he is far from trying to disband the organization. Trump has gotten serious about reconsidering American trade policies toward foreign countries, especially China. The jury is out on whether Trump will actually pursue an America First foreign policy à la Kennan or Buchanan, but he has at least intermittently practiced diplomacy in a new key. Rand Paul praised him for meeting with Putin in July 2018 and expressed scorn for the new Russophobes.[55] It would testify to Trump's commitment to conservative realism if he elevated Rand Paul to the post of secretary of state or national security adviser. So far of course this has not happened.[56]

In 2000, Kenneth Waltz, the founder of the school of structural realism, wrote the article "Structural Realism after the Cold War," in which he predicted the disappearance of NATO after the Cold War. Unlike George Kennan, Waltz originally failed to see that NATO would find a new reason for existing even without a Soviet threat. Waltz reasonably asks how one can offer a guarantee if one cannot explain "guarantee against whom?"[57] Put another way, how can an alliance have meaning without a clear adversary? But arguing against those who would place the primacy of international institutions above the nation-state, Waltz writes,

> The survival and expansion of NATO tell us much about American power and influence and little about institutions as multilateral entities. The ability of the United States to extend the life of a moribund institution nicely illustrates how international institutions are created and maintained by stronger states to serve their perceived or misperceived interests. The Bush administration saw, and the Clinton administration continued to see, NATO as the instrument for maintaining America's domination of the foreign and military policies of European states. . . . The European pillar was to be contained within NATO, and its policies were to be made in Washington.[58]

Waltz supports the argument made by Buchanan that we unnecessarily alienate Russia if we work to bolster and expand NATO. "The American arms industry," he writes, "expecting to capture its usual large share of a new market, has lobbied heavily in favor of NATO's expansion. The reasons for expanding NATO are weak. The reasons for opposing expansion are strong. It draws new lines of division in Europe, alienates those left out, and can find no logical stopping place west of Russia."[59] We may wonder whether Trump has absorbed such lessons and, perhaps even more relevant, whether he fully understands the historical context in which he came to power. Part of his electoral success can be traced back to the geopolitical failures of the Bush and Obama eras; and without exaggerating continuities, the alternatives suggested by candidate Trump, however tentatively during his electoral campaign, have something in common with the older American conservative realism of Kennan and Buchanan. The million-dollar question is whether the present administration will return to that understanding of the world, in earnest.

6

THE CONTRADICTIONS OF CATHOLIC NEOCONSERVATISM

Jesse Russell

The Catholic branch of the neoconservative movement has a very long geneal-ogy. One could begin examining it by mentioning the heresy of Americanism among Irish Catholics living in America in the eighteenth and nineteenth centu-ries who wanted to assimilate into Anglo-American Protestant liberalism.[1] One could also turn to the work of such moderately liberal early twentieth-century Catholic political thinkers as the American Father John Courtney Murray and the French Neo-Thomist philosophers Jacques Maritain and Yves R. Simon.[2] But Catholic neoconservatism as a definable and coherent movement begins with the reaction to 1960s radicalism.

Blowing in the Wind: Early Radical Roots

Before their entry into the Ronald Reagan regime, the Catholic neoconservatives were an amorphous bunch of thinkers adrift in the post–Vatican II, post-Kennedy era. In this period, some Catholics had made it to the heights of American politi-cal power but also began to lose their ethnic and religious cohesion. The story of Catholic neoconservatism is a "coming to America" immigrant story and shares some parallels with the Jewish neoconservative experience.[3] Moreover, the Cath-olic neocons, in a similar fashion to Jewish neoconservatives such as Norman Pod-horetz and Irving Kristol, not only went from being leftists to moderate conser-vatives but also were able to bring along some of their coreligionists on their political journey.[4]

The Vietnam War was a catalyzing event for the Catholic neoconservatives. After a stint as a Holy Cross seminarian from whence he went on to become a reporter at the Second Vatican Council (1962–1965), Michael Novak covered the Vietnam War for the *National Catholic Reporter*. He also served as the Catholic contributor to *Vietnam: Crisis of Conscience*[5] and interpreted the North Vietnamese cause as "a struggle for independence" similar to the American Revolution. Novak then called for an immediate American withdrawal from Southeast Asia.[6] Interestingly, however, the human rights credo that drove the young Novak to oppose the Vietnam War incorporated liberal ideas that the neoconservative Michael Novak would invoke to advocate wars in the Middle East for the sake of freedom and democracy. This transposition can be seen in onetime Lutheran pastor Richard John Neuhaus, who was once at the center of Christian radicalism. Neuhaus would form with Rabbi Abraham Joshua Heschel the group Clergy Concerned about Vietnam (later renamed Clergy and Laymen Concerned about Vietnam), which advocated for rights and freedom as a form of revolutionary struggle. Ironically, this was the same posture that inspired the later Neuhaus to endorse the war on terror and to call for liberating the oppressed peoples of the Middle East.

The Vietnam War was just one of the outlets for the early Catholic neoconservative revolutionary ethos; the other was the civil rights movement, which attracted Michael Novak. Like many of his generation who became Reaganites and neoconservatives, Novak never abandoned the foundational principle of the civil rights movement: the implicit notion that membership in Western nations is predicated not on ethnicity, religion, or historical claims but rather on commitment to the ideal of equality. Richard John Neuhaus was even closer to the center of Christian civil rights radicalism. The Lutheran pastor attended the epochal March on Washington in August 1963 as well as the 1965 Selma to Montgomery Freedom March. Like the New Left, Novak and Neuhaus viewed history as a process that was furthered by marginalized ethnic groups.[7] Catholic neoconservatives would maintain their civil rights ethos as they moved (slightly) to the Right.

They typically spoke about having had an epiphanic moment during which they embraced the neoconservative cause. In his memoirs, *Lessons in Hope: My Unexpected Life with St. John Paul II*,[8] the papal biographer and third member of the "Four Horseman" of the Catholic neoconservatives, George Weigel, although an early opponent of the Vietnam War, claims to have experienced a revelation during the lifting of Americans from the Saigon embassy in Operation Frequent Wind on April 29, 1975.[9] Humiliated by America's abandonment of the South Vietnamese, Weigel would thereafter become a convinced hawk who would provide the most vocal Catholic support for both Gulf Wars.

While Novak states in *Writing Left to Right* that he came out as a conservative with his April 20, 1976, *Wall Street Journal* article, "A Closet Conservative Confesses," he had joined the neoconservative fold as early as 1972.[10] Then he published an article in *Commentary* commemorating the life of Reinhold Niebuhr, one of the most important early influences on the neoconservatives. This essay was fittingly titled "Needing Niebuhr Again."[11] This often forgotten piece is critical to understanding the Catholic neoconservative movement. Echoing his attack on the White Anglo Saxon Protestant establishment in *The Rise of the Unmeltable Ethnics: The New Political Force of the 1970s*,[12] Novak's "Needing Niebuhr Again" decries Anglo-Saxon "racial pride" and argues for "realism" as opposed to both the "old" and "new" moralism.

George Weigel would recycle "Niebuhrian realism" in his foreign policy writings in the 1980s in which he argues for a realpolitik, pragmatic approach to politics. He calls for a view that favors "what works best" to prevail while at the same time holding individual Christians to a high personal moral standard. The old moralism that often conflicted with this realism would be the traditional Christian teachings regarding economic and social policy, which went back to the Middle Ages. Niebuhrian realism likewise rejected the new moralism of left-wing Christians who quoted the Gospels in support of socialism and pacifism. Novak rightly points out that the new moralism quickly degenerated into a hysterical emotivism that "used indignation, outrage, and feelings of guilt to energize reform."[13] Novak's appeal to Niebuhr would ultimately be abandoned as Catholic neoconservatives went on to other mentors.

For Richard John Neuhaus, it was the abortion issue that moved him rightward. Neuhaus's 1971 chronicle of his experience in Africa, *In Defense of People: Ecology and the Seduction of Radicalism*,[14] which was a response to Paul Ehrlich's 1968 *The Population Bomb*,[15] represented his first explicit attempt to distance himself from "radicalism." The Supreme Court's decision to legalize abortion in *Roe v. Wade* in 1972 precipitated a split among Christian activists of the Left and further solidified Neuhaus's conviction that the Democrats had become the party of death. Neuhaus's strong opposition to eugenics and population control and the practices of abortion, sterilization, and birth control would be issues over which the Catholic neoconservatives would not compromise, even if it meant serious division with other neoconservatives.[16] Neuhaus would continue to court Catholics, and slowly during the Reagan era he created at least an informal alliance among neoconservative Catholics, Protestants, and Jews.

Opportunities in the 1980s

The 1980s saw the political ascendancy of the Catholic neoconservatives as "Mr. Conservative," Ronald Reagan, successfully hoisted America out of the Vietnam era and jump-started the American economy while encouraging American optimism. At the same time, a Polish pope began to court the media and refurbished the public image of Catholicism that had languished under his predecessor Pope Paul VI (1963–1978). But the Catholic Left in the United States held sway over the American Church. This was in no small measure due to Joseph Cardinal Bernardin of Chicago, who pushed a radical reading of Vatican II. In addition to other public statements by liberal Catholic celebrities, two critical political documents came out of the Bernardin Church in the United States: the condemnation of the Reagan military buildup, *The Challenge of Peace: God's Promise and Our Response*,[17] and *Economic Justice for All*.[18] The latter was a not too subtle critique of the Reagan administration's policies that contained a number of economic ideas for those who were seeking a "third way" economic model.

Catholic neoconservatives worked to provide a political, economic, and military policy that would fit the needs of the Reagan Republican era. While the Catholic neoconservatives labored under the shadow of the American Catholic Left, dominated by Joseph Cardinal Bernardin and his acolytes, it was also essential for them to discredit the Catholic Old Right. Patrick Allitt documents in *Catholic Intellectuals and Conservative Politics in America, 1950–1985*[19] that until the Second Vatican Council, Catholics in America celebrated three major figures: Pope Pius XII, Cardinal Francis Spellman of New York, and Senator Joseph McCarthy.[20] Certainly, Pope Pius XII, the last pope representing the older tradition, deeply sympathized with monarchy and more generally the Right. Cardinal Spellman and Senator McCarthy were both patriotic Americans whose fierce opposition to Communism attracted the Right. It would be difficult to regard these figures as liberals or even "proto-neoconservatives."[21]

The twentieth century, moreover, gave many examples of traditionally conservative Catholic parties such as Action Française in early twentieth-century France, which scorned democratic pluralism as well as Communism. Such parties and the regimes that they created were seen as obstacles to the neoconservative project because they offered an unwanted countermodel to the Left. It was therefore essential for the Catholic neoconservatives to craft a new conservatism that took its cue from a selective, post–World War II reading of Anglo-American liberalism.

Catholic social teaching from its modern inception with Pope Leo XIII's 1891 *Rerum Novarum* had been dominated by both reactionary and moderate left-wing critiques of capitalism and socialism. Not surprisingly, the first sphere in which the neoconservatives tried to make their weight felt in the 1980s was economic policy. In 1982, Michael Novak, who was then at the American Enterprise Institute, published *The Spirit of Democratic Capitalism*.[22] A dense and by no means felicitously written tome, Novak's book hardly represents an original contribution to economic thought. Rather, like Weigel, Neuhaus, and later Robert George, Novak was able to market neoconservative ideas to American Catholics while claiming to be a learned Catholic theologian. Drawing selectively on Max Weber's *The Protestant Ethic and the Spirit of Capitalism* and the political writing of John Locke, Novak argues that capitalism springs from the application of human reasoning. (For window dressing, he avails himself of the Aristotelian-Scholastic term "practical intellect.") Capitalists imitate and complete God's act of creation, "bringing forth the potentialities the Creator has hidden."[23] This unleashing of the power of capitalism in Western Europe during the Enlightenment, according to Novak, has released the "spirit of democratic capitalism," which is "the spirit of development, risk, experiment, adventure." Through their activity, capitalists have "introduced a novel pluralism into the very center of the social system."[24] Contrary to two hundred years of Catholic political teaching, Novak also maintained that liberal democracy, as practiced by the United States, offered humanity the noblest form of government. The alleged tolerance and pluralism of liberal democracy, in Novak's view, prevented "grave dangers to the human spirit," which "lurk in the subordination of the political system and the economic system to a single moral cultural vision."[25] In such passages Novak is at least indirectly attempting to overturn the traditional Catholic position that Catholic teachings should be the supreme moral authority of the state.

Novak's magnum opus appeared at the onset of the Reagan revolution and became a best seller at least partly because of when it was published. It reached the book market as many were prospering in the later 1980s and during the Clinton boom of the 1990s. Among its uses to Catholic neoconservatives, *The Spirit of Democratic Capitalism* provided a counterpoint to the Bernardin wing of the American Catholic Church. It also was cited against the socialist-tinged church in Europe that reflected the spirit of John Paul II's social encyclicals.

The Spirit of Democratic Capitalism and its defense of American welfare state capitalism found an ideological companion in Richard John Neuhaus's *The Naked Public Square*, which appeared in 1984. Neuhaus's work would serve as the political breviary of religious neoconservatives. *The Naked Public Square* is often interpreted as a manifesto of right-wing religious extremism, indeed as a call for theocracy.[26] But contrary to Neuhaus's left-wing critics who may not have read his work, *The Naked Public Square* was intended to launch a new religious Right. It would be different from the old one that was too weighed down with illiberal sentiments for neoconservative tastes. Neuhaus makes it clear in *The Naked*

Public Square that the new religious Right would base its arguments not on the Bible but on natural reason. He condemned the "strictness and dogmatism of reactionary religious groups"[27] and those who would call for "Constantinism,"[28] a term used by the Left to attack the alliance between Christianity and state power that began during the reign of Constantine the Great. Shedding traditional American conservative Protestant antipathy to Catholicism and, to a lesser degree, Judaism, Neuhaus called for a public square defined by "biblical, Judeo-Christian religion"[29] and led by "nonfundamentalist evangelicals."[30] In place of a Christian theocracy, Neuhaus hoped to weld his projected union of Protestantism, Catholicism, and Judaism into a powerful political coalition. He laid out the qualities that define "the project we call America," which included "a devotion to liberal democracy, a near obsession with civil liberties, a relatively open market economy, the aspiration toward equality of opportunity, a commitment to an institutionalized balancing of powers and countervailing forces, and a readiness to defend this kind of social experiment, if necessary, by military force."[31] Promoting liberalism if necessary by military means would come to characterize not only its Catholic formulation but all neoconservativism in the twenty-first century.

Meanwhile, George Weigel would tackle foreign policy from a neoconservative perspective laced with Catholic theological references. Like the economic and social argument in the Catholic Church in America, issues of war and peace concerned left-leaning bishops who made no bones about their contempt for Ronald Reagan's increase in defense spending. In response to the National Conference of Catholic Bishops' *Challenge of Peace: God's Promise and Our Response,* Weigel penned *Tranquillitas Ordinis: The Present Failure and Future Promise of American Catholic Thought on War and Peace.*[32] His work is neoconservatism's first major attempt to recruit patristic and medieval Catholic theology for a defense of neoconservative politics. Weigel argues seemingly in accordance with Augustine's conception of *Tranquillitas Ordinis* and other Christian sources that American global military hegemony conforms to the just war theory that marked the Catholic justification for military force. Weigel contends that Catholic thought, properly understood, can help "advance the international peace of political community, freedom, charity, justice, and truth."[33] Although Weigel is correct that the Catholic Left's pacifist approach runs contrary to Catholic tradition, his insistence on an escalating military buildup for the sake of advancing "human rights" would probably seem alien to a traditional Catholic theologian.

The Ascendance of the 1990s

The Catholic neoconservatives were able to ride the coattails of the Reagan revolution into the early 1990s. Still, they often appeared as outsiders in terms of their disconnectedness from the Catholic hierarchy. As they tried to enhance their specifically Catholic profile, they hitched themselves to John Paul II's pontificate. The first effort in this direction came with their management of the American reception of John Paul II's commemoration of the one hundredth anniversary of Pope Leo XIII's *Rerum Novarum*, *Centesimus Annus*. John Paul had disappointed the neoconservatives with his encyclicals *Laborem Exercens* (1981) and *Sollicitudo Rei Socialis* (1987), which, like earlier Catholic social teachings, had focused on protecting labor over capital. Rumors out of the Vatican and from the neoconservative-friendly politician Rocco Buttiglione indicated that *Centesimus Annus* would be more sympathetic to capitalism than were previous papal pronouncements.[34] With the euphoria of the defeat of Communism in Eastern Europe washing over the West, it seemed especially critical for the Catholic neoconservatives to explain Catholic social teaching as neoconservative. It had to be shown to be a liberal counterweight to the church's reactionary past while at the same time standing athwart the leftward drift of bishops in the West. Receiving a purloined copy of the encyclical, each of the neocons published an article the day before its official release on May 2, 1991. Novak released a piece in the *Washington Post*, Weigel in the *Los Angeles Times*, and Neuhaus in the *Wall Street Journal*.[35] There is little question that John Paul II's *Centesimus* contains some positive and cautious endorsements of "free market" economy "as the most efficient instrument for utilizing resources and effectively responding to need." That said, the encyclical also excoriates the "structures of sin" in Western capitalism, "which impede the full realization of those who are in any way oppressed."[36] Although *Centesimus* was not a full-throated affirmation of capitalism, as some have noted,[37] the Catholic neoconservatives were able to argue with at least minimal credibility that a new era in Catholic social teaching had arrived.[38]

The 1990s also witnessed a battle on several fronts between the Catholic neoconservatives and both the Right and the Left. The neoconservatives gained a powerful platform for their ideas in what was to become the most pronounced voice of religious neoconservativism: *First Things*, which was born from the split between the neoconservatives and the paleoconservatives after the Cold War. *First Things* magazine became an influential publication throughout the 1990s and early twenty-first century as a platform for neoconservative ideology addressed to Jewish neoconservatives and self-described traditional Christians. The magazine soon adopted a specifically Catholic tone as its editor, Richard John Neuhaus, would be accepted into the Catholic Church on September 8, 1990. Neuhaus was then ordained as a priest a year later, after studying under the tutelage of Father Avery Dulles, son of President Eisenhower's secretary of state, John Foster Dulles.

Furthermore, despite losing elections to the charismatic William Jefferson Clinton in the 1990s, the Catholic neoconservatives were able to capture their own prize: molding the American view of Pope John Paul II. Despite his reactionary associations (John Paul's birth name "Karol" was derived from the last Hapsburg emperor, Blessed Charles of Austria, for whom John Paul II's father served as a Calvary officer) and his apparently left-leaning economic views, John Paul was, in many ways, the first American pope. As a cardinal, Karol Wojtyła developed a friendship and professional alliance with President Jimmy Carter's national security advisor, Zbigniew Brzezinski. (The future Polish pope would meet with Brzezinski on his visits to the United States.) But the American politician with whom John Paul developed the closest working relationship was Ronald Wilson Reagan, someone who happily listened to neoconservatives advisers.[39]

The Catholic neoconservatives also marketed themselves as leaders of conservative Catholic discourse. They did this at least partly in the context of presenting themselves as the authorized interpreters of John Paul II's thought in the United States. George Weigel also positioned himself simultaneously with favorable coverage from the neoconservative media as an interpreter of Eastern European Catholic politics. He did this most successfully in *The Final Revolution: The Resistance Church and the Collapse of Communism* in 1992.[40] *The Final Revolution* also drew the attention of those in the Vatican with pro-American sympathies such as Vatican press secretary Joaquin Navarro Valls and Bishop Stanislaw Dziwisz, John Paul's personal secretary. Weigel admits in *Lessons in Hope* that he collaborated with Joaquin Navarro Valls to offset the effect of *New York Times* reporter Tad Szulc's biography *John Paul II: The Biography*.[41] In Szulc's work, the Polish pontiff is depicted as theologically conservative but tending toward the Left on economic questions. Such a position went contrary to the neoconservative reading of John Paul. While the neoconservatives themselves had adopted the appellation "conservative," it was essential for them to control what that term meant. This was especially the case in dealing with a two-thousand-year-old institution that was in cultural flux. In any case, Catholic neoconservatives needed to make it appear that John Paul II approved of their brand of American conservatism.

Weigel's friend and Vatican public relations official Joaquin Navarro Valls tried to alter Tad Szulc's depiction of John Paul II as someone who was theologically conservative but leaned toward the socialist Left in economic matters. He tried to do this in his own efforts to depict the pope. Then Weigel released *Witness to Hope: The Biography of John Paul II* in 1999,[42] which was followed by *The End and the Beginning: Pope John Paul II—The Victory of Freedom, the Last Years, the Legacy.*[43] This latter work complimented the earlier *God's Choice: Pope Benedict*

XVI and the Future of the Catholic Church,[44] a work that was ostensibly about Benedict XVI but that also dealt with John Paul II. (At least half of the last book was dedicated to the late Polish pontiff.) Weigel's seminal biography, *Witness to Hope*, which was heavily quoted during John Paul's canonization procedure, presents John Paul as a kind of Hegelian hero, who was fated to spread liberal and democratic capitalism. Weigel, in fact, reaches for the Hegelian term "world historical" in characterizing John Paul II in his biographies.[45] This popular depiction of John Paul II marked a success for Catholic neoconservatives as they worked to achieve public recognition. It also ensured that Vatican pronouncements about certain political issues would be packaged in neoconservative dressing for American audiences.

The 1990s also saw the entrance of a fourth member, Professor Robert George of Princeton University, of what would later be called the Four Horsemen. In a series of books, beginning with *Making Men Moral: Civil Liberties and Public Morality*[46] and including *The Clash of Orthodoxies: Law, Religion, and Morality in Crisis*[47] and *In Defense of Natural Law*[48], George attempted to provide an academic pedigree for Richard John Neuhaus's task of ensuring a strong Christian voice in the public square. George's efforts focused on providing Natural Law arguments derived from Scholastic and Classical philosophy in support of defending human life and Christian marriage. Like the "Whig Thomism" (that presents St. Thomas Aquinas as one of the fathers of Anglo-American liberalism) identified with Michael Novak in *This Hemisphere of Liberty*, Robert George presented himself as a conservative Catholic philosopher influenced by both St. Thomas Aquinas and the American liberal tradition. Significantly George omitted Aquinas's insistence that the church have supreme moral authority and that Divine Law direct human morality.[49] The question is whether George would have gained his prominence as a neoconservative-promoted Catholic conservative if he had tried to expound such positions.

The Triumph of the Bush Era and the Beginning of the End

Like heroes in a Greek tragedy, the Catholic neoconservatives fell from power and influence after they reached the heights of their success. During the first term of George W. Bush's presidency, the Catholic neoconservatives were able to score a series of crucial domestic and foreign policy victories. But with the advent of the second Gulf War in 2003 and the unmistakable opposition to the war coming from John Paul II's Vatican, the Catholic neoconservatives lost their credibility as representatives of the papacy. Their association with George W. Bush became a liability since both the papacy and the American presidency in the twenty-first century changed in ways the neoconservatives had not foreseen.

The Catholic neoconservative support for the 2003 Iraq War found a precedent for the first Persian Gulf War in 1990. Already then Catholic neoconservatives were forced to combat American Catholic bishops who opposed President George H. W. Bush's war. They were also forced to oppose John Paul II, who also specifically condemned the invasion of Iraq for "casting a shadow over the whole human community."[50] In response to the opposition from both Catholic and Protestant clergy to the Iraq War, George Weigel and Rutgers University's James Turner Johnson wrote *Just War and the Gulf War.*[51] Outside of Iraqi fatalities and the mysterious Gulf War syndrome that affected American troops, the war, according to these authors, was a smashing success. Later the split between the Catholic neoconservatives and the papacy over the 2003 Iraq War would further weaken the prestige of Catholic neoconservatives.

Like their non-Catholic colleagues, the Catholic neoconservatives had labored throughout the 1990s to push President Clinton into invading Iraq.[52] While Saddam had been an American ally in the 1980s, he had also been in the crosshairs of the neoconservatives. A member of the Project for the New American Century, or PNAC, George Weigel was one of the signatories of the neoconservative think tank's "Statement of Principles," which argued for expanded American global rule through "military strength."[53] According to PNAC's statement of principles, one of the areas of the world in which American military strength was needed was the Middle East—especially Iraq, the destruction of which, it was argued, was necessary for peace in the Middle East. The events of September 11, 2001, famously gave the neoconservatives a blank check to remake the Islamic world, and, at least initially, they had the support of the American people in their efforts.

John Paul II and the Vatican, however, were adamant in their opposition to the Second Gulf War. Thus, in the lead-up to this invasion, the neoconservatives did everything in their power to convince the Vatican to support President George W. Bush's decision to topple the Iraqi government. Along with neoconservative William Bennett and conservative gay rights activist Andrew Sullivan, Novak went to the Vatican in the winter of 2003 to persuade John Paul II to support the war. The Americans, however, were not given a papal audience, and the Catholic neoconservatives had to go it alone during the Iraq War. Then they were forced to break ranks with the pope on whom they had based their own reputations as Catholic spokesmen. The Catholic neoconservatives struck back with what ammunition they had. Weigel turns to mockery in *Lessons in Hope*, stating that there "was little serious just war thinking inside the Leonine Wall," which was the result of "a conceptual vacuum" in Catholic thought.[54] In *God's Choice*, Weigel again blames the Vatican's refusal to support the war on "poor coordination of the Vatican's message."[55] Never does Weigel admit that John Paul II opposed both Iraq wars. But Michael Novak was more honest, writing in his autobiography that he experienced a "great struggle of conscience" when "the pope did all he could to avert the second war in Iraq."[56] The clear discord between John Paul II and then Benedict XVI, on the one side, and the Catholic neoconservatives, on the other, during the Iraq War caused irreparable damage in the relationship between the two.

As it became clear that the liberation of Iraq was by no means a "mission accomplished," the Catholic neoconservatives crafted a series of books in support of George W. Bush and the war on terror. In 2005 George Weigel released *The Cube and the Cathedral: Europe, America, and Politics without God*,[57] a simplified but more theologically weighted version of the work by foreign policy strategist Robert Kagan, *Of Paradise and Power: America and Europe in the New World Order*.[58] *The Cube and the Cathedral* maintains that the European refusal to support American interventionist policy is rooted in Christian decline. In his book, Weigel points to declining birthrates and the omission of the mention of God in the European Constitution. Yet, as the war dragged on and hundreds of thousands of American servicemen and women returned from the Middle East with what became popularly known as PTSD (post-traumatic stress disorder), Weigel needed to craft a better-developed argument to convince Catholic readers that the war on terror was a necessary struggle, indeed a clash of civilizations.

The clash of civilization, in Weigel's presentations, was not an ethnic or religious conflict. Rather, it was a Kulturkampf between liberalism and authoritarianism. In 2007 George Weigel released *Faith, Reason, and the War against Jihadism*[59] at the height of the surge and immediately before John McCain's loss to Barack Obama in the presidential election of 2008. Released in tandem with Norman Podhoretz's *World War IV: The Long Struggle against Islamofascism*,[60] *The War against Jihadism* is an attack against not only "jihadists" but also "postmodernists"[61] and "xenophobes" such as Patrick J. Buchanan. Weigel sees the war on terror as a means of establishing "Enlightenment political theory" and, above all, "religious freedom" in the Islamic world.[62] This point is especially critical for understanding the Catholic neoconservative vision of the war on terror. The Catholic neoconservatives tried to fold religious language and ideas into a largely liberal political argument aimed at garnering support for a liberal "crusade" against Arab authoritarianism. In the end, however, the Catholic neoconservative argument failed as Barack Hussein Obama became president, ushering in a leftist ascendancy.

The second major setback for the neoconservatives in managing the image of the pope was the election of Joseph Ratzinger as Pope Benedict XVI. In 2007, Pope Benedict XVI issued an encyclical *Summorum Pontificum*, regularizing the ancient

Latin Mass that had been supplanted by the *Novus Ordo Missae* in 1969. In this announcement the pontiff stated, "What earlier generations held as sacred, remains sacred and great for us too, and it cannot be all of a sudden entirely forbidden or even considered harmful."[63] Pope Benedict thus gave the lie to the neoconservative notion that the church was modernizing itself irreversibly. But Pope Benedict's regularization of the Latin Mass was not enough to draw the ire of Catholic neoconservatives. Benedict's overture to Catholic traditionalists, in the form of lifting the excommunications of four bishops of the traditionalist Society of St. Pius X (SSPX), indicated a turning toward the Right on the part of Rome. The society was founded by the late French archbishop Marcel Lefebvre, a churchman who flaunted his reactionary political and religious views. For the sake of damage control, George Weigel wrote a commentary in *Newsweek* entitled "Did the Pope Heal or Deepen a Catholic Schism?" Here Weigel said the obvious when he linked the SSPX to nineteenth- and early twentieth-century French reactionary thought.[64]

Pope Francis, the first pope from the New World, turned out to be even more radically different for the neoconservatives than the pope he replaced. The first shot fired across the neoconservative bow was the Apostolic Exhortation *Gaudium Evangelii*, in which the Holy Father condemned trickle-down economics. In *Gaudium Evangelii*, the pope argued that "some people continue to defend trickle-down theories which assume that economic growth, encouraged by a free market, will inevitably succeed in bringing about greater justice and inclusiveness in the world."[65] The impression that Catholic teaching on economics had forever changed with John Paul II's *Centesimus Annus* began to crumble; and in response to *Evangelii Gaudium*, Michael Novak penned "Agreeing with Pope Francis," which was printed in the *National Review*.[66] Novak argued unconvincingly that Pope Francis was conditioned by his experience in Latin America and that in any case his words were mistranslated into English. As the Holy Father gave a host of sound bite statements and photo opportunities that declared his sympathy with Marxism, the neoconservative attempt to control Francis proved even more futile.

But this opposition to capitalism was not enough to complete the divorce between the neoconservatives and the papacy. Throughout a series of interviews and casual pronouncements, Pope Francis also revealed an at least tacit endorsement of homosexual relations, transgenderism, and the use of birth control. He has also remained relatively silent on the issue of abortion to the chagrin of traditional Catholics.[67] Pope Francis also shocked the traditionalist camp when he appeared to endorse divorce and remarriage in his 2016 Apostolic Exhortation *Amoris Laetitia*.[68] The strong opposition of John Paul II and Benedict XVI to homosexuality and abortion and their defense of Christian marriage had been obviously more congenial to Catholic neoconservatives. John Paul II had, in fact, written an encyclical at the height of the Clinton era, *Evangelium Vitae*, or "The Gospel of life," in which the pontiff strongly condemned abortion and argued for a "culture of life."[69] Moreover, the pro-life argument had been one of the most effective tools for recruiting Catholics into the Republican fold. As the Roman pontiff began sending mixed signals on abortion and marriage, the Catholic neoconservatives felt obliged to distance themselves.

Finally, even the old grand dame of Catholic neoconservatives, Father Richard John Neuhaus, gave his pet project, *First Things*, an illiberal cast in 2017 and 2018. The editors began questioning free market capitalism and published the strongly worded article "Mammon Ascendant: Why Global Capitalism Is Inimical to Christianity."[70] *First Things* drew further comment in 2018 when it published a positive review of the memoirs of Father Edgardo Mortara. This was the young Jewish boy who was clandestinely baptized as a sickly infant and then taken by Pope Pius IX and raised as a Catholic. (Mortara eventually became a Catholic priest.) The publication of this review prompted an angry and nervous rebuttal from the remaining Catholic neoconservatives. These Catholics hoped to preserve an alliance with neoconservative Jews as an essential element of their cultural capital (i.e., being allied with Jews created the impression that the Catholic Church had shed its reactionary cast).[71] What was most noteworthy here is that a Catholic and supposedly neoconservative journal, *First Things* magazine, presented a "pre–Vatican II" or traditionalist argument in favor of a premodern church. With the Catholic neoconservative journal par excellence departing from the party line, the Catholic neoconservatives received another critical blow.[72]

The downfall of the Catholic neoconservatives was further accelerated by the election of Donald J. Trump, whom Robert George and George Weigel attacked in a May 2016 *National Review* piece, "An Appeal to Our Fellow Catholics."[73] In their diatribe, Weigel, George, and their fellow cosigners warned that Donald Trump would endanger the moderately socially conservative and small government coalition that the neoconservatives had built. They fretted that Trump's "vulgarity" and "appeals to racial and ethnic fears" were contrary to "any genuinely Catholic sensibility."[74] While in the past the Catholic neoconservatives had been successful in promoting or damaging politicians, this time their rhetoric did not work. Trump earned the nomination, and a majority of white Catholics voted for Donald Trump over Hillary Clinton in the 2016 presidential election.

Michael Novak's signature was curiously missing from "An Appeal to Our Fellow Catholics." After the 2016 election the veteran Catholic neoconservative wrote two pieces, one in *First Things*, "Silver Linings for Never Trumpers,"[75] and the other, "What on Earth Happened on November 8?"[76] in *National Review*. Both commentaries welcomed the populist uprising that Trump's victory represented for the country. It is difficult to tell what Novak's being out of step with his group indicated. Was he returning to his working-class origins that he celebrated in *The Rise of the Unmeltable Ethnics*, or was he switching to what he thought was a rising political force? One thing was certain, however: Novak's comrades in arms in the neoconservative movement could no longer sway American Catholics.

Like the earlier generation of Jewish thinkers who influenced them, the Catholic neoconservatives appear to have made a political journey. While the course generally went from "left to right," the Catholic neoconservatives still retained elements of their earlier positions. Like the Jewish neoconservatives, they repackaged with some change in the contents their older positions and called it "conservatism." But it was always possible to discern in their later political and moral statements the progressive welfare state politics of an earlier generation, and this was true in their defenses of capitalism as well as in their other polemical activities. What Catholic neoconservatives wished to discourage was any lurch toward what they saw as the economic Left; and they were often at war with the Catholic hierarchy whom they scolded for pushing "democratic capitalism" in the direction of something un-American.

Likewise they remained faithful in their minds to the human rights ideology that had accompanied their youthful political crusades. In line with this apparent transformation, Catholic neoconservatives shaped or reshaped the image of Pope John Paul II as a "world historical" figure who was promoting democratic capitalism and liberal democracy. Whatever the media visibility of these figures, they remained dependent on a larger movement of which they were only a piece. Although their neoconservative sponsors used them for alliance-building purposes, the more powerful non-Catholic neoconservatives also viewed the Catholic neoconservatives as expendable. Not surprisingly, Catholic neoconservatism declined in importance as neoconservatism went from being the only visible or significant form of establishment conservatism to being its still dominant but no longer all-inclusive form.

7

TRUMP, NEOCONSERVATIVES, AND THE MISREPRESENTATION OF THE AMERICAN FOUNDING

Nicholas W. Drummond

Donald Trump's presidential campaign messages of "America First" and "Make America Great Again" vowed to put the interests of "the people" before the interests of elites, noncitizens, and foreigners.[1] As Trump reiterated in the State of the Union (2018): "My highest loyalty, my greatest compassion, and my constant concern is for America's children, America's struggling workers and America's forgotten communities. I want our youth to grow up to achieve great things. I want our poor to have their chance to rise."[2] In terms of actual policy, Trump promised the end of interventionist wars, tougher enforcement of immigration laws, the construction of a border wall, and the restructuring of trade deals like the North American Free Trade Agreement).

Neoconservatives have been critical of all these proposals, but Trump's immigration policy has received the harshest denunciations. In this chapter, I discuss a repeated theme of these critics—that Trumpism is a betrayal of America's founding principles. Through textual analysis of primary sources, I demonstrate this claim to be inaccurate because it relies on Straussian scholarship that ignores the anthropological requirements of America's political system.[3] Cultural and racial diversity have enriched the country in many ways, but if the Founders knew America would become a heterogeneous republic, they would have designed a very different political system. Some Straussians do acknowledge the Founders' aversion toward diversity, but their analysis gives insufficient attention to the enabling relationship James Madison identified between heterogeneity and plutocracy.[4]

The Straussian Founding

The name Leo Strauss probably means very little to most Americans, but it is a name they should investigate because the interpretation of the Founding associated with this immigrant professor from Germany has significantly influenced U.S. politics. Although Strauss had relatively little to say about America, his disciples reshaped America's national mythology and political ethos, and in doing so, have facilitated its demographic and cultural transformation. Americans may be more tolerant and inclusive because of these changes, but the diverse country we are today is not the republic envisioned by the Founding Fathers. This alone should concern Americans because the person who designs something may have a better understanding of its limitations.

Straussians are unified by their shared respect for ancient Greek philosophers and for Strauss himself, but they have divided into two rival camps offering distinct but overlapping interpretations of the Founding.[5] The East Coast contingent includes such widely celebrated scholars as Allan Bloom, Harvey Mansfield, and Thomas Pangle. They tend to regard the American republic as a Lockean project of individualism and rational self-interest. Instead of establishing a republic based on virtue, natural law, or religious ideals, the Founders are said to have envisioned a modern commercial regime built on the "low but solid ground" of self-preservation and the acquisition of property.[6] A "homogeneous citizenry" would not be required to sustain this republic because America was a creedal nation in which law-abiding citizens "found a fundamental basis of unity" in accepting rights enumerated by the Declaration and protected by the Constitution.[7] Thus, the great hope of this project was for divisive affiliations like "class, race, religion, national origin, or culture" to diminish in importance because citizens would become "universal, abstract" individuals.[8]

The West Coast Straussians include prominent scholars such as Harry Jaffa, Charles Kesler, and Larry Arnn. They tend to believe the Founders were influenced by an "Aristotelian-Locke" whose philosophy incorporated natural law and Judeo-Christian values.[9] The Founding was thus a noble project of culminating political thought, codified by Thomas Jefferson's Declaration, and fully applied by Abraham Lincoln's assertion that America was "a new nation . . . dedicated to the proposition that all men are created equal."[10] Instead of establishing the shallow and materialistic regime depicted by the East Coasters, the Founders are thought to have designed a republic for virtuous and religious citizens who strive for moderation, justice, and liberty.[11] Despite these differences, the West Coasters share their rival's view that America was a creedal nation. Citizens who differed by race, class, religion, or national origin could unify as one people if they embraced the "universal principles" of the Declaration.[12]

The Straussian version of the Founding has been critical for American politics because of its adoption by neoconservatives.[13] These advocates may not be true disciples of Strauss, but they employ the universalistic language of the Straussians and they invoke the names of the Founders. Ironically, this is done to promote neoconservative policies that the Founders would have found problematic, like mass immigration and wars intended to convert other countries to American-style democracy.[14] In this regard, the neocons resemble Al-Farabi, the Middle Eastern philosopher admired by Strauss who recommended the deceptive strategy of gradually leading the "vulgar" masses away from "accepted opinions" by dressing their opinions in familiar robes.[15]

The Neoconservatives

Neoconservatives are best known today for being war hawks associated with the Bush administration's military occupation of Iraq in 2003.[16] Before Trumpism, they were despised by the Left for establishing "a dystopian national security state" and for murdering "hundreds of thousands of citizens" in the Middle East.[17] Yet, in response to Trump's ascendancy, the neocons have sought an alliance with the establishment Left because of converging views about foreign policy, trade, and immigration.[18] Mutual concerns about Trump's demagoguery may also be unifying this Left-Right coalition.[19]

What exactly is neoconservatism and how has it influenced the Right? In a seminal essay answering this exact question, the "godfather" of the neoconservatives Irving Kristol said, "The historical task and political purpose of neoconservatism [is] to convert the Republican Party, and American conservatism in general, against their respective wills, into a new kind of conservative politics suitable to governing a modern democracy."[20] Given that Kristol traces the origins of this movement to "disillusioned liberal intellectuals in the 1970's," it might be the case that neoconservatives reshaped the conservative movement to fit their own interests and values.[21] A more academic interpretation is that Kristol and other neocons have successfully executed the strategy of entryism, which is when a political group "enters a larger [organization] with the intention of subverting its policies and objectives."[22] Incidentally, this strategy was popularized by Leon Trotsky, a Marxist intellectual esteemed by some neoconservatives.[23]

In his discussion of the American roots of neoconservatism, Kristol makes no reference to the Founding Fathers. Instead, he associates his political "persuasion" with the "20th-century heroes . . . TR, FDR, and Ronald Reagan."[24] His seminal essay also mentions the influence of Strauss, an intellectual whose teachings and writings have guided neocons like Abram Shulsky and Bret Stephens.[25] Other neoconservatives like Robert Kagan and Paul Wolfowitz may deny Straussian influence on their thinking, but the universalistic and human rights themes of the Straussian Founding permeate their writings and speeches.[26]

The Straussian Founding is particularly evident in the neoconservative critique of Trump's immigration policies. For example, Stephens has called Trump "a loudmouth vulgarian" whose policies constitute a rejection of America's "founding creed," which Stephens reduces to (1) "all men are created equal," and (2) Emma Lazarus's 1883 poem, "give us your tired, your poor."[27] Jennifer Rubin has said "antagonism toward immigrants and a preference for White Europeans over brown and black people remain the default setting for Trump and increasingly for his party."[28] Rubin supports "robust legal immigration" from all corners of the globe because "it demonstrates fidelity to the Founders' vision that the country be defined not by race or ethnicity (blood and soil) but by adherence to the ideals of the republic."[29] Former president George W. Bush has described Trump's hard-line views on immigration as "nativism," emboldened "bigotry," and "blasphemy against the American creed."[30] He supports this critique by appealing to the Founders and the values they bequeathed us: "We become the heirs of Thomas Jefferson by accepting the ideal of human dignity found in the Declaration of Independence. We become the heirs of James Madison by understanding the genius and values of the U.S. Constitution."[31]

Diversity and the American Founding

There is no denying that Trump has said controversial things about immigrants, but neoconservatives who appropriate Straussian ideals to attack Trump's immigration policies are misrepresenting the Founders.[32] Uncomfortable as it may be for scholars to admit, the Founders established a republic that assumed racial and cultural homogeneity, and they attempted to preserve this homogeneity with governmental control of naturalization. This sentiment is most evident in *The Federalist Papers*, no. 2, where John Jay describes the unity of the American people as follows: "A people descended from the same ancestors, speaking the same language, professing the same religion, attached to the same principles of government, very similar in their manners and customs, and who, by their joint counsels, arms, and efforts, fighting side by side throughout a long and bloody war, have nobly established general liberty and independence."[33]

Scholars have accused Jay of exaggerating America's homogeneity, but some of these scholars are guiltier of exaggerating the country's heterogeneity. They do so by overstating the political, ethnic, religious, and linguistic differences of Americans; or by highlighting social forms of diversity (e.g., diet choices, fashion, and sexuality) that likely exist in all nations and probably most small cities; or by including within their demographic calculations three groups excluded from citizenship—slaves, Indians, and Tories who fled America after the Revolution.[34] America in 1787 was clearly not a small, homogenous republic of uniform manners, but that hardly means its internal divisions were as salient as they are today.[35]

The best data we have on the demographics of this period (1790) indicate that (1) approximately 60 percent of whites were ethnically English; (2) around 86 percent of whites hailed from the British Isles; and (3) most of the remaining whites traced their ancestry to Western Europe.[36] Furthermore, according to the census of 1790, America's population of 3,893,637 disaggregates as follows: 3,140,207 (80.65%) were white; 694,280 (17.83%) were slaves; and 59,150 (1.52%) were free nonwhites.[37] The nonwhite citizen population was therefore about 1.85 percent of the total population. As for culture, divisions certainly existed that were associated with region, economics, and sectarianism, but Jay dismissed these differences because America's majority culture was Protestant Anglo-Saxon, which meant the country was "a band of brethren, united to each other by the strongest ties."[38] Although George Washington and Madison viewed the possibility of Jewish and Catholic integration favorably, Madison echoed Jay's sentiment when he said Americans were "mutual guardians of their mutual happiness" because they were "knit together . . . by so many cords of affection."[39] This included the "kindred blood" that made Americans "fellow citizens" capable of living "together as members of the same family."[40] Madison also said Americans were British in their "language . . . usages . . . & . . . manners."[41]

Alexander Hamilton likewise regarded American culture as predominantly British, and he said the country was sufficiently homogenous for the Constitution to work as designed.[42] He also warned that national security required "the energy of a common National sentiment," which would be eroded by immigrants of "foreign bias" who harbored antiliberal values and were attached to the "customs and manners" of their native countries. An "influx of foreigners" was therefore likely to produce a heterogeneous compound," which would "complicate and confound public opinion" and "introduce foreign propensities."[43] These concerns were shared by other Founders such as Jefferson, Benjamin Franklin, and James Winthrop.[44] Madison likewise believed that naturalization should be limited to those immigrants who "really meant to incorporate into our society."[45] He declared on the floor of Congress that citizenship was a privilege and should be restricted to "the worthy part of mankind" who could "increase the wealth and strength of the community."[46] Madison never mentioned race or culture during this speech, but he supported the bill under review, which limited naturalization to "free white persons . . . of good character."[47] Known to be an avid opponent of slavery, he nevertheless believed the long-term solution to America's "original sin" was the recolonization of freed slaves.[48] This separatist mind-set can also be found in Jefferson and even Abraham Lincoln.[49] Racial integration would end badly for the country because of white prejudice and black resentment, and because both races acquired vices from the institution of slavery.[50] Madison's regard for America's indigenous peoples was equally pessimistic: "Next to the case of the Black race within our bosom, that of the red on our borders, is the problem most baffling to the policy of our Country."[51]

West Coast Trumpians

West Coast Straussians do acknowledge some concerns the Founders had about excessive heterogeneity. For example, Thomas West notes that America's forefathers opposed racial diversity, were suspicious of illiberal cultures, and rejected mass immigration because of the difficulties of assimilating too many people at one time.[52] West believes the latter two concerns are legitimate. He contends that since 1880, most immigrants and their descendants have become Democrat voters who reject the Founding ideal of limited government in favor of a growing "centralized and bureaucratized modern administrative state."[53] He also thinks assimilation is failing today because rapid mass immigration is overwhelming a country whose people no longer proudly regard their "way of life" as "best in the world."[54] On the contrary, Americans since 1960 have taught immigrants that the United States is racist, sexist, and intolerant, which means nonmajority groups require politically designated benefits rather than equal rights.[55]

From West's perspective, the only thing that can save the Founders' republic is "an indefinite moratorium on almost all immigration combined with significant penalties for employers of illegal aliens as well as for the illegals themselves."[56] Neoconservatives would call these policies a betrayal of the American creed, but West believes his views are perfectly compatible with the Declaration itself, which says "one people" can dissolve itself from others and "assume among the powers of the earth a *separate* and equal station to which the Laws of Nature and of Nature's God entitle them."[57]

Michael Anton thinks the Founders' republic has been rejected by the identity politics of the Left, and he worries that demographic changes will secure a permanent electoral victory for Democrats.[58] He also believes Americans have every right to implement Trump's hard-line immigration policies because "we are originally a nation of settlers, who later chose to admit immigrants, and later still not to, and who may justly open or close our doors solely at our own discretion, without deference to forced pieties."[59] The forced pieties Anton has in mind are (1) diversity is our strength, and (2) America is a nation of immigrants. Neoconservatives such as Lindsey Graham and John McCain consider Anton's views a betrayal of America's founding principles, but Anton supports his stand by invoking the preamble to the United States Constitution, which includes a specific reference to securing "the blessings of liberty *to ourselves and our posterity.*"[60] In other words, "the Constitution and the social compact it enshrines are *for us*—the American people—and not for foreigners, immigrants (except those we choose to welcome), or anyone else."[61]

Anton's emphasis on intergenerational duty can be supported textually. Hamilton spoke of "framing a government for posterity as well as ourselves," and Jefferson said the republic was established to secure the "rights of ourselves and our posterity."[62] Washington, Adams, and Madison all regarded the republic as an inheritance that would indebt future generations to their forefathers.[63] According to Madison, Americans obtained a "precious heritage . . . from the virtue and valour of their fathers," and they had a "sacred obligation" to transmit "to future generations, that precious patrimony of national rights and independence, which is held in trust by the present, from the goodness of Divine Providence."[64]

The Science of Politics

A major gap in the scholarship of West Coast Straussians is the Founders' perspective on diversity as it relates to class politics and plutocracy. This shortcoming may derive from an undue emphasis on natural rights philosophy rather than political science. With this possibility in mind, it may be helpful to consider Hamilton's warning to Marquis de Lafayette about the impending direction of the successful French Revolution: "I dread the reveries of your Philosophic politicians who appear in the moment to have great influence and who being mere speculatists may aim at more refinement than suits either with human nature or the composition of your Nation."[65] Madison echoed this sentiment when he said that political thinking should be guided by what is "compatible with the course of human affairs."[66]

When it came to designing the new republic of 1787, the Founders relied on the emerging "science of politics" rather than on Locke, philosophy, or divine revelation.[67] Practical thinkers like Madison and Hamilton identified principles of government through (1) experiential service, (2) the study of ancient and modern regimes, and (3) the study of influential thinkers like Baron de Montesquieu and David Hume, who also engaged in case study analysis to develop advanced political theories.[68] It was this reservoir of empirical knowledge that gave the Founders hope that a new kind of self-governing regime was possible, one that would avoid the pitfalls that had ruined so many republics and confederations of the past.[69] This scientific approach also provided the Founders with a pragmatic understanding of diversity.

Diversity and Plutocracy

The question of diversity was the center of gravity during the Constitutional Debate (1787–1788). Ratification required convincing the states that America would not suffer the fate of extensive republics like ancient Rome and Greece.[70] The predominant theory was Montesquieu's argument that large republics were unsustainable because of diversity, wealth inequality, and socioeconomic complexity, all of which eroded civic virtue and impaired the public's capacity to vigilantly check elites.[71] A large republic would therefore succumb to plutocracy unless the people—hateful and envious of the patrician class—threw their weight behind a populist demagogue who promised liberty but delivered tyranny.[72]

Founding thinkers like Hamilton and Madison were impressed by two solutions that Montesquieu proposed for overcoming this problem: a confederate republic based on Lycia and a tripartite government based on England's constitutional monarchy.[73] At the Philadelphia Convention, these two models were synthesized into a federation system, where state governments would share power with an energetic national government that now had the authority to nullify state laws.[74] Federal authority would be limited by the enumeration of powers in the Constitution and by the internal checking of the national government's legislative, executive, and judicial branches.[75] Not everyone agreed this political system would preserve liberty. Anti-Federalists warned that constitutional provisions like the supremacy clause and the necessary and proper clause would enable the national government to annihilate state governments, which meant America would eventually become a consolidated state, and thus suffer all the problems anticipated by Montesquieu's thesis.[76] However, in contrast "to the prevailing Theory," Madison argued that larger size could be a republic's salvation rather than its ruination.[77] An extensive territory meant a greater diversity of affiliations (e.g., religious sects, regional interests, economic professions, economic class, and factions under the sway of demagogues). Consequently, subgroup loyalties would break apart majority factions that might otherwise legislatively oppress minority interests. Extensive size also meant a larger pool of "enlightened" and "virtuous" candidates to serve as representatives in the federal government.[78]

Scholars have made much of Madison's turning Montesquieu on his head, but a fuller explanation of his thesis appeared in a letter written to Jefferson shortly after the Philadelphia Convention. Madison cautioned against an excessively large republic because of its diversity. He warned that "a defensive concert" of the people "may be rendered too difficult against the oppression of those entrusted with the administration."[79] The outcome would be despotism by means of "divide et impera," a threat Madison emphasized in the 1790s when he thought plutocratic forces were "reviving exploded parties and taking advantage of all prejudices, local, political, and occupational, that may prevent or disturb a general coalition of sentiments."[80] Excessive diversity worried Madison because he regarded the checks and balances of America's political system as "auxiliary precautions."[81] The primary defense against despotism was the "vigilant and manly spirit" of sufficiently patriotic citizens.[82] If diversity eroded the "mutual confidence and affection" of the people, then Madison believed this checking force would short-circuit.[83] His solution was therefore a "sphere of a mean extent"—that is, a republic that was large enough to mitigate majority factions without being so large that plutocracy emerged.[84]

Madison did argue that it was possible to "extend the sphere" with federative governance and by nurturing social homogeneity.[85] The latter could be done with a true Republican Party, education, progressive taxation, and communicative activities like road building, commerce, and the circulation of newspapers.[86] However, Madison never indicated that the size of a republic could expand indefinitely or that his solution to class warfare could operate in a racially and culturally diverse country. On the contrary, the preponderance of evidence supports the opposite conclusion.

The American Republic Today

The research findings of this chapter point to two concluding thoughts. First, there may be plenty of good reasons to criticize Trump. His critics may not be entirely wrong when they identify him with the populist demagogue whom Montesquieu and the Founders warned against.[87] That said, Trump's immigration policies would not have offended the Constitution's authors, who were not really celebrants of diversity. Had the Founders known that America would become the diverse country it is today, they would have established a different form of government. What this regime would look like extends beyond the scope of this chapter. But we can assume that if Madison were around, he would be warning us that cultural diversity has rendered America vulnerable to plutocratic elites ruling over a divided citizenry.[88] He and other Founders might even recommend that we imitate their actions in 1787: scrap the Constitution and begin anew. By now, the United States is so fractured along moral, ideological, and cultural lines that the old federal framework may have been rendered obsolete.[89]

For those interested in this topic, an appropriate place to begin would be the Anti-Federalists. Many of these thinkers rejected the Constitution because they believed preserving liberty in a republic the size of America required a decentral-ized political system in which the domestic affairs of diverse peoples could be lo-cally governed.[90] Localism would ensure that representatives had real affinity for their constituents and a true understanding of their particular needs. Failing that, corrupt or incompetent representatives could be held accountable by culturally similar constituents who understood local politics, wanted the same things, and retained the social capital necessary to form defensive concerts against tyranny. Some Anti-Federalists also favored a decentralized system because people could escape despotism by moving to more congenial states.[91]

8

WHY THE ALT RIGHT IS NOT GOING ANYWHERE (REGARDLESS OF WHAT WE CALL IT)

Richard T. Marcy

In a 2018 talk, the noted cognitive psychologist Steven Pinker referred to the Alt Right as a group of "highly literate, highly intelligent," and "media savvy" individuals—a very bold and provocative statement coming from a Harvard University professor, and one that seemed to suggest that the Alt Right is a movement that we should continue to take seriously.[1] Perhaps predictably, Pinker was then subsequently attacked by a number of media outlets that sought to correct him on this pronouncement, suggesting not only that he is wrong about members of the Alt Right (i.e., they are a group of ignorant racists) but further that the Alt Right is in a great decline anyway, thereby posing less of a future threat.[2] The striking contrast in these statements raises a number of important questions, not the least being whom and what are we talking about when we say "the Alt Right"? How effective are the contributions of each of these different individuals and groups in furthering their movement—for example, does Richard Spencer fill the same role and have the same amount of influence as Matthew Heimbach of the Traditionalist Worker Party, or an anonymous troll on 4chan for that matter? And most importantly, is the Alt Right movement still a threat to the status quo (i.e., the mainstream Left and Right)?

While it is clear that there are certain parts of the Alt Right that do appear to be on the wane (for example, Richard Spencer's brand seems to be tarnished in the public eye since the 2017 Charlottesville rally), the early pronouncement of the movement's demise may be wishful thinking. There is still quite a bit we do not know about the Alt Right. The mainstream press has tended to focus on sensational individuals and groups, removing them from a larger, historical context, and the Alt Right as a whole. Clearly, Richard Spencer is only one part of the movement, and his role in it is often difficult to discern and is still up for question—the degradation of his brand may or may not reflect the downfall of the entire movement.

Over the past couple of years, a number of individuals and groups have adopted the term "Alt Right" (such as Patrick Casey of Identity Evropa and Jared Taylor of American Renaissance), with a large number being given the label through the media. As a result, it is sometimes difficult to determine who is truly of the Alt Right, let alone how effective the movement is and may become. While some (particularly in the Alt Right) might argue that the conflation of all these members and groups is a tactic intended to group all branches under one loathsome umbrella, it is also possible that this conflation arises out of a lack of awareness of, or disinterest in, some of the differences between these individuals and groups.

There also seems to be a lack of attention paid to the strategic goals of some Alt Right tactics (Angela Nagle being a notable exception here).[3] One example of this would be the coverage of the Alt Right's public trolling campaigns, with some journalists appearing to take members of the Alt Right completely at face value. This could be yet another example of an overall strategy by some journalists to ensure that everyone in the Alt Right is contextualized in a similar way; but it could also just indicate a general lack of interest—it is enough for most journalists to just cover the more abhorrent actions of the Alt Right. This lack of attention however, can lead to further issues (an illustrative example here might be the "It's okay to be white" campaign, in which members of 4chan lured some in the media into a compromising overreaction).[4] This gap in reporting has not been helpful in achieving a deeper understanding of the Alt Right movement, which is clearly needed for an accurate assessment.

This selective engagement is proving to be a problematic omission in today's political communications. While in the past it was politically and technologically possible to quarantine some controversial ideas by denying them access to popular channels of communication, some of the issues raised by groups within the Alt Right (for example, those related to immigration and diversity) have been hard to keep out of public discussion. This public access has been facilitated by social media, with its multiple channels and its unique challenges for vetting and censoring information (such as the Streisand effect), and has helped bolster Alt Right legitimacy in the face of opposition from the traditional media.[5]

The avoidance by many journalists and academics to fully engage these issues has led to what some, such as Steven Pinker and Noam Chomsky, have described as "gifts to the Right." The unwillingness of the political establishment to engage particular members of the Far Right on these contentious issues has helped drive their discussion underground. As a result the political opposition appears to be conceding arguments that it seems unwilling to address.

As the Alt Right comprises a number of different groups, each serving its own strategic purpose and distinct audience, it might be useful to unpack some of the different roles that individuals and groups are playing within the movement; we might then better understand the strategies and tactics of those individuals and subgroups. This exploration would also allow us to investigate some of the psychological and sociological assumptions underpinning these strategies, to further determine their potential effectiveness.

It might also be useful to place these approaches within a larger historical context—namely, the history of past artistic and sociopolitical avant-gardes. Quite a bit of analysis has noted the ways in which the Alt Right has drawn from the theoretical base of past avant-garde political movements in the course of constructing its political program (for example, its use of Situationist theories of media criticism).[6] This chapter hopes to contribute to this literature through an examination of the strengths and weaknesses of adopting past artistic and sociopolitical avant-garde strategies as tools for expanding influence. In detailing the various strategies and tactics of Alt Right subgroups, this chapter will conclude with some tentative predictions regarding the future viability of these groups as well as suggestions for further research directions.

The Alt Right as an Avant-Garde

Throughout the past decade, Richard Spencer has repeatedly referred to past avant-garde traditions, and in a number of different ways, whether through the naming of his internet podcasts (e.g., "Vanguard"), his references to wanting to become an "avant-garde theatre director,"[7] or his direct discussions of prior artistic and sociopolitical avant-gardes (such as the Situationist International; Spencer brought up these subjects in interviews with Jonathan Bowden in early podcasts, knowing that Bowden was himself well versed in the history and philosophy of past avant-gardes).[8] Other Alt Right members, like Greg Johnson (head of Counter Currents, a key Alt Right website), have called for creating a "manifesto" for the movement (a manifesto being another staple of avant-garde practice).[9] While it seems clear that the history and philosophy of past artistic and sociopolitical avant-gardes have influenced the Alt Right, less has been written in the academic literature on the relationship between the strategies of past avant-gardes and the present behaviors of Alt Right leaders and groups.

Avant-garde practices and their role in political change have been largely neglected in the political and psychological literature of the past three decades as the turbulence of the 1960s has faded.[10] Arguably one of the more influential avant-gardes of recent times has been the Situationist International (SI), a movement of the Left that many scholars have suggested had a profound influence on the events of May 1968 in Paris, France.[11] As a widely reported moment in this period, this event would go on to shape mainstream politics and culture for years.

The power of avant-gardes is often overestimated in terms of their short-term political influence (particularly when compared with the sensational media coverage that they often acquire), but is also typically underestimated in terms of their more indirect ability to shift political opinion over the long term, as well as create political space for close, but less extreme, actors to capitalize on.[12] This approach is often confused through comparison with more conventional approaches to political power and thus the efficacy of its tactics in gaining attention is also often overlooked. Unlike more mainstream political efforts, which work toward some form of consensus to garner political respect, the extreme provocations of avant-garde groups are often intended to create an extreme position through which less extreme (but closer) political positions can be made to appear politically acceptable (i.e., what some might characterize as a shifting of the Overton Window within the public's consciousness).[13]

For example, the stated purpose of the SI as an avant-garde was not to exercise direct political influence by becoming another part of the establishment (e.g., another political party), but rather to position itself in such a way as to be able to "outmaneuver" the enemy and subvert the status quo through cultural change. The SI helped bring about social change through front-line activist events (for example, through sensational, media-covered events); the development and dissemination of social theory (through the publication of influential texts); the execution of subversive cultural approaches (like *détournement* and derives) intended to undermine mainstream culture; and the direct recruitment of particular segments of the public that were amenable to their ideas (such as university students and professors).[14]

It would seem as if a number of Alt Right members are taking pages from this avant-garde playbook, whether with front-line activist events (as in the case of demonstrations and other media appearances), the development and dissemination of coherent social theory (as in the works of Jared Taylor and his allies),[15] the application of subversive cultural approaches (as in the use of détournement by Alt Right video creators like Walt Bismarck,[16] as well as in the creation of politically incorrect memes by anonymous trolls), and the active cultivation and recruitment of a support base (i.e., the "silent majority" of the Alt Right that resides in the online world).

While the use of these tactics alone is no guarantee of success, their execution represents a necessary precondition for achieving ultimate political objectives. Without these forms of engagement with the public, whether online or in the real world, it would be difficult for Alt Right players to alter public consciousness. The degree to which these strategies and approaches are working is a key consideration for trying to assess the Alt Right's potential for growth.

Given some of the parallels between past avant-gardes and the present Alt Right, particularly the importance of fundamentally similar strategies, it would seem sensible to examine the assumptions and tactics under which these subversive groups have operated. Since the immediate goal of these past avant-gardes was often cultural and metapolitical (as a prelude for future mainstream political influence), it is important to explore how these approaches worked in the past.[17] As this is in many ways a goal of the mind as well as one tied to a social and political outcome, it is important that we also look at the psychological processes that might underpin these avant-garde strategies.

Avant-Garde Roles within the Alt Right

When Steven Pinker spoke of the highly intelligent members of the Alt Right, he was careful to note that he was referring to what he had read by some members, often anonymous, posting on internet discussion boards. Suffice it to say, he was not likely referring to those members that can be seen on YouTube screaming racial epithets. This is no small point as anyone previously identified with the Alt Right had often been conflated into one overarching political group (i.e., white supremacist) with one strategic approach (i.e., protest demonstrations), despite the fact that there has been, and continues to be, important points of variability—in both political beliefs and strategic approaches—across those that have been identified with the Alt Right.[18]

Much of the journalistic and academic coverage of those individuals and groups in the Alt Right has highlighted their political philosophies and/or political objectives. While this coverage has contributed to our understanding of what these different members of the Alt Right believe and want, there has been less analysis of the tactics through which Alt Right members have tried to influence the public, especially from psychological and sociological perspectives. To aid in our understanding of the strategic actions that different groups have employed, it might be useful to start with the different roles that individuals and groups have been playing within the overall Alt Right movement. Here we might use the following terms: *front-line activists* and other *subversive cultural producers* (for example, "trolls"), *intellectuals*, and the *silent majority* (of the Alt Right).

These functional role categories relate to general models of social change, as well as cognitive models that can be employed by leaders and groups to accomplish their goals. For example, each of these roles has an integral part to play in what the psychologist Kurt Lewin saw as a three-step organizational change model of "unfreezing norms," "realignment," and "refreezing norms."[19] Similarly, each of these steps has a relationship to individual and group-level psychological processes that help facilitate change. Marcy has introduced a cycle that represents the types of cognitive tools that radically innovative leaders have selected to effect social change; namely, "sensebreaking" of public mental models has to occur first, which is then followed with "sensegiving" tactics to provide people with new information in which to create new cognitive relationships.[20] This process then culminates in "sensemaking," which allows the person affected by the change to move forward. Front-line activists and subversive cultural producers help serve this cycle through their unfreezing of norms by means of *sensebreaking* tactics; intellectuals in the movement help serve a process of realignment through *sensegiving* tactics, with the silent majority (and general public) being both the target and the vehicle of the refreezing or establishment of new norms through their own *sensemaking*.

For an avant-garde movement to be maximally effective, each of these roles needs to be successful in reaching and influencing its respective audience, without the role-players coming into conflict. This is a tall order for leaders of avant-garde groups—threats of co-optation, along with ego conflicts, leave many in movements such as the Alt Right hesitant about reaching out for collaborators.[21] To begin a critique of the Alt Right and its present and future potential, it does not appear as if the various roles and groups within the Alt Right are always working in concert, with some openly mocking and even fighting with each other.[22] While criticism *within* social movements is often a healthy mechanism for working through theoretical and practical problems, airing that criticism in public can leave an impression of disorder and weakness, which detractors often exploit.

The Sensebreakers: Front-Line Activists and Subversive Cultural Producers

For the Situationnistes, sensebreaking of public consciousness involved a number of different tactics. Among the most obvious were controversial media appearances, along with the use of détournement.[23] In one famous media appearance, Guy Debord was asked in an interview what it meant to be a Situationist, to which he replied, "We're not here to answer cuntish questions," and walked off the stage.[24] This example of Debord's public rejection of conventional civility illustrates a strategy of refusing to collaborate with elite agendas while simultaneously provoking shock to direct public attention toward the SI's ideas.[25]

Situationist use of détournement was employed across a number of media forms. In *Can Dialectics Break Bricks?* Situationist René Viénet stripped all of the dialogue from a Chinese kung fu (martial arts) film and replaced it with lectures on Marxist theory. Viénet presented the Japanese invaders in the film as the establishment and the Chinese as the revolutionary working class.[26] Other Situationnistes turned comics and other forms of mass culture away from their intended meanings through the strategic removal and replacement of key text within the comics.

This adaptation of mass market cultural materials served to destruct the implicit social relationships in such materials. Further, the deliberate choice of popular cultural materials in this subversion process attracted a much wider audience than one would be able to reach by presenting ideas more straightforwardly through obscure references and complicated texts. The process underlying these subversive approaches breaks the "sense" previously connoted by status-quo-oriented comics or movies while simultaneously providing a new mental model of social relationships (i.e., sensegiving). This recontextualization of familiar themes breaks the audience's understanding of existing social relationships while immediately prompting a cognitive shift through ideas.[27]

The Alt Right appears to have adopted some of these approaches in spreading its ideas. Walt Bismarck has "détourned" Walt Disney movies to help spread Alt Right ideas related to IQ and immigration, while innumerable anonymous trolls have helped create and spread contentious memes through the internet. Richard Spencer has given countless provocative interviews, unreservedly expressing highly controversial viewpoints on racial differences and the dispossession of white people in the United States. These interviews, along with the rallies that he and others in the Alt Right have held, have drawn considerable media attention, thereby aiding in transmitting Alt Right ideas to the public. For the most part, these appearances have presented an uncompromising stance—a direct assault on the tenets of the status quo.

Given the falling of Spencer's star, particularly as a result of the Charlottesville debacle, it would be easy to regard his group as being in decline. More difficult, however, is determining whether the larger role that he has been occupying (i.e., front-line activist) with a few others in the movement (Patrick Casey, James Allsup, etc.) is still effective in pushing an Alt Right agenda, and whether this might have implications for the larger movement.

Drawing from the example of past avant-garde front-line activists may be helpful here. Many past avant-gardes did not go on to achieve political power themselves, but instead helped shift public consciousness before fading into the historical background. This provided room for other, often more moderate, voices to gain political ground. The Situationnistes, and many avant-gardes before them, did not morph into political parties as their political goals became realities. Rather, they enabled other political factions to leverage their ideas to achieve political objectives. This appears to be happening with some groups within the Alt Right movement.

By staking out a more extreme and uncompromising position in the media, Alt Right spokesmen have expanded the spectrum of political discourse and have helped provide cover for other less extreme but still recognizably right-wing voices that would have been marginalized before. Less than three years ago, conversations regarding immigration, race, and IQ were much more constrained, with little discussion of these subjects taking place in the public square. This is now changing, with the prominent social psychologists Jonathan Haidt, Jordan Peterson, and Steven Pinker fielding questions and commenting on these once-forbidden topics.

If the effectiveness of Alt Right front-line activism were assessed only in terms of being able to raise discussion of formerly taboo subjects in public forums, and breaking the paradigm of allowable discourse, then certainly the Alt Right movement should be viewed as at least a partial success. The question might then be asked whether this highly combative approach is sustainable and whether it can lead to further political achievements. If viewed from the perspective of past avant-gardes, history would suggest that sustainability of a front-line activist role is difficult to maintain, given the daunting task of working directly against the status quo,[28] nor is sustainability even central to the purpose of an avant-garde. Rather, the successful employment of this role depends not on achieving some form of public support or career advancement but primarily on its ability to change public discourse.

If front-line activists are the bad cop in the "good cop/bad cop" routine, then it is important to keep in mind that it is usually the good cop that moves on and continues to influence those who listen, while the bad cop fades into the background, once his or her purpose has been achieved. It is also important to note that who the good cop is at this moment may not be entirely clear with respect to the Alt Right movement. Alt Right groups have a tendency to vehemently dismiss as "Alt Lite" those who sound a bit like them but wander too far in the direction of the establishment. While this style of contestation between actors often makes for an effective bad cop, thereby pushing the Overton Window even further, it also needs to be made clear that *both* cops should be working in concert. The Alt Right's failure to maintain this delicate relationship may be a strategic weakness.

The role of an avant-garde front-line activist is often too contentious to gain mainstream acceptance and respectability (that is in fact the strength of the position—to be uncompromising is to potentially create greater shifts in consciousness); therefore, it is vital that a more mainstream successor be planned for. In the early days of the second wave of the Alt Right, that successor was Donald Trump—it is unclear who that person or group is now. Some in the Alt Lite have taken the mantle (such as Jordan Peterson), but this does not appear to be a deliberate move on the part of groups within the Alt Right. There seems to be some confusion about strategic roles, one of the more notable examples being the short-lived bid by Richard Spencer for a congressional position back in 2016. While Spencer seems to be aware of the strategic and tactical differences between being the leader of an avant-garde and taking a more mainstream political stance, he has also sent out his own mixed signals at various times, straddling the fence between being a provocateur and being a more mainstream spokesman.[29] This has led to some confusion on the Alt Right and among the public at large about Spencer's avant-garde brand.

Capitalizing on the strength of particular strategic roles, working in concert with other roles in the movement, and having a positive vision beyond a critique of the existing status quo are tasks that the Alt Right appears to be doing less well in. While the Situationnistes under Guy Debord composed all of the functional roles that have been outlined to be an effective avant-garde (front-line activists, intellectuals, etc.), the Alt Right movement has been less centralized and less well coordinated. Separate groups have filled different roles, often in conflict and even in competition with each other. Whereas this lack of coordinated roles, as well as clear leadership, has allowed the movement a high degree of flexibility, it also betrays an inherent weakness in that the lack of coordination has resulted in weakened attack power. Confused roles have also allowed a high degree of infighting that has sapped the movement's strength.

If the Alt Right is to be more effective in the future, its leaders will need to coordinate their functional roles more efficiently and with less acrimony. For example, within the front-line activists are groups that have appeal to what is commonly referred to as highbrow ethnonationalists (such as the followers of Richard Spencer and Jared Taylor) and others that are more lowbrow (such as the now-defunct Traditionalist Worker Party). These subgroups have typically been ill at ease with each other. To be more effective, the Alt Right would need to create a vision that accounts for all these subgroups, rather than a medley of independent visions that pit one group against the other.

Some Alt Right leaders who are moving in this direction and trying to avoid petty disputes have reached out to others in the movement. Richard Spencer joined forces with Arktos, thereby further bridging the gulf between some roles (front-line activists and intellectuals). Millennial Woes, a prominent Alt Right blogger, has taken the controversial step of embracing the "lost" of the movement (and the wider culture)—the lost being, as he notes, "the basement dwelling neck beards" that the Left has highlighted as exemplars of the Alt Right in attempts to shame it and, of which, the Alt Right has also shunned and denied acceptance.[30] Rather than distance themselves further from these members, or even continue to ignore them, Millennial Woes has advocated coming to terms with these often socially disenfranchised, tossed-aside individuals and bringing them into the fold. While this tactic could further damage the social image of the Alt Right, it could also elicit greater public empathy, as well as enhance group solidarity within the movement.

The Sensegivers: The Intellectuals of the Alt Right

The Situationnistes were a coordinated avant-garde, tightly controlled by their leader Guy Debord. They had members who filled all the functional roles in the movement, including those of the intellectuals. At the level of strategies and tactics, intellectuals played a necessary role in the spreading of Situationist ideas. Like those filling other strategic roles, intellectuals leveraged multiple social change tools through their writing (e.g., sensebreaking and sensemaking), but the role in which they were arguably the most vital was sensegiving.

Although most intellectuals typically do not remain anonymous and also depend on a reputation built through engagement with the public, they are distinct in the strictest sense from front-line activists; their audience is typically narrower, but nonetheless influential—namely, the intelligentsia and educated classes—and their success depends on the persuasiveness of their scholarship. While the primary goal of a front-line activist is to influence the masses through advocacy—which includes providing information that supports particular political objectives, while often omitting/distorting information that does not affirm these objectives—there is an expectation that a social movement's intellectuals adhere to more rigorous standards than front-line activists. The degree to which a movement's intellectuals represent these standards may be the degree to which they can influence their peers. Some of these standards include credibility (not only in their communications but also in their backgrounds) and coherence (regarding the internal logic of what they present).

In the case of the SI, credibility was established through its primary journal that promulgated its main ideas and theories. The movement also built a substantial reputation through its initial incubation as an art movement before it moved on to sociopolitical issues. The SI attracted high-quality members and was extremely exclusive, often disciplining capable members for minor infractions. It built a fearsome reputation through its apparent expertise in some areas of research. Prominent Situationnistes also published widely reviewed books, such as the *Society of the Spectacle*, which furnished critical studies of modern society.

In the case of the Alt Right, intellectuals such as Jared Taylor have been writing and publishing books for more than two decades. As a Yale graduate who is fluent in Japanese, as well as English and French, Taylor is often described as a "courtly presenter of ideas," along with being known, even by his detractors, as a man who is bringing a measure of intellectualism and seriousness to the Alt Right movement through a "cultivated, cosmopolitan" approach.[31] In the defense of his arguments, he often cites findings from peer-reviewed academic studies, further contributing to his credibility as a researcher. The achievement of "expert" status is no small matter since there are few forms of power available to someone who is challenging the status quo. Institutional forms of reward and punishment are typically not available to such a dissident, leaving him with only his claim to knowledge as an expert to convert others to his views.[32]

This use of peer-reviewed academic articles is also greatly contributing to a growing public sense of coherence in Alt Right theory. The reluctance of many politicians, journalists, and academics to discuss the findings of some of these peer-reviewed articles on race, IQ, and diversity has resulted in a dearth of critical engagement. As Adolph Reed lamented in *Trumpland*, the Alt Right has "internally consistent explanations to offer,"[33] which are not often discussed outside its own ranks. While this gap has not been entirely ignored in mainstream journalism, the battle over Alt Right ideas has gone on mostly in social media. Through this medium, the Alt Right may be making gains in bringing its arguments to a larger audience.

Due to the controversial nature of their writings about race, IQ, and immigration, Alt Right intellectuals have received extremely negative attention from the mainstream press. Regardless of the obloquy to which Alt Right authors have been subject, there is a public forum under which some Alt Right intellectuals have been quickly gaining prominence, namely YouTube. Here, debates over some of the Alt Right's most controversial stands have been taking place at a breakneck pace.[34] It is difficult to determine what effect these debates might be having on general public discourse, but one thing is clear: the desire to engage with these issues is strong in view of the readership that many of these debates have been attracting. Some Alt Right discussions have attracted hundreds of thousands of views, and some videos are topping almost half a million.[35]

Furthermore, it seems as if these issues are becoming more and more commonplace for discussion throughout the internet, with a culture emerging from these debates that clashes with establishment opinions. If the YouTube community at all represents the public at large, particularly for millennials, these discussions will likely have political implications. We may not yet have seen the full effects of these internet discussions because of social desirability biases (i.e., people failing to disclose opinions that run counter to socially acceptable ones), much in the same way that the Trump vote was obscured in polling in 2016.

The Sensemakers: The Silent Majority of the Alt Right (and the Public at Large)

Who exactly are the targets of the sensebreaking and sensegiving tactics of the front-line activists and intellectuals? For the Situationnistes, a key demographic for conversion turned out to be university students. This "silent (and/or anonymous) majority" were largely student activists, who were initially working at the fringe of the movement, together with other students, in their personal networks. These students used graffiti on city buildings and bridges to the same effect as Alt Right trolls now use memes—to spread provocative ideas through public channels. Students also disseminated and popularized Situationist theory through pamphleteering, one of the more famous pamphlets being *On the Poverty of Student Life.*[36] These political actions by anonymous students who were "redpilled" by Situationist sensebreaking and sensegiving (e.g., media demonstrations and theoretical publications) eventually helped bring about the student occupation of the Sorbonne in May 1968. This in turn led to further massive demonstrations and general strikes throughout France.

For the Alt Right, the "silent majority" comprises a number of subgroups, two of the most conspicuous of which are trolls and lurking fellow travelers. Given their outrageous antics, the trolls have evoked the most public attention and shock, while lurking fellow travelers have been a less covered phenomenon. It is unclear just how large the Alt Right "silent majority" is and whether the sampling that has been done thus far is capturing the opinions of primarily trolls, which have a unique agenda, or whether it includes fellow travelers as well. There is also the issue of not appearing respectable—the contentious nature of these issues is likely to keep some people from responding honestly to such polls (i.e., social desirability bias).

The size of the silent majority warrants some attention. Many of those presently holding Alt Right beliefs are far from being the rural, uneducated, generational racists that the media typically describe.[37] In considering the possibility of the Alt Right as a threat to the status quo, we might turn to the potential effects of minority influence on majority groups, with some studies suggesting that long-term influence is greatest when minorities present an uncompromising position.[38] An "uncompromising position" clearly describes the Alt Right's approach to messaging. While we can only speculate about the effects of this messaging, some studies of white millennials suggest that larger numbers of them share less socially acceptable beliefs than had been previously imagined (if we account for social desirability bias, these percentages may be even higher).[39] Coupling all of this with a study that suggests that as little as 25 percent of a group's membership has to be shifted in order to change group opinion[40] leads one to conclude that the Alt Right could become a formidable threat to mainstream political opinion at some point in the future.

It would be best to note that the central method applied in this study—namely, looking at the Alt Right as an avant-garde movement through a psychological lens—is only one approach to understanding a multicausal phenomenon. While clearly some members and groups within the Alt Right are drawing from an avant-garde legacy, multiple tactics have been embraced to further an Alt Right agenda, and it may be necessary to apply a multidisciplinary focus to properly understand where the movement is going. This chapter has tried to shed further light on the Alt Right through one particular approach, that of organizational and cognitive psychology within an avant-garde context.

Thus far only one psychological study on the personality profiles of members of the Alt Right has taken place.[41] This is a promising start, but there are many more Alt Right issues that could be explored through a psychological perspective: identity, leadership, and status quo deviance, as well as the assumptions and appeal of a general political discourse centering on diversity, race, and IQ.

As to whether the Alt Right will continue to be a threat to the political establishment, it would seem from the evidence that it will remain so for some time. Although its front-line activist arm is somewhat in disarray and some activist groups (such as Richard Spencer's) are in decline, other front-line groups (such as Identity Evropa) are already replacing them.[42] And its intellectual branch has seemingly not lost ground—if anything, it seems to be gaining ground and is growing in its influence to provide coherent, if not highly controversial, arguments (i.e., sensegive) to very serious social issues. Similarly, there is little evidence that the "silent majority" has diminished or shifted from an Alt Right perspective, and may just be waiting to see which leaders emerge from the Charlottesville debacle to identify themselves with a surging, nonestablishment Right. Whatever we might ultimately call this movement—Alt Right, Identitarian, and so on—it is likely to stay around.

9

THE UNWANTED SOUTHERN
CONSERVATIVES

Boyd D. Cathey

No discussion of Southern conservatism, its history, and its relationship to what is broadly termed the "American conservative movement" would be complete without an examination of events that have transpired over the past fifty or so years and the pivotal role of the powerful intellectual current known as neoconservatism.

From the 1950s into the 1980s, Southerners who defended the traditions of the South, and even more so, of the Confederacy, were welcomed as allies and confreres by their Northern and Western counterparts. William F. Buckley Jr.'s *National Review* and Russell Kirk's *Modern Age*, perhaps the two leading conservative journals of the period, welcomed Southerners into the "movement" and onto the pages of those organs of conservative thought. Kirk dedicated an entire issue of *Modern Age* to the South and its traditions (Fall issue, 1958), and explicitly supported its historic defense of the originalist constitutionalism of the Framers. And throughout the critical period that saw the enactment of the Civil Rights and Voting Rights Acts, Buckley's magazine defended the "Southern position," arguing forcefully on constitutional grounds that the proposed legislation would undercut not just the guaranteed rights of the states but also the protected rights of citizens. Southern authors such as Mel Bradford, Richard Weaver, Clyde Wilson, Tom Landess, and James J. Kilpatrick lent their intelligence, skill as writers, and arguments to a defense of the South.

Yet by the 1990s, that "Southern voice" had pretty much been exiled—expelled—from major establishment conservative journals. Indeed, friendly writers from outside the South who were identified with what became known as the

Old (or Paleo) Right (that is, the non-neoconservative Right) were also soon purged from the mastheads of the conservative "mainstream" organs of opinion: noted authors such as Joe Sobran (from *National Review*), Sam Francis (from the *Washington Times*), Paul Gottfried (from *Modern Age*), and others were soon shown the door.

Perhaps the first major example of this critical process came in early 1981, after the election of Ronald Reagan as president. Conservative Republican stalwarts Senators Jesse Helms and John East, both from North Carolina, joined by Democrat Howell Heflin of Alabama, lobbied hard for the nomination of the distinguished Southern scholar Mel Bradford to head the National Endowment for the Humanities. Bradford was originally tapped for the position by Reagan.

According to the intellectual historian David Gordon, Reagan's wish "to elevate [Bradford] to the prestigious post did not stem solely from Bradford's academic credentials. The president and he were acquainted, and he had worked hard in Reagan's campaign for the Republican presidential nomination. Respected conservatives such as Russell Kirk and Senator Jesse Helms also knew and admired Bradford."[1] But the selection met with strong opposition from various neoconservative writers and pundits, including the syndicated columnist George Will and prominent figures like Irving Kristol and Norman Podhoretz, who objected strongly to Bradford's criticisms of Abraham Lincoln. They circulated to the press and to Republican political leaders quotes from Bradford characterizing Lincoln as "a dangerous man" and "indeed almost sinister." He was even accused of comparing Lincoln to Hitler. More, Bradford's support for the 1972 presidential campaign of Governor George C. Wallace was brought up negatively. In the end, it was the neoconservative choice William Bennett who was selected for the post later in 1981.[2]

What had happened? How had the movement that began with such promise in the 1950s, essentially with the publication of Kirk's seminal volume *The Conservative Mind* (1953), descended into internecine purges, excommunications, and the sometimes brutal triumph of those who only a few years earlier had shown links to the Marxist Left?

To address this question we must first examine the history of the non-Stalinist Left in the United States before and after World War II. And we need to pinpoint significant differences between neoconservatives who made the pilgrimage from the Left into the conservative movement, and those more traditional conservatives, whose basic beliefs and philosophy were at odds with those of the newcomers. As a mostly neglected but useful source of information, we might look at a long list of critical interpreters of American conservatism, starting with Richard Weaver, Russell Kirk, and Mel Bradford, and continuing through Paul Gottfried, Gary Dorrien (*The Neoconservative Mind*, 1993), and Stefan Halper and Jonathan

Clarke (*America Alone: The Neo-Conservatives and the Global Order*, 2004). I also bring in my own experience as a witness to the transformation under discussion. That transformation saw the triumph of a pattern of thinking that went back to only partially recovered onetime adherents of certain deviationist forms of Marxist Leninism.

The complex history of that ideology and, in particular, of the aggravated differences between developing factions in the dominant power structure in Russia would have profound effects on the Communist movement in the United States. After the death in 1924 of the leader of the newly formed Union of Soviet Socialist Republics (USSR), Vladimir Lenin, a political struggle between the two major leaders who emerged, Joseph Stalin and Leon Trotsky, revealed the fissures in Marxist Leninist theory and practice. While both men had served the Communist revolution in Russia (1918–1921), Trotsky advanced a Marxist Leninist position that would stress global proletarian revolution and a dictatorship of the proletariat based on working-class self-emancipation and a form of mass (workers') democracy. Unlike Stalin, who posited the establishment of "socialism in one country" as a prerequisite for furthering the socialist cause elsewhere, Trotsky advanced the theory of "permanent revolution" among the working class. Trotsky desired that revolution would be worldwide and pay homage to "democracy." This would set it apart from Stalin's more insular emphasis on Russian geopolitical interests.[3]

In the United States, the prominent American Marxist Jay Lovestone (born Jacob Liebstein, of Jewish parentage, in what is now Lithuania) would play a pivotal role not only in the early history of the Communist Party USA but also in the eventual emergence of what is now known as neoconservatism.[4] Lovestone's allegiances were with Trotsky and another adversary of Stalin, Nikolai Bukharin. Their faction of Communism stressed internationalism, workers' revolution, and opposition to what was perceived as the overly bureaucratic concentration of power in the hands of high party members.[5]

Eventually expelled from the Communist Party in 1929, Lovestone began a pilgrimage to the right that brought him finally into the ranks of fierce anti-Communist union activities and eventually counterespionage action on behalf of the CIA. Thus the title of Ted Morgan's exhaustive biography, *Jay Lovestone: Communist, Anti-Communist, Spymaster* (1999), chronicles his subject's intellectual journey and also indicates a direction taken by other American leftists, beginning in the late 1930s and continuing until their entry into the ranks of staunch anti-Communist movement conservatism in the 1970s.

Indeed, the final breaking point for many of those disillusioned with the failure of Marxism who would within a few decades gain a foothold in the American conservative movement probably came with the recrudescence of anti-Semitism under Stalin in post–World War II Russia (e.g., the infamous "doctors' plot"). Horrified and disillusioned by the further derailment of the socialist revolution, these "pilgrims from the Left"—who were mostly Jewish in origin—moved toward an explicit anti-Communism.

Although many had self-identified as "democratic socialists" and later with the Democratic Party, where their voice was significant until the 1960s, the movement of many of their prominent leaders to the right continued and gained momentum as the Democratic Party seemed to embrace more extreme positions over the Vietnam War and New Left. Notable among them were Podhoretz and Kristol, both of whom had sons who would figure prominently in the current neoconservative establishment.

Embraced by an older generation of conservatives, and invited to write for conservative publications, the neoconservatives soon began to occupy positions of leadership and importance. More significantly they changed views associated with the older movement to mirror their own vision. For even though they were shell-shocked by the effects of Soviet Communism, they nevertheless brought with them a worldview drawn from the Left. And they brought with them relentless zeal for furthering this worldview.

A remarkable admission of this genealogy came in 2007, in the pages of *National Review*. Here one finds the expression of sympathies clearly imported from the onetime Far Left and presented in a onetime Old Right publication. As explained by the contributor Stephen Schwartz: "To my last breath, I will defend Trotsky who alone and pursued from country to country and finally laid low in his own blood in a hideously hot house in Mexico City, said no to Soviet coddling to Hitlerism, to the Moscow purges, and to the betrayal of the Spanish Republic, and who had the capacity to admit that he had been wrong about the imposition of a single-party state as well as about the fate of the Jewish people. To my last breath, and without apology."[6]

Integral to their quest for power within the conservative movement, members of the conservative "new class" were also motivated by a strong desire for professional advancement. This too made it necessary that older, more traditional conservatives give way. Although not a Southerner (albeit sympathetic to Southern conservatives), the respected Old Right scholar Paul Gottfried is a case in point. Advanced by the relevant departments as a candidate for a chair in the humanities at the Catholic University of America, he saw his nomination, like that of Bradford, torpedoed by massive neoconservative intervention. This may have occurred, he subsequently learned, because his neoconservative opponents had someone else in mind for the position that he had sought and was on the point of obtaining.

By the late 1990s the neoconservatives had taken over most of the major conservative organs of opinion, journals, and think tanks. They also, significantly, exercised tremendous influence politically in the Republican Party (and to some degree within the Democratic Party, at least during the presidency of Bill Clinton). Irving Kristol, one of the intellectual godfathers of neoconservatism, carefully distinguished his doctrine from traditional conservatism. It was "forward-looking" and progressive in its attitude toward social issues like civil rights, rather than reactionary like the earlier conservatism. Its adherents rejoiced over the civil rights bills of the 1960s, unlike Buckley's *National Review* at the time. Neoconservatives were also favorable to the efforts to legislate more equality for women and for other groups who had hitherto been kept from realizing the American Dream.

Rather than simply attacking state power or advocating a return to states' rights, the new conservatives, according to Kristol, hoped to build on the existing federal administration. They believed that the promise of equality, which neoconservatives found in the Declaration of Independence, had to be promoted at home and abroad; and American conservatives, they preached, must lead the efforts to achieve global democracy, as opposed to the illogical and destructive efforts of the hard Left, or the reactionary stance of the Old Right.[7] It goes without saying that this neoconservative vision would clash glaringly with traditional Southern conservatism and its foundational principle of states' rights and opposition to what was perceived to be government social engineering.

Neoconservative rhetoric and initiatives did not go unopposed in the ranks of more traditional conservatives. Indeed, no less than the father of the conservative intellectual movement of the 1950s, Russell Kirk, publicly denounced the neoconservatives in the 1980s. Singling out the Jewish intellectual genealogy of major neoconservative writers, Kirk boldly declared in 1988: "Not seldom has it seemed as if some eminent Neoconservatives mistook Tel Aviv for the capital of the United States."[8] Kirk's resistance, and the warnings of Paul Gottfried, Sam Francis, Patrick Buchanan, and others of like mind, emphasized the sharp differences between the Old Right and the ascending neoconservatives.

From the perspective of the Old Right, the neoconservatives were "unpatriotic" in the sense that they placed their globalist values of equality and liberal democracy above their allegiance to any historic nation. Indeed, they converted their bizarre nationalism into a kind of world faith. According to this post-Christian faith, America was the "exceptional nation," which held a duty to go round the world and impose its vision, as articulated by neoconservatives, on unenlightened countries. The term "American exceptionalism" enjoyed favor with Lovestone and his breakaway, radical socialists. These partisans insisted that the United States existed independently of the otherwise ironclad Marxist laws of history because of its economic abundance and the lack of rigid class distinctions in our society. Lovestone and his followers believed that the strength of a self-reforming American capitalism rendered unnecessary a Communist revolution. America was uniquely open to gradualist approaches for righting social and racial inequalities.[9]

As the former Marxists made their trek rightward more than a half century ago, the linguistic template and ideas associated with "American exceptionalism" were deployed to signify the universal superiority of their conception of the American experience. Further, these retread Marxists read their conception of a reformed and crusading American democracy back into the American Founding. For example, the neoconservative favored political thinker Allan Bloom offers this opinion in *The Closing of the American Mind*: "And when we Americans speak seriously about politics we mean that our principles of freedom and equality and the rights based on them are rational and everywhere applicable." Americans must engage in "an educational experiment undertaken to force those who do not accept these principles to do so."[10]

Although the two groups may seem at times in major disagreement, both the multicultural Left and the neoconservative Right share a basic commitment to certain ideas and tropes. Both use comparable phraseology—about "equality" and "democracy," "human rights" and "freedom," and the desirability of exporting "our values." Despite this overlap, both the dominant Left and the neoconservative Right try to give discrete meanings to the foundational doctrine of equality that the two sides share with equal enthusiasm.

In their defense of the civil rights legislation of the 1960s and their advocacy of moderate feminism and equal rights for women (now extended to same-sex marriage and even transgenderism), the neoconservatives mirror the political stances of the Left. They also seem to agree with the Left's overarching premises while also criticizing the Left for being excessive in how it implements its policies. Thus we have such neoconservative notables as Ben Shapiro, Jonah Goldberg, George Will, Guy Benson, and others essentially endorsing same-sex marriage and wishing to accommodate transgenderism but also insisting that they are moderate "conservatives" who are recognized by reasonable liberals as such.[11]

From the showcasing of such figures one gains the impression that the most recent reversal of traditional moral standards—same-sex marriage, or transgenderism—is actually conservative. Or, in foreign policy that it is critically necessary to send American soldiers to fight in faraway jungles or deserts to establish democracy, in order to prevent one group of rebels in Asia or Africa from killing off another group of rebels in that territory—that other group being willing to do the bidding economically and politically of the United States. This crusade takes place supposedly in the name of spreading global equality and freedom and other benefits of American democracy.

Not surprisingly, the Southern conservative historian Mel Bradford stressed the incompatibility of the neoconservative vision with the older republican constitutionalism of the Founders and Framers. According to Bradford, our old republic was not founded on abstractions about equality or democracy, or on some imperative to impose our democracy on the rest of the world.[12] We were not intended to be "the model for the rest of the world," to paraphrase Allan Bloom. Those notions in the case of the neoconservatives were a hangover from their immersion in a universalism that owed its origin to the radical Left. Traditional Southerners by contrast regarded as the basis for their unity, kinship, and blood an attachment to community and ancestral land. Moreover, both states' rights and a central religious core annealed the older republican tradition as understood by Southern traditionalists.

Understanding the old republican legacy, as interpreted by Bradford and likeminded Southerners, is essential for differentiating Southern traditional conservatism from the neoconservative vision. North Carolinian Richard Weaver aptly described the society created in the Old South, a century before the Declaration of Independence and the Constitution, as one based on a communal or "social bond" individualism.[13] By that, Weaver meant that colonists from Europe brought with them to the South a community-oriented individualism that offered enumerated liberties and autarky to each of its members within the parameters of a hierarchical society anchored in commonly accepted traditions.

Settlers on America's Southern shores, according to Southern conservatives, were not seeking to create an "exceptional nation" dedicated to spreading the gospel of equality and democracy. They were only trying to preserve the order in which they already lived. Paramount for Southerners was the defense of localism and coexisting with other communities and states within a federalized union. According to this Southern conservative understanding of American history, the Northern victory in 1865 overthrew the original republic and paved the way for the present-day success of what the author Sam Francis called the managerial state—and what we now characterize as the Deep State.

In the so-called conservative wars of the 1970s and 1980s, Southern conservatism found itself fighting side by side with a dwindling contingent of the Old Right. That was understandable, seeing that the Old Right treated the South and even the Confederacy with some sympathy. By contrast, the neoconservatives never hid their contempt for the white South as a quagmire of reaction and racist attitudes. This now predictable linkage between the white South and reactionary bigotry was reflected in the efforts of neoconservative TV celebrity Ben Shapiro to defame conservative Republican candidate Corey Stewart in the Virginia Republican primary for the U.S. Senate. Not only did Stewart's support for Confederate heritage become a negative issue for Shapiro and other neoconservatives. He also made much of the fact that Stewart at one time associated with a former congressional candidate, Paul Nehlen, who later made statements that some observers characterized as anti-Semitic.[14] The tarring of Stewart through guilt by association with someone's hypothetical anti-Semitism followed a customary neoconservative script. Southern whites who stray to the right of the neoconservatives are pummeled with charges of racism and anti-Semitism.

Historian and Fox News media star Victor Davis Hanson also cannot quite master his hatred of Southern white society. In a critique of Massachusetts senator Elizabeth Warren for her insistence on her claimed remote Native American ancestry, Hanson compared modern hard-core leftists to Southerners on the eve of war in 1861. He predictably dredged up images of Southern white racism, accusing Warren of "harkening back to the old South's 'one drop rule' of 'invisible blackness.' Supposedly any proof of sub-Saharan ancestry, even one drop of 'black blood,' made one black and therefore subject to second-class citizenship." Further: "The yellow star rectifies this strange situation in which one human group that is radically opposed to the people of white blood, and which for eternity is unassimilable to this blood, cannot be identified at first glance." Hanson's linkage between Nazis and traditional Southern conservatives was unmistakable but also unlikely to render him unpopular with his like-minded sponsors.[15]

It may be relevant to mention that neoconservative revulsion for white Southerners of a traditionalist persuasion does not seem to be grounded in an unforgiving attitude toward the South for having once practiced slavery and segregation. As Gary Dorrien and other historians have noted about the origins of neoconservatism, this movement's strong identification with the civil rights revolution came mostly long after the event.[16] In the 1970s, neoconservative authors were openly critical of black civil rights leaders for opposing Jewish public educators in New York City and for failing to support Israel. It was the campaign to unseat the Southern conservative front-runner for the directorship of the National Endowment for the Humanities in 1981 that turned neoconservative journalists into raging enemies of supposed Southern bigotry. This emotion was not, however, entirely feigned. Neoconservatives have fairly consistently associated the white South with anti-Jewish prejudice; and the invective they unleashed on Bradford may well have been motivated by hostility to someone whom they saw as culturally different from and possibly hostile to their own Jewish subgroup.

Given their profound repugnance for defenders of the white South, it seems unlikely that establishment conservatives would be welcoming them back into their movement very soon. But other developments occurred that suggest that such a welcome may be unnecessary. With the civil rights revolution and the subsequent abandoning of the South by the Democratic Party, a change took place in political party identification in the former Confederacy. From the mid-twentieth century when figures such as Senators Harry Byrd Sr. of Virginia, Richard Russell of Georgia, and Sam Ervin of North Carolina—all Southern Democrats— defined Southern conservative politics, the political leadership of the South has undergone transformation.

Ervin is now remembered mostly as the "Watergate senator" who helped bring down Richard Nixon. A Bible-quoting, storytelling, and well-educated conservative Democrat who rose to become North Carolina's senior U.S. senator, "Senator Sam" was an archetypal traditional Southern conservative. His speeches on the Constitution and his autobiography, *Preserving the Constitution: The Autobiography of Senator Sam J. Ervin* (1984), are like a journey back into the mind of the Framers. Ervin defended an American republic and American society that have all but vanished. As a leader of the opposition to the 1964 Civil Rights Act, he warned against the long-range consequences of federal overreach. Ervin upheld strict constructionism, and his understanding of states' rights may be seen as an effort to create a bulwark against the modern social-engineering state. His strictures against the Watergate break-in were also directed against the same target, unchecked centralized government.[17]

Ironically, despite its Northern and Jewish roots, neoconservatism gained adherents in the states of the old Confederacy and today seems to dominate Southern Republican politics. Neoconservatives were able to co-opt a long tradition of Southern patriotism that had evolved after defeat in the War between the States, subsuming it in the service of an internationalist agenda. In this they were aided by favorable conservative media, and, in particular, by the generally neoconservative-oriented Fox News channel. This network offers neoconservative views on a wide range of themes, from American intervention in Syria and an often awkward outreach to racial minorities, to militantly pro-Likud policies for the Middle East.

Although some political leaders in the South continue to claim the conservative mantle, they stand worlds apart from men like Ervin, Jesse Helms, and Harry Byrd. A Senator Lindsey Graham of South Carolina, or a Senator Bob Corker of Tennessee, demonstrates the pervasive influence of neoconservative thinking. Like many other Southern solons in Washington, these Republicans have advocated vigorous American intervention across the globe and accept the enunciated tenets of an American exceptionalism that would, in effect, impose American-style democracy and equality on nations that appear backward or "undemocratic." Southern political leaders who are sometimes ranked as "conservatives" also affirm such once-taboo practices as same-sex marriage, couching their acceptance as a matter of individual choice. In June 2015, after the Supreme Court rendered its *Obergefell v. Hodges* decision, Senator Graham announced that he no longer favored a constitutional amendment defining marriage as between one man and one woman because it might hurt the Republican brand among independents and millennial voters: "No, I would not engage in the Constitutional amendment process as a party going into 2016. Accept the Court's ruling."[18]

Graham also joined South Carolina governor Nikki Haley and other political and cultural leaders in calling for the removal of the Confederate Battle Flag from the grounds of the South Carolina state capitol. This came after the shooting in a black church in Charleston in 2015 by a lone gunman who displayed Confederate iconography.[19] The connection between the flag on the capitol grounds and the shooter was tenuous at best, but it afforded the occasion for nervous Southern politicians to discard an indelible image of Southern heritage identified by the media as a hate symbol. The position taken by many Southern Republican politicians was one more reminder of the difference between traditional Southern conservatives and their putative newer incarnations.

Neoconservatives have also enjoyed success in bringing over to their side Southern evangelicals. Their positions have often dovetailed with those of Southerners who profess Dispensationalism or "end times theology," in which the State of Israel is seen to possess the divine mandate given to it in the Old Testament. Perhaps most notable here has been Pastor John Hagee, pastor of Cornerstone Church in San Antonio, Texas, with his international media network.[20] Hagee's role and activities are similar to those of other church figures, and their influence among Southern evangelicals is significant. Because of their unswerving theological devotion to the Israeli state and its policies, these advocates and their followers have been open to neoconservative influence generally.

Among traditionally conservative Southern Baptists, moreover, there has been a tendency to adapt to the leftward drifting media. A notable example can be found in the reaction to the violent confrontation between demonstrators from the militant Left and those from the militant Right that occurred in Charlottesville, Virginia, on August 12, 2017. A scheduled march by various partisans in defense of a threatened monument to General Robert E. Lee was met by counterprotesters from Black Lives Matter, the Antifa movement, and others on the left. One counterprotester was killed in the resulting melee. The media denounced only the right-wing "extremist" demonstrators but avoided mentioning the complicity of the Left in the violence that erupted.[21]

Whereupon several Evangelical Protestant leaders announced the formation of a group, Unifying Leadership, and sent an open letter to President Donald Trump. Spearheaded by such prominent Southern Baptists as Steve Gaines, president of the Southern Baptist Convention; Danny Akin, president of Southeastern Baptist Theological Seminary in Wake Forest, North Carolina; and Baptist social activist Russell Moore, the group urged President Trump to denounce the

"Alt-Right" movement and "white nationalism." (Trump had previously condemned provocateurs on *both* sides at Charlottesville, an act that raised the hackles of the Washington establishment and prominent neoconservatives.)

The signers also asked the president to "join with many other political and religious leaders to proclaim with one voice that the 'alt-right' is racist, evil, and antithetical to a well-ordered, peaceful society." Other leaders of American Evangelical Protestantism soon added their signatures to his document.[22] This followed a condemnation by the Southern Baptist Convention earlier that year of what was termed "white supremacy." Thus in addition to their ultra-Zionist position, Baptist and Evangelical Protestant leaders made common cause with neoconservatives in highlighting the danger of white racism that the government must continue to address.

The surprise election of Donald Trump with his vision to "make *America great again*" was an indication that a somnolent and older grassroots tradition, a native populism that owed more to William Jennings Bryan than to George W. Bush, was on the rise again. The future president's apparent questioning of the shared Left/Right consensus on America's duty to spread democracy and equality together with his later refusal to follow the consensus narrative on the Charlottesville incident suggested that he was not in the mold of establishment Republicans.

The rise of Trump threw both the neoconservatives and their Southern followers off stride, at least temporarily. Despite his New York origin and his brashness of manner and language, the electoral earthquake occasioned by Trump's triumph had wide-ranging consequences beyond the election of a president. Such stalwart neoconservatives and establishment Republicans as Bill Kristol (Irving's son), George W. Bush aide Peter Wehner, Steve Schmidt (who ran John McCain's 2008 presidential campaign), former New Hampshire senator Gordon Humphrey, and Max Boot (major foreign policy adviser to McCain) joined the Never Trump opposition. Boot, in a *Washington Post* column, announced that he was leaving the Republican Party and blasted what he termed the "Trumpian revolution" that was working "to transform the GOP into a European-style nationalist party that . . . believes in deportation of undocumented immigrants, white identity politics, protectionism and isolationism backed by hyper-macho threats to bomb the living daylights out of anyone who messes with us."[23]

Indeed, the alacrity and eagerness with which white Southerners voted for the new president have been frequently noted, and not always favorably. But since white Southern support for the GOP has been surging for decades, none of this should have been entirely unexpected. Certainly Trump did not go out of his way to appoint Southern conservatives to his administration, but he has also not been hostile to them and even came out in defense of preserving Confederate monuments.[24]

There has also been a revival of interest in preserving "Southern heritage," which has found followers in all social classes. This mounting interest has been fueled by the campaign to pull down monuments and plaques commemorating the Confederacy and by the efforts to remove the Confederate Battle Flag from public buildings in the South. In this crusade neoconservatives have been largely opposed to anything that treats the Southern white past favorably. But opposition to the leftist anti-Confederate project has surfaced nonetheless. During the furious debate over threatened monuments, much to the surprise and shock of both pollsters and many political leaders, nearly two-thirds of Southerners favored keeping them in place.[25]

What is evident, however, is that Southern conservatives, properly understood, have no place in contemporary establishment conservativism. Their orientation and those who express it have become a hindrance to the "movement" as it reaches out and tries to form alliances and frame dialogues with the opposition, always on the left. Nevertheless, what has happened to this ousted part of the Old Right warrants our attention if we seek to understand where the conservative movement has gone since the 1960s.

10

REPUBLICAN VOTERS AND CONSERVATIVE IDEOLOGY

George Hawley

Most Republican Voters Are Not Conservative

When Republicans battle for presidential nominations, we expect candidates to compete for the mantle of "true conservative," or more specifically, "Ronald Reagan conservative." Candidates use every opportunity to lambast their opponents for their apparent lack of conservative purity. The 2016 GOP primary was different; Donald Trump chose not to play that game and was pilloried by the conservative intelligentsia. Leading conservatives apparently believed the modal Republican voter was a "true conservative," dedicated to constitutional government, limited intervention in the economy, traditional family values, and neoconservative foreign policies. Thus, they thought pointing out Trump's ideological impurity would derail his candidacy. To these conservatives' frustration, their attacks did not matter. They did not matter because Republicans in the electorate care about conservative principles far less than conservatives in the Beltway believed. The public's conservatism, as the conservative movement understands the term, is more symbolic than substantive.

The Conservative Movement's Attack on Trump

The conservative attacks on Trump began early in the campaign. Some preceded the announcement of his candidacy. The conservative radio show host Mark Levin declared Trump a nonconservative in 2011.[1] That same year, the conservative blogger and activist Andrew Breitbart expressed concern that Trump might run for president as a Republican, which was a problem because Trump was "not a conservative."[2] In the months leading up to Trump's announcement of his candidacy, conservative pundits mocked the idea. In April 2015, when asked to place a bet on which candidate would likely become the Republican nominee, George Will said he was willing to give Trump a 1 percent chance "in the hope that he will be tempted to run, be predictably shellacked, and we will be spared ever more this quadrennial charade of his."[3] The next day, Jonah Goldberg wrote the following: "All I see is a guy who's been preening for attention with bogus talk about running for president for years who's deeply offended that nobody believes him or cares anymore."[4] When Trump formally became a candidate, the conservative columnist Kevin D. Williamson described Trump as a "witless ape" with a "messiah complex." Williamson then remarked, "The problem with messiah complexes is that there's no way to know whether you are going to rise on the third day unless somebody crucifies you. Trump has announced, and I say we get started on that."[5]

Attacks on Trump's lack of consistent conservatism increased after he formally threw his hat into the presidential ring. The popular and influential radio personality Glenn Beck declared in June 2015: "He is a progressive, and you can prove that by the things that he believes in. A progressive believes in high tariffs. A progressive believes the government is the answer. Donald Trump has shown time and time again he believes the government is the problem, and if it is run properly, it is the answer. That's what a progressive believes."[6] A few days later, the conservative journalist John Fund questioned whether Trump was a closet leftist: "But just maybe Trump is a double agent for the Left. He is nearly a cartoon version of what a comedian such as Stephen Colbert considers a conservative—the kind of conservative Colbert played on Comedy Central until this year. He reinforces all the Left's negative stereotypes of conservatives as ignorant blowhards."[7] Later in that article, Fund clarified that he did not think Trump was literally a left-wing double agent; instead, "he is playing the useful idiot for the Left. He might as well be doing it on purpose." Michael Reagan, son of Ronald Reagan, made a similar remark, saying, "The liberal media treasure Trump even more because he spends so much time helping them discredit the Republican Party and conservatism."[8]

Writing in *The Atlantic* in early July, Conor Friedersdorf pointed out that Trump has an amazing ability to switch positions on a dime and make contradictory statements with what can appear to be passion and sincerity: "He seems as if he is fearlessly stating his core convictions, consequences be damned, even when he is being a shameless poseur."[9] Matt Walsh, a popular conservative blogger, not only attacked Trump but also attacked all self-described conservatives who supported him: "Like Obama voters in 2008, you have become not proponents of a set of ideas, but advocates for an individual. You are supporters of personality, not policy. This is particularly true in your case, because Trump's policies are either: A) non-existent, or B) completely anathema to anything that could possibly be considered conservatism."[10]

Anti-Trump sentiment reached a peak when *National Review*, weeks before the Iowa caucus, dedicated an entire issue to denouncing Donald Trump. The cover dramatically carried the words "Against Trump." The magazine made the entire issue available for free online. The issue drew from a wide range of thinkers on the right. The first signed essay of the symposium was written by the talk show host Glenn Beck (who endorsed Ted Cruz for the nomination). Beck is one of the most influential conservative talk show hosts in the United States. The issue also included the talk show hosts Michael Medved and Erick Erickson. Many of the contributors were leaders of the neoconservative wing of the movement, such as William Kristol and John Podhoretz. Thomas Sowell, perhaps the most celebrated living conservative scholar, also wrote an essay. There was even a nonconservative contributor—David Boaz, who is the executive vice president of the libertarian Cato Institute. The ecumenical nature of the issue demonstrated that there were strong reasons to oppose Trump, regardless of where one belonged within the big tent that is American conservatism.

In the unsigned editorial that began the issue, *National Review* made it very clear that conservatives of all stripes must resist the temptation to support Trump, and did so in the harshest terms: "Trump is a philosophically unmoored political opportunist who would trash the broad conservative ideological consensus within the GOP in favor of a free-floating populism with strong-man overtones."[11] The essay went on to describe the damage a Trump nomination would cause conservatism in almost apocalyptic tones: "If Trump were to become the president, the Republican nominee, or even a failed candidate with strong conservative support, what would that say about conservatives? The movement that ground down the Soviet Union and took the shine, at least temporarily, off socialism would have fallen in behind a huckster. The movement concerned with such 'permanent things' as constitutional government, marriage, and the right to life would have become a claque for a Twitter feed."[12]

Many of these same charges were repeated in the signed essays that followed. The various arguments were not always in agreement with each other, and many seemed contradictory. Several contributors noted that Trump was, and may still be, a liberal. Katie Pavlich noted, "Trump's liberal positions aren't in the distant past—he has openly promoted them on the campaign trail. Trump isn't fighting for anyone but himself, which has been his pattern for decades."[13] Mona Charen asked, "Is Trump a liberal? Who knows? He played one for decades—donating to liberal causes and politicians (including Al Sharpton) and inviting Hillary Clinton to his (third) wedding."[14]

Trump was also chastised for reasons unrelated to his history of liberal positions—some of which he never disavowed. Two essays attacked him for his "populism," which is ostensibly incompatible with conservatism. Two essays compared Trump to Mussolini. Hitler's name was brought up three times. He was also called a racist. Medved noted that Trump's candidacy would only strengthen the Left's argument that the conservative movement was largely motivated by racial animus: "Even those who take Trump at his word—accepting his declaration that he qualifies as the least racist individual in the nation—can imagine the parade of negative ads the Democrats are already preparing for radio stations with mainly black audiences and for Spanish-language television."[15] Beyond the mere political calculation, Russell Moore argued that conservatives should reject Trump's rhetoric on women and minorities out of principle: "Beyond that, Trump's vitriolic—and often racist and sexist—language about immigrants, women, the disabled, and others ought to concern anyone who believes that all persons, not just the 'winners' of the moment, are created in God's image."[16]

The charge that Donald Trump is not a movement conservative is unquestionably true. He has never shown any interest in conservative political theory, nor does he lambast policy proposals purely because they are not congruent with conservative ideas. According to conventional wisdom, this was supposed to hinder his ability to capture the Republican nomination. Those who follow national politics often assume that the kind of person who regularly votes in a Republican primary is a conservative who is looking for the most conservative candidate that can plausibly win the general election. When conservative opinion leaders assess what ails the Republican Party, a common refrain is that the party has abandoned its conservative principles, and to abandon conservative principles is to "betray" the voters who put Republicans in power.[17]

This view has some support. A Gallup poll conducted in late 2015 showed that 60 percent of Republicans wanted the GOP to nominate a candidate who was either conservative or very conservative.[18] But leading figures of the conservative movement may not define conservatism the same as your average voter. To assume that the average Republican voter is familiar with the conservative canon, understands the argument that there is a logical connection between free markets and tradition, or can even identify which specific policies are associated with conservatism requires overestimating the electorate's political sophistication.

There is evidence that many Republicans in office agree with the idea that their base of support is conservative across the policy spectrum, on economics, social issues, and foreign policy. They fear the wrath of talk radio. There is also a real fear that an elected Republican can be defeated in a primary for angering certain elements of the conservative base; Eric Cantor's 2014 primary defeat at the hands of a political neophyte seemed to demonstrate this. Nevertheless, the notion that pure conservatism is a common trait among Republican voters, let alone the overall population, is questionable.

Ideological Constraints in the Electorate: The Debate within Political Science

There has long been a disconnect between how pundits and other strong ideologues in the media view the ideological inclinations of the electorate and how political scientists view these same convictions. No one with a passing familiarity with the political science literature on American electoral behavior will be surprised to learn that ideological purity is a rare trait among voters. Yet the failure of Republican primary voters to repudiate Trump's ideological inconsistency is apparently shocking to many opinion leaders. In 1964, Philip Converse published an influential article that investigated the degree to which mass publics exhibited ideological "constraints," which he defined as "the probability that a change in the perceived status (truth, desirability, and so forth) of one idea-element would *psychologically* require, from the point of view of the actor, some compensating change(s) in the status of idea-elements elsewhere in the configuration."[19] In other words, logically, a person's views on one issue should correlate with his or her views on related issues, and a changing attitude on one of those issues should correlate with changes in the others. In his empirical examination, Converse found that there was shockingly little evidence that much of the population exhibited these kinds of logical constraints. Only at the elite level do we ever find coherent political belief systems. In the subsequent decades, a great deal of research provided additional evidence for Converse's argument.[20]

Not all scholars agreed with Converse's conclusions,[21] and one can reasonably argue that ideological consistency in the electorate has increased.[22] As elites have become more polarized and are thus giving more consistent ideological cues to the public, the public also seems to have become more consistent in its ideological stances.[23] But the assumption that ideology should be treated as a one-dimensional scale (running between liberal and conservative) may also be problematic, and if it is, such a finding creates a new source of headaches for scholars who wish to carefully examine this issue.[24] At the elite level there tends to be a strong correlation between conservative attitudes on economic issues and conservative attitudes on social issues, but this correlation is weaker among the general public.[25]

Although it is reasonable to say that most Americans are not consistent ideologues, it may be unfair to claim that they have no meaningful political attitudes or that their attitudes are cobbled together in a haphazard manner. Stephen Ansolabehere and his colleagues made a compelling argument that policy issues play an important role in shaping vote choice.[26] Alan Abramowitz and Kyle Saunders additionally found that ideological orientation, as opposed to social identity, has become an increasingly important determinant of party identification.[27] Even so, the growing congruence between ideological stance and party ID has not really translated into new constraints when it comes to issues—when we look at most peoples' list of policy preferences, we still see very little logical coherence across multiple issues.[28]

In spite of new caveats, Converse's thesis still holds up pretty well.[29] There is evidence that some of the perceived lack of political sophistication within the electorate is due to poor wording of survey questions and measurement errors on the part of political scientists.[30] But even if we take this into account, we continue to find that hard-core ideologues, with consistently conservative or liberal policy preferences, are not the norm. A 2008 study by David E. RePass found that only about 7.4 percent of potential voters were both strong conservatives and strong Republicans.[31] Hillygus and Shields examined what they called "cross-pressured voters," those voters with policy preferences that are not aligned with the platform of their preferred party. They concluded that more than a quarter of "partisans embrace issue positions that are inconsistent with their preferred political party."[32] Donald Kinder and Nathan Kalmoe also weighed in on this debate. In their 2017 book, *Neither Liberal nor Conservative*, these political scientists revisited Converse's hypothesis, using a massive amount of public opinion data. They concluded that Converse's theory is just as valid today as it was in the 1960s.[33]

Even if we could find congruence between policy preferences and vote choice and party identification, however, our concerns about the reasonability of the electorate may not be alleviated. People may not determine their party identification or their vote choice based on policy considerations. Instead, once their party identification is well established, their policy preferences subsequently become aligned with the positions taken by their preferred party.[34] To complicate this issue even further, the direction of the causal arrow on this question may not be consistent over time; during some periods, policy preferences seem to drive party identification, and during other periods, the relationship appears to be reversed.[35]

Resolving these issues is well beyond the scope of this chapter. I bring up these debates because some of the best political science research gives us a strong reason to be suspicious of the claim that the modal Republican voter is a strong conservative, and that conservatism is what drives his or her party identification and vote choice. To a limited extent, major figures associated with the conservative movement have also acknowledged this; within the conservative movement, at least among intellectual conservatives, it is recognized that there is a meaningful difference between social conservatives and economic conservatives. In spite of the efforts of fusionists like Frank Meyer and others, this distinction has never gone away entirely, and these differences can only be painted over in the hope that these two wings of the movement can hold together well enough to form a powerful political coalition—the logic being that, whatever their differences, economic and social conservatives still prefer each other to the progressive egalitarianism embodied by the modern Democratic Party. That still assumes, however, that within the broad Republican coalition we can find a significant percentage of voters who are at least consistent traditionalists or consistent supporters of free-market economics. We will consider this in the pages ahead, but first we should consider whether most self-described Republicans even consider themselves to be conservative.

Most Republicans Are Self-Described Conservatives

For many decades, the American National Election Survey (NES) has been among the most useful tools for scholars of American politics. It combines a large number of observations with a large number of useful questions, and it can provide a detailed snapshot of where the American public stands on important political issues. For this study, I rely on the 2012 NES because it was completed well before the 2016 presidential election cycle. Had I examined 2016 data, one might reasonably question whether Trump's candidacy had influenced the views of Republican voters.

In the Republican category, I include people who initially identify as a Republican as well as independents who, when pushed, admit that they lean more toward the Republican Party than the Democratic Party. This is because so-called independent leaners tend to be no less committed to their party than people who expressly and immediately declare themselves supporters of a particular party.[36]

The first general question is whether most Republicans describe themselves as conservative. The NES includes a helpful scale that allows us to see where Americans fall ideologically. Respondents were asked to place themselves somewhere on a seven-point ideological scale, between "extremely liberal" and "extremely conservative." If we collapse this into a dichotomous variable, so that the "extremely conservative," the "conservative," and the "slightly conservative" respondents are all merged into a single category, and moderates and all varieties of liberals are categorized as a separate category, we see that a large majority of Republicans consider themselves conservative—about 74 percent. When we break conservatism down into those three possible categories, however, we see that extreme conservatives are relatively uncommon, even among Republicans (only about 8 percent described themselves in that manner). Far more called themselves conservative (about 42 percent) or slightly conservative (about 24 percent). In fact, self-described moderates were more than twice as common as self-described extreme conservatives (about 22 percent called themselves "middle of the road"). This is unsurprising, as other important research has indicated that ideological polarization, while present at the elite level, has never been pronounced in the electorate.[37]

As a verification check on the finding that most Republicans view themselves as conservatives of some sort but rarely identify as "extreme conservatives," we can consult the 2014 General Social Survey (GSS). This survey has been conducted regularly since the early 1970s and includes a large battery of questions related to personal demographics, cultural practices, and political and policy attitudes. The GSS also includes a question about ideology, using very similar wording to the NES. It also found that a large majority of Republicans consider themselves conservative. Also like the NES, it found that only about 8 percent of them considered themselves "very conservative."

Terms like "moderate" and "conservative" are subjective, however. Someone could be far right of the median voter on a large number of issues and still consider himself or herself to be a moderate. A person may also be a self-described conservative despite having few points of agreement with the mainstream conservative movement—by "conservative," a person may simply mean something like "levelheaded," or even just vaguely patriotic. An often neglected fact of American politics is that a large percentage of self-described conservatives do not support the conservative movement's policy agenda. This was an important point in *Ideology in America*, by Christopher Ellis and James Stimson.[38] We must recognize that there are two very different conceptions of ideology: symbolic ideology and operational ideology. Symbolic ideology may have only a tenuous relationship to policy preferences. Americans are, on average, very attached to symbolic conservatism: they love the flag, consider themselves religious, and are moved by talk of liberty and the Constitution. Operational ideology is focused on the actual things people want government to do. Here we find that Americans, including Republicans, are much more liberal. Among political and intellectual elites, symbolic and operational ideologies are infrequently in conflict. Among the general public, the two are frequently in conflict, which can lead observers to overstate the degree to which Americans are politically conservative.

Given that self-placement on the ideological scale may not be useful for discerning where the public stands on the issues, the more interesting question is how Republicans think about actual policies.

Consistent Conservatism Is Rare When It Comes to Policies

To keep its various factions united, the conservative movement has always accepted a degree of ideological diversity. Nonetheless, the typical conservative journalist or intellectual will contend that a true American conservative must agree with the three core principles of contemporary conservatism: limited government intervention in the economy, the promotion of traditional values, and support for the American military. When it comes to more specific policies, there is much variation in how these principles should be put into practice, but the principles themselves are nonnegotiable. This of course is true if we are looking at conservative elites, but is it true of Republicans in the electorate? We can organize these issues into three general areas: economic issues, social issues, and foreign policy issues.

Economic Issues

We begin with the signature issue of the GOP: taxes. Conservatives fondly remember President Reagan for his major tax cuts, and the revolt against George H. W. Bush was presumably the result of his decision to break his promise of "no new taxes." From this, we might plausibly infer that Republicans are uniformly opposed to any new taxes or hikes in the tax rate. Yet, this does not appear to be true. According to the NES, Republicans in the electorate are actually very open to the idea of higher taxes for high earners. When asked whether they would support higher taxes on millionaires, almost 62 percent of Republicans responded that they would favor such a policy. Another question lowered the income level at which taxes should be raised in order to reduce the budget deficit, specifically asking whether income taxes should be raised on anyone who makes more than $250,000 a year. A near majority (49.87 percent) of Republicans favored such a policy; an additional 18 percent were ambivalent. Only about 32 percent opposed a new tax increase on those whose income exceeds that threshold. Many Republicans are even open to the idea of a higher tax rate on corporations in order to reduce the budget deficit—about 42 percent of Republicans expressed support for such a policy, compared with 36 percent who were opposed.

One might argue that this analysis considers too large a group. A significant percentage of the electorate identifies as Republican, but the average Republican is not particularly active and involved. Perhaps if we look at a particular class of Republicans, one that is very active and vocal, we will find a stronger degree of fiscal conservatism on the tax issue. The NES also helpfully asked respondents if they were supporters of the Tea Party. If there is any element of the electorate that is likely to be extremely conservative on fiscal matters, we can expect it to be this group. Yet even Republicans who support the Tea Party are divided on the question of taxes. Within this group of respondents only 49.36 percent said they opposed raising taxes on people making more than $250,000 annually.

There are many Republicans in the electorate who are doctrinaire economic libertarians. But they are not the norm. Even the Tea Party faction of the GOP is not unified in its opposition to higher taxes. It is possible that the Republicans who oppose new taxes are passionate about this issue, whereas those who are open to the idea of higher taxes are generally indifferent. Nonetheless, the fact that a large percentage of Republicans are willing to support higher taxes, at least theoretically, is underappreciated.

Even if Republicans are not unified in their opposition to higher taxes, perhaps they agree that government spending needs to be cut. Yet we see little evidence that most Republicans want to see major federal spending cuts. Conservatives have long argued that a Republican president should abolish the Department of Education, presumably to return control of education back to state and local governments. Yet very few Republicans actually want to decrease federal spending on education. About 19 percent wanted federal spending on education to be cut, compared with about 47 percent that wanted it increased and about 34 percent that think current spending levels are about right. Less than 10 percent of Republicans wanted to see spending cuts to Social Security.

Other scholars have similarly found that fiscal conservatism among Republicans is less common than is frequently assumed. In a 2007 study, Stephen Miller found that the relationship between party identification and economic beliefs is not particularly strong.[39] On average, Republicans and Democrats are very similar to each other when it comes to economic policy preferences. Although both Republicans and Democrats tend to reject classical elements of socialism—such as wage and price controls—there is a general liberal consensus that the United States should have a system that is best described as "welfare capitalism."

Social Issues

If average Republicans are not die-hard budget hawks, perhaps they are strong conservatives on those social issues that have been so divisive in American politics. Such a finding would be congruent with the argument that middle- and lower-income Republicans vote against their economic interests because they are devoted to the religious Right and its social agenda. This was the thesis of Thomas Frank's best-selling book, *What's the Matter with Kansas?* These voters may not care about taxes, but maintaining American virtue is high on their agenda. We can easily examine the degree to which this is true.

Every four years, the GOP platform includes language indicating support for new abortion restrictions. Court decisions such as *Roe v. Wade* were partly responsible for the rise of the religious Right in the 1970s, as well as the avalanche of votes this movement brought to the Republican Party. Perhaps no other issue has inspired such heated rhetoric and strong passions in the United States since the civil rights movement.

Although the faction of voters that would ban abortion in all circumstances is a vocal element of the conservative coalition, they represent a small minority of all Republicans. As of 2012, only 18 percent of NES respondents agreed with the statement "by law, abortion should never be permitted." In fact, there were far more *pro-choice* purists in Republican ranks than those who consistently take a pro-life stance. About 29 percent of Republicans agreed that, "by law, a woman should always be able to obtain an abortion as a matter of personal choice." In other words, almost three in ten Republicans believe there should be *fewer* restrictions on abortion than is the case today. A slight majority of Republicans believe abortion should be permitted, but with restrictions; about 37 percent want fairly harsh restriction, such as allowing abortion only in the case of rape, incest, or danger to the mother; and an additional 16 percent would allow it in other circumstances as well but do not favor total legalization of abortion in all possible circumstances. On average, Republicans are much more pro-life than non-Republicans (a majority of non-Republican respondents declared that they thought abortion should always be legal in all cases), but that does not mean that Republicans are uniformly opposed to abortion.

We see similar patterns when we turn our attention to other social issues. The issue of gay marriage was extraordinarily divisive during the Bush presidency. Throughout those years, a number of states passed laws prohibiting gay marriage, and it was widely believed that the evangelicals who turned out to oppose gay marriage played a role in securing Bush's second term as president. Although Republicans may have been uniformly against legal recognition of gay marriage a decade ago, that is not the case today. In fact, as of 2012, a majority (about 64 percent) of Republicans actually favored some kind of legal recognition for same-sex couples (about 21 percent favored full marriage rights, and about 43 percent favored civil unions). Only about 35 percent of Republicans believed there should be no legal recognition of gay couples. Unlike abortion, which will likely remain a divisive issue indefinitely, the issue of gay marriage appears to be permanently settled; even if the Supreme Court decision that legalized gay marriage nationwide were overturned, the legal recognition of gay relationships now has massive, bipartisan support from the American public.

Compared with abortion and same-sex marriage, the issue of marijuana legalization is now less politically contentious—several states have legalized marijuana for medical and even recreational use, with little pushback from the national conservative movement. A number of leading conservatives have even advocated for the legalization of marijuana on libertarian grounds.[40] That said, we might nonetheless expect that most Republicans in the electorate are opposed to legalization. It is true that opposition to legalization remained the modal response among Republicans as of 2012 (about 48 percent held this position). But about 28 percent favored legalization, and about 23 percent neither favored nor opposed legalization.

Gun control is another deeply divisive issue in the United States, and the National Rifle Association is one of the most influential lobbying groups in the country. Conservative media are nearly uniform in their uncompromising stance on the Second Amendment. Perhaps here we can find a conservative consensus among Republicans. Yet we actually see that many Republicans are in agreement with progressives on this issue, and very few are interested in removing existing laws. When asked whether laws should make it more difficult to access a gun, should make it easier to access a gun, or are about right as they are, an impressive 26 percent of Republicans said that it should be more difficult to get a gun. Only about 8 percent thought it should be easier. The rest felt gun laws were fine as they are. Although, as of 2012, a majority of Republicans did not favor new restrictions on guns, there was little interest in abolishing laws that already exist.

On several of the most contentious, and supposedly partisan, social issues, we do not see that most Republicans are doctrinaire conservatives. Large minorities within the GOP actually prefer a more liberal position when it comes to abortion, gay marriage, and guns. Much smaller minorities prefer the most extreme conservative option available to them. Although, on average, Republicans tend to be more conservative on these issues than Democrats and independents, they are not particularly conservative.

Foreign Policy Issues

Foreign policy is the final leg of the conservative stool, and it must also be addressed. On this subject, we might again expect a large amount of Republican agreement. That is indeed what we find. The number of Republicans who say they want to decrease military spending is small. However, Republicans have become increasingly willing to declare that foreign policy decisions made by the last Republican administration were mistakes.

Republicans remain very supportive of the military. The NES includes "feeling thermometer" questions for a large number of social groups, institutions, and individuals. On a feeling thermometer, the range is between zero and one hundred, and higher values indicate that the respondent has warmer feelings toward the group in question. Among Republicans, the military consistently gets warmer scores than most other groups. In 2012, the mean score for the military was 85.5. This is much higher than the mean score for the Tea Party (about 52), conservatives (about 69), and even Christians (about 78). Republicans, at least rhetorically, very much still "support our troops."

However, although Republicans continue to hold the military in high esteem, they, on average, have begun to show signs of war weariness. In 2012, about two-thirds (66.5 percent) of Republicans concluded that the Iraq War was not worth the cost. We similarly saw that Republicans were generally opposed to the use of the military to make sure Iran does not develop nuclear weapons. An overwhelming majority (95 percent) of Republican respondents believed that Iran was trying to develop nuclear weapons. However, when asked what they wanted to do about this supposed threat, most favored a nonmilitary response. About 69 percent said that they favored direct diplomacy; about 74 percent said they favored an increase in economic sanctions; only about 40 percent were willing to favor an airstrike on Iranian nuclear sites; and only about 21 percent said they were willing to support a ground invasion to prevent Iran from developing these weapons. In other words, although many of the leading conservative intellectuals and pundits believed President Obama's strategy toward Iran was too accommodating or even qualified as "appeasement," Obama's foreign policy decisions on this subject were similar to those favored by ordinary Republicans in the electorate. When it comes to foreign affairs, it would not be a stretch to say that your average Republican was closer to President Obama than to the editorial staff of the *Weekly Standard.*

We should not overstate this, of course. There are more recent data indicating that many Republicans subsequently became more hawkish. The data I cited were from 2012, before the rise of the Islamic State and renewed fears of terrorism. A Pew study conducted in 2015 indicated that most Republican voters would prefer a candidate who took a hard line on foreign policy.[41] More than two-thirds (69 percent) of Republicans stated that they would be more likely to support a GOP candidate who wanted to end the nuclear agreement with Iran. A slight majority (53 percent) even indicated that they would be more likely to support a Republican candidate who supported using ground troops to fight ISIS. Unfortunately, that wording was vague, and a differently worded question might have yielded different results—did these respondents actually favor an invasion of Syria, or did they mean the use of troops again in Iraq, where the United States already had a presence on the ground? The best explanation for the discrepancy between the 2012 NES results and the 2015 Pew results is that views on foreign policy and terrorism are probably context dependent. In times when terrorism is a salient fear—as it certainly was in the fall of 2015—a Republican candidate's fortunes in a primary appear to be strengthened by taking a hawkish position. In other circumstances, this is less of a certainty. The main takeaway from these findings on Republican feelings about foreign policy is that they are inconsistent over time when it comes to specific policies; they may even be ambivalent when it comes to the overall tone of American foreign policy.

Consistency within and across Policy Domains

It may be the case that, to keep the conservative coalition together, some degree of fusionism is indispensable at the elite level. Different conservative groups with different interests need to be able to talk to each other and cooperate. In the electorate, however, there may not be such a need for this kind of ideological consistency. Your average voter has no reason to be concerned with coalition building. He or she simply has preferences on economic and social issues, which may or may not be related, and votes accordingly. For the sake of simplicity, in this section I use those NES questions that allowed answers of "yes," "no," or "don't know" responses, rather than lengthier scales—it is easier to identify the conservative answer to such a question, but more difficult to identify the precise dividing line between liberalism and conservatism on a seven-point scale.

To begin with, we should measure what percentage of Republicans are consistent in their attachment to economic conservatism. That is, on every question related to taxes, they express their opposition to higher rates. It turns out that this is very much a minority position. Less than a quarter of all Republicans (about 21 percent) claimed that they were against any new tax increases for any group. Even if we restrict our sample to Republicans who describe themselves as supporters of the Tea Party, we still do not find across-the-board opposition to new taxes. Only about 38 percent of Tea Party Republicans said they opposed all new taxes. This does not mean that Republicans in office are free to raise taxes, of course. That 21 percent is likely a powerful segment of the Republican coalition. Some of the most influential lobbying groups in Congress are heavily focused on the tax issue, and there are grassroots lobbying organizations, such as Americans for Prosperity, that can quickly mobilize opposition when nonconservative economic policy is considered. Nonetheless, although strong economic conservatives are a vocal and powerful minority within the GOP, they are a minority.

Consistent social conservatives are just as rare. Only about 14 percent of Republicans gave a traditionalist conservative response on the question of gay marriage (opposing all forms of legal recognition), marijuana (opposing legalization), abortion (opposing legalization except in cases of rape or incest), and guns (opposing new laws that make purchasing firearms more difficult). One might argue that this is unfair, as the more questions one includes on such a measure, the more likely it is that a respondent will choose at least one nonconservative answer. The most logical question to remove from consideration is the question on marijuana, as it is generally low salience and a number of conservatives have called for its legalization. If we drop this question from consideration, the number of consistent social conservatives increases, but not by much—about 20 percent gave conservative answers on the questions about guns, abortion, and gay marriage.

Perhaps if we restrict our attention to a particular subset of Republicans, we will find more uniformity on social issues. In this case, it makes sense to restrict the analysis to evangelical Christians, as this group is presumably the main constituency for social conservatism in American politics. If we look just at evangelical Christian Republicans, we still find that only about 35 percent held consistently conservative positions on issues of gay marriage, abortion, and guns. The majority held a moderate or liberal position on at least one of those issues.

So we see that both consistent social conservatives and economic conservatives are a minority among self-described Republicans. That being the case, it necessarily follows that consistently conservative Republicans, who prefer a conservative position on both social and economic issues, must be an even smaller percentage of all Republicans. Of course, as the number of questions that must be answered in the conservative direction increases in order for a person to be classified as a consistent conservative, the number of people who receive such a classification decreases. Increasing the number of questions additionally increases the odds that measurement error will throw off the results. Thus, I classify a consistent conservative as anyone who answers two out of three questions related to taxes in a conservative direction and two out of three questions related to social issues in a conservative direction as a consistent conservative. When we use even this fairly generous definition of a consistent conservative, we find that only about 17 percent of Republicans in this 2012 sample answered a majority of questions related to social issues and economic issues in a conservative manner.

Of course, one could argue that there is a problem with this methodology, as I examined all self-described Republicans in this sample, including those who identified as weak Republicans and who identified as independents who leaned Republican, as well as those who do not vote. For purposes of this study, it will be useful to examine the relative conservatism of Republican primary voters. Even when we restrict ourselves to this much smaller sample of self-described Republicans, we still find that only a minority (about one-quarter) can be classified as consistent conservatives when it comes to both social and economic policy. I must again include the caveat that these data are from 2012. However, there is little reason to expect that the policy preferences of Republicans have shifted in any systematic way since that time. Indeed, given the high levels of interest and turnout in Republican primaries and caucuses in 2016, we can reasonably expect that strong conservatives were an even smaller minority in the most recent election.

Note that in my examination of conservative consistency among Republican voters I have included only two of the three legs of modern conservatism. I have not added questions of foreign policy. If a true conservative is always against higher taxes, takes conservative stances on social issues, and is a foreign policy hawk, these numbers are even smaller. If we contend that conservatives must also be supporters of the Iraq War to properly wear the label, then only about 8 percent of all Republicans and about 12 percent of Republican primary voters pass the test.

The finding that ideological conservatism is uncommon seems to defy our everyday observations of the political world. After all, there seem to be signs all around that the United States is politically polarized, with huge numbers of people firmly on the far left or far right. Can the signs of polarization be reconciled with the often liberal policy preferences expressed by ordinary Republicans? One thing to keep in mind is that the polarization of the electorate has been overstated. Morris Fiorina and his colleagues persuasively made this argument in their book, *Culture War? The Myth of a Polarized America*.[42] This work made the case that ideological and partisan polarization is primarily an elite phenomenon; among the electorate more broadly, there is little evidence that Americans are increasingly divided along red and blue lines.

Yet this also seems unsatisfying. If we look at Americans who are not part of the political elite, we can still find a lot of bitter partisanship; political candidates, party leaders, and talk radio and cable news hosts are not the only angry voices in American politics. Lilliana Mason's research sheds light on the apparent paradox of an electorate that seems bitterly divided and polarized despite the relatively small percentage of voters that support extreme policies. Building on the work of other scholars,[43] Mason argued that partisanship should be considered the result of social identity, rather than policy preferences.[44] Americans feel a strong emotional connection to their parties, and strongly dislike the opposing party, but these feelings of partisanship are only loosely connected to policy preferences. Instead, we form attachments to parties based on our social group memberships (such as our race and religion), and our parties subsequently become a part of our personal identity. Most Republicans do not support their party because they have strong feelings about the estate tax; they are Republicans because the GOP is the "correct" party for people with their other social identities (white, native born, Christian, etc.). The Republican Party can expect widespread support from a large number of enthusiastic voters, even if those voters have very little interest in conservative public policies per se. This suggests that they are not going to abandon the Republican Party anytime soon, but they may be open to a GOP that stands for something other than conservatism—they may even prefer a less conservative GOP.

The existing survey data lead us to conclude that very few Americans are consistent conservatives, at least as the organized conservative movement defines the term. This finding will not surprise scholars of American politics, but many pundits, politicians, and consultants are under the impression that there is a great grassroots army of conservatives and that voters rally around the movement and embrace all of its elements. It is true that more Americans describe themselves as conservative than describe themselves as liberal; this has long been the case. But calling oneself a conservative is not the same thing as endorsing the policy positions pushed by the official voices of the conservative movement. If we use policy preferences as our measure, then we can emphatically declare that most Americans are not conservatives. We can even confidently state that most Republicans are not conservative.

This disconnect between the reality of voter preferences and the rhetoric of conservative think tanks, journalists, and advocacy organizations helps us understand why so many leading voices on the right mistakenly declared Trump's candidacy dead in the water. The truth is that most Republican voters do not insist that candidates pass a specific conservative litmus test. These voters would not personally pass such a test. If there is a conservative consensus, it exists only at the elite level. That being the case, it is clear that elites play a critical role in keeping the Republican Party's elected officials within conservative boundaries. Republican leaders clearly listen to what the leading voices of the conservative movement have to say, and rely on them when forming policy.

This arrangement, where the leaders of the conservative movement keep the Republican Party wedded to conservative principles, has worked well for conservatives—even if conservative pundits lament the large number of "Republicans in name only" in Congress. However, as we have seen, this system is vulnerable to Republican candidates who are not reliant on the conservative movement in any way—either in formulating policy or in securing donations. Up until now, the number of such Republicans has been small. The few examples we have, such as Ron Paul, were not threatening to the conservative movement, as Paul's libertarian ideology is even more unappealing to American voters than conservatism.

In fairness to mainstream conservative commentators, at least some have recognized and admitted the weak hold that the movement has on the electorate, including Republican voters. Talk show host Rush Limbaugh is one surprising personality who made this point. In January 2016, in reaction to the bafflement many conservatives expressed about Trump's high level of support, Limbaugh stated that "the degree of conservatism in the Republican Party has been overestimated."[45] When conservative talk radio show hosts make such statements, they are usually referring to Republican politicians in office or party leaders. Limbaugh, however, was referring to Republicans in the electorate. Limbaugh went on: "It's not just conservative principles that hold people who are conservative together. There are many different things, and the full-blown conservatives are a little bothered by this because it makes 'em think maybe they're not that important. It could be bothersome."[46]

"Bothersome" is an understatement. Donald Trump's primary victory, as well as the conservative "Never Trump" movement's failure to peel away many voters in the general election, set a dangerous precedent for conservatives. The conservative movement's power comes exclusively from its hold on the GOP. It never succeeded in persuading many Americans to support conservative policies. This fact has always been lurking in public opinion data, but before Trump's election, the myth of conservative voters kept many Republican politicians in line. It is likely that the conservative movement has been a liability to the GOP, rather than an asset. If that becomes widely acknowledged, and a new wave of GOP candidates reject conservative orthodoxy, the mainstream conservative movement may become irrelevant.

AFTERWORD
The Never-Ending Purges

Paul Gottfried

Note to the reader: Lest there be any misunderstanding about what follows, it may be useful to begin with some disclaimers. Nothing in this afterword is intended to be an endorsement of a particular political position. I am not writing as a political advocate for an ideologically restricted circle; I am not taking a position for or against race realists, economic libertarians, or the intensely anti-Communist foreign policy of *National Review* in the 1950s and 1960s. What I am trying to demonstrate is, first, the intolerance exhibited by the conservative movement toward its own dissenters, and second, the extent to which the media contributed to this behavior. Such an investigation seems warranted because the facts of this study have been concealed for decades.

In the winter and spring of 2018, conservative movement websites abounded with defenses of Kevin D. Williamson, a forty-five-year-old journalist who had been a regular contributor to *National Review* but who had also worked for Jeffrey Goldberg as a writer for the *Atlantic*. Williamson, a hulking giant of a man with a beard and bald head, presents himself as a libertarian but his métier seems to be serving up inflammatory prose. In 2016, he won applause from both Never-Trumpers at *National Review* and the left-liberal establishment by mocking Trump and even more ferociously Trump's voters. In a memorable invective, he expressed contempt for the white working class that was tempted to support Trump and even wished them a speedy death. At this point Williamson won the affection of the mainstream media as well as that of *National Review*'s editorial board, which has been denouncing Trump regularly since he announced his candidacy for the presidency in 2016.[1]

Williamson obviously went too far, however, when he opined in a six-word tweet four years ago that women who aborted their unborn babies should be hanged. Although politically correct in other respects, Williamson has expressed strong opposition to abortion beyond the first trimester. Moreover, his tweet, which he insists we should not take literally, cost him his position at the *Atlantic*. Williamson's firing unleashed a storm of denunciation not only from the *National Review* but also from other prominent conservative movement publications and websites. The mainstream Left, or those members of it who had fired Williamson, was allegedly suppressing open discussion of critical moral and social issues; and what happened to Williamson was thought to portend further attempts by the other side to stifle free speech and dissenting opinions.

What happened to Williamson could be compared to what had occurred a few years earlier at the publication that angrily rose to his defense. In 2012, about five and a half years before Williamson lost his job at the *Atlantic, National Review* editor Rich Lowry fired a star writer and editor, John Derbyshire, for expressing insensitive opinions on the Takimag website.[2] Derbyshire had advised his children not to stop and assist black youths who were signaling that their car had broken down. Derbyshire, a respected mathematician and an exceptionally elegant essayist, was astonished at how quickly the conservative movement reduced him to an "unperson."[3] This firing, however, was only one of a multitude of such incidents, going back to the 1950s, in which *National Review* and other fixtures of the conservative movement empire had released and sometimes subsequently humiliated employees and former allies who had taken deviationist stands. It is astonishing how rarely this behavior received notice. Those whom the gatekeepers of the socially and professionally acceptable Right cast into perdition are expelled as "extremists."

On the fiftieth anniversary of the founding of *National Review* in 2005, senior editor Jonah Goldberg presented the authorized account of how the magazine's founder, William F. Buckley, had sanitized the postwar conservative movement. In the commentary "Golden Days," Goldberg indicates the care with which Buckley scraped off the dross from what became a major political and cultural force in American life.

> Buckley employed intellectual ruthlessness and relentless personal charm to keep that which is good about libertarianism, what we have come to call "social conservatism," and what was necessary about anti-Communism in the movement. This meant throwing friends and allies off the bus from time to time. The Randians, the Rothbardian anarchists and isolationists, the Birchers, the anti-Semites, the me-too Republicans: all of these groups in various combinations were purged from the

movement and masthead, sometimes painfully, sometimes easily, but always with the ideal of keeping the cause honest and pointed north to the ideal in his compass.[4]

Whatever ideal William F. Buckley assigned to his movement, Goldberg proceeded to admit, existed "only on paper." Further, "conservative dogma remains unsettled, and conservatism remains cleaved ideologically." That said, the movement launched by Buckley was for Goldberg a breathtaking success—and one that had occurred with minimal commotion.

E. J. Dionne, in an equally lavish tribute in the *Washington Post*, proclaimed that Buckley was not only deserving of his friendship but also someone who had "determined to rid the right of the wing nuts." The guiding spirit of *National Review* had evolved into "the scourge of the very anti-Semitism that had once infested significant parts of the right." Dionne blasted the conspiracy theories of the John Birch Society, which he applauded Buckley for having helpfully unmasked. Unfortunately, these remarks contain little if any truth.[5]

For example, the *National Review* staff devoted a special feature on October 19, 1965, to denouncing the Birch Society, but not as an anti-Semitic operation (of which there was scant evidence). The editors excoriated the society for not supporting the war in Vietnam and thereby giving up on the struggle against Communism.[6] As a point of information: the best man at Buckley's wedding, Revilo Oliver, was an outspoken anti-Semite, as well as a formidable classicist and Sanskrit scholar.[7] Oliver continued to write for Buckley's publication well into the 1960s. Most of those who were expelled from his magazine and, more broadly, from Buckley's movement in the early days were Jewish libertarians such as Ayn Rand, Frank Chodorov, Murray Rothbard, and Ron Hamowy.[8] Although the conservative movement had once included "anti-Semites" such as Oliver, it seems overblown to describe Buckley's excommunications as a crusade against bigotry. In fact, Goldberg's mentor had gone after those who were identifiably Jewish but who opposed his crusade against the Soviet empire. In Rand's case, Buckley turned against someone whose atheism offended him.

Even more astonishing is Goldberg's suggestion that throwing allies off the bus occurred only rarely in the conservative movement. These critical junctures helped shape the movement that Goldberg is now defining. They were no more exceptional than the purges in the American Communist Party that *National Review* would have noted during its passionately anti-Communist days. Moreover, the expulsions took place with such regularity that it might be helpful to divide them into different periods in accordance with the changing interests of the conservative establishment.

Being thrown off the bus had implications for its target that went beyond not being encouraged to write essays for *National Review*. As the conservative media empire rose to prominence, thanks largely to steady infusions of money from such patrons as the Australian press baron Rupert Murdoch and the Koch brothers, banishment by one of its organs carried dire consequences. Someone banned from the *Wall Street Journal*, the *Weekly Standard*, or *National Review* would not likely be welcome at an affiliated movement publication or among the staff of Fox News, a channel that enjoys the same sponsorship as most of the rest of media conservatism. Whittaker Chambers's acerbic judgment about conservatives that they fail to "retrieve their wounded" may not be harsh enough.

One figure who has never undergone total expulsion is Patrick Buchanan. This exception is understandable. Buchanan has been a widely read journalist since the 1960s and was a close friend of Republican presidents. His very limited appearances on Fox may have also been conditional on his willingness to be agreeable. During his most recent TV appearances, Buchanan (to my knowledge) never contradicted his host. This may have helped preserve his exceptional status for as long as it lasted.

There was another reason for the provisional tolerance accorded Buchanan. He lost a berth at a rival Democratic channel, MSNBC. Before that time, the channel's directors accommodated him and featured him on a regular basis. He may have been tolerated there because like other members of the Old Right, Buchanan lost favor with the conservative movement in the early 1990s owing to his poor relations with neoconservative gatekeepers.[9] The Heritage Foundation, the American Enterprise Institute, *National Review*, *Wall Street Journal*, and other movement fixtures all gradually broke with Buchanan. This became the practice even while Buchanan's books were soaring on the *New York Times* best-seller list.

For the less fortunate, however, expulsion has usually been catastrophic. The accompanying campaign of vilification has often left those it has targeted socially and professionally ruined. Typical victims of this process were the Southern conservative M. E. Bradford and the populist journalist and critic of managerial democracy Samuel T. Francis. The elimination of Bradford as front-runner for the National Endowment for the Humanities directorship in 1981 and, ten years later, the removal of Samuel Francis as the star columnist by the already neoconservative-controlled *Washington Times* followed a now-familiar course. Those condemned as outcasts by movement leaders suffered repeated journalistic attacks and went from being conservatives to "bigots" sometimes overnight. Liberal journalists readily joined these campaigns and often seemed to be working in tandem with their neoconservative acquaintances, in order to rid respectable conservatism of "wing nuts." Printed assaults against the designated extremists were so devastating that their victims never regained any standing as respectable writers.

My own professional history provides a minor example of such attacks. In my case, they were mostly surreptitious, although it became clear long in advance of my character assassination that my adversaries did not wish me well. Mine, however, was not a typical purge proceeding. Unlike others who suffered a comparable fate, I never left a paper trail on certain abrasive issues such as Jews in the media or American involvement in World War II. Although I have been stigmatized by the usual sources (quite implausibly) as an ally of white nationalists,[10] this certainly was not the reason that I initially incurred the movement's displeasure. In the 1980s, I made powerful enemies during the conservative wars waged in that period. I insisted too loudly that generic leftists had taken over the Right; and I compounded my sin by calling attention to the foolishness of the global democratic foreign policy that the movement's new masters were imposing on their obliging servants.

I had no illusion about what would come next after neoconservatives slandered me to the administration at Catholic University of America, and I had to forfeit a graduate professorship that otherwise in all likelihood would have been mine. I never thought these attacks once they commenced would soon stop. After the incident at Catholic University, certain predictable afflictions followed. I could no longer place my writings in most "movement conservative" publications. The editors, also not incidentally, refused to review my books, and my name has rarely appeared in any authorized conservative magazine since the late 1980s. One of the few times my name did turn up in such a publication was in 2003, when David Frum, writing in *National Review*, identified me with the nonaligned Right as an "unpatriotic conservative." According to Frum, his friends had done nothing to harm me professionally or to justify my outbursts. I had fabricated my narrative because I was a troubled person.[11] My case was exceptional because aside from suggestions that I had taken leave of my senses, no campaign was waged against me as an "anti-Semite" or, until recently, as some kind of "racist." And because I was a tenured academic, my ostracism did not affect me to the same extent that it did other targeted dissenters on the right. M. E. Bradford, Samuel Francis, and Joseph Sobran, all of whom died soon after their public humiliation, come to mind here.

Certain distinctions may be in order. Not all of those who were made to leave the bus suffered their fate for the same reason. In *National Review's* early days, those whom Buckley expelled from his movement rejected his Cold War politics and usually called themselves libertarians. Misrepresenting these expulsions was easy enough because Buckley's followers, like E. J. Dionne, collaborated in producing the authorized accounts of the events in question. Intellectuals and authors on the right rarely fell from grace for the official reasons, the ones that surfaced in the media. This became even more the case when the neoconservatives took over the conservative movement.

Undesirables thereafter fell into two camps. First there were the Southerners like M. E. Bradford and his followers, who made no apologies for the Confederacy and expressed misgivings about the civil rights revolution. Second were the critics of the aggressive liberal internationalist foreign policy associated with the neoconservatives. Those in the two camps coalesced for a time as a "paleoconservative" insurgency, and they were soon joined by libertarians of a socially traditionalist stripe, such as Murray Rothbard and, for a time, Lew Rockwell.[12] The movement smeared all these dissenters as "anti-Semites." Joseph Sobran, once senior editor of *National Review*, noticed the shifting meaning of "anti-Semite," from someone who hates Jews to someone whom certain Jews in high places decided they didn't like.

The journalists John O'Sullivan and Peter Brimelow became less welcome than they had been previously at *National Review* in the late 1990s for opposing Third World immigration. *Commentary*, the *Wall Street Journal*, *Policy Review*, and other publications that were close to the neoconservatives were strongly pro-immigration, and O'Sullivan and Brimelow, who had moved demonstratively in the opposite direction, were out of step. Pro-immigration advocates Linda Chavez and John Miller took to task Samuel Francis for his statements, made in response to an apology by the Southern Baptist Convention for their coreligionists' one-time endorsement of slavery. Francis had correctly but imprudently noted that the Bible does not condemn slavery.[13] Francis, a mainstream right-of-center journalist with a biting wit and distinctive literary style, went by the end of 1995 from being a nationally syndicated writer to a professional pariah. Chavez and Miller then found an ally a few months later in the reliable neoconservative author Dinesh D'Souza, who denounced Francis as an isolated representative of white racism, although D'Souza had borrowed from Francis and from the self-described "race realist" Jared Taylor passages for his book *The End of Racism*.[14]

Although he eventually found employment on the staff of *National Review*, Jason Richwine lost his job as a researcher at the Heritage Foundation because of the discovery of detailed references in his doctoral dissertation, approved at Harvard University, to the relatively low IQs of recent immigration groups.[15] At the time of his firing and longtime blackballing by movement foundations and magazines, Richwine had not achieved any prominence in what has been euphemistically styled "the conservative policy community." He was therefore expendable to the newly named director of the Heritage Foundation, Jim DeMint, a skittish Southern Republican. DeMint was not dealing here with a journalistic celebrity, for example, someone of the stature of Charles Murray, whose work included focusing in on the cognitive differences between ethnic and racial groups.

Yet nothing approaching Richwine's fate befell the author of *The Bell Curve*, who has enjoyed the protection of the American Enterprise Institute, *National Review*, and *Commentary*. It is evident that the young Richwine was not in the same league as the far better connected Murray in terms of his value to the movement. Significantly, despite the fact that such conservative movement heavy hitters as Murray, Michael Barone, and Richwine's collaborator at Heritage Robert Rector weighed in on his side, Heritage would not rescind its decision. The foundation's directors were apparently convinced that Richwine was simply not worth a dog-fight with those leftist journalists who had cornered him.

Much can be forgiven and even shoved down a memory hole for those who have influence. Although Norman Podhoretz as editor of *Commentary* inveighed for decades against gays, as documented by Gary Dorrien in *The Neoconservative Mind*,[16] this did not prevent Podhoretz's allies from attacking Patrick Buchanan as a "homophobe" in 1992. This transpired after Buchanan, speaking at the Republican National Convention, made reference to the lifestyles among some members of the opposition party. But this was no different from how neoconservatives had viewed gays a few years earlier. As late as 1984, the neoconservative hero Jeane Kirkpatrick, in an address before the Republican National Convention, sneered at the Democrats for their "San Francisco values."[17] Kirkpatrick's gibe elicited resounding applause from neoconservative journalists. Homophobia, we may assume, was not the *real* cause for the animus against Buchanan. He is a harsh critic of the Zionist lobby and is perceived as an isolationist. As late as the spring of 1992, it seemed possible that Buchanan could win the presidential nomination against the politically weakened, tongue-tied George Bush Sr.

Similar double standards were discernible in the character blackening committed against M. E. Bradford in 1981, in which neoconservative journalists, particularly George Will and the editors of the *Wall Street Journal*, played key roles. Bradford's offense was to have characterized Lincoln as a tyrant and to have likened his invasion of the South to Hitler's attack on Germany's neighbors and Cromwell's invasion of Ireland. The attacks against Bradford, which focused on a footnote in one of his books, were remarkably selective, given his voluminous output as a literary scholar.[18] The outrage was also dishonest, given the lack of reaction then or later to a signature essay that Podhoretz had placed in *Commentary* in 1963, "My Negro Problem—and Ours."[19] Unlike Bradford, who never disparaged black people, Podhoretz explained to his readers how he was managing his "hatred" for Negroes. These effusions, however, did not serve to disqualify the cofather of neoconservatism (along with Irving Kristol) from leadership in the conservative movement. Nor did his stated revulsion for those of different skin color diminish Podhoretz's considerable influence in the Reagan administration.

Also going after Bradford in 1981 were Buckley and Heritage president Edwin Feulner. Both of these movement dignitaries, whose fortunes were bound up with the neoconservative ascendancy, visited newly elected president Reagan.

They asked the chief executive to reconsider the nomination of Bradford and presented their Southern friend of many decades as someone who would disgrace the NEH directorship. While on their visit to the White House, the same conservative luminaries plugged the candidacy of a liberal Democrat, William Bennett, whom the neoconservatives were prepping for the office they intended to deny Bradford.

The assault on the courtly Texan Bradford, as Keith Preston indicates in his contribution to this anthology, stemmed from multiple causes, starting with crass material interest. The neoconservatives hoped to put their own favorite in a position that would yield financial resources. If things worked out as they hoped (and as indeed they did), they would have hundreds of millions of dollars in grants to distribute to their foot soldiers. Their destruction of Bradford's reputation and, ultimately, life was collateral damage. As documented in the second edition of *The Conservative Movement*,[20] grants of hundreds of thousands of dollars went to Eric Foner, scion of a famous Communist family who has since morphed into a figure of the academic Left. Someone who then seemed to be working cheek by jowl with the neoconservatives, Foner published a rant against Bradford as a prejudiced Southerner in a newspaper column that managed to be widely distributed and even reached members of Congress.

These incidents illustrate the difficulty of attributing all purges from the conservative movement to changes in ideological direction. Equally important were the social dynamics and the political and material goals of movement players when the purges unfolded.

Although not all expulsions occurred for the same reasons, every one of them was spun in the same way: as a dismissal of "right-wing" fanatics. Since, according to their accusers, those who "left" the bus engaged in racism and anti-Semitism—and in some cases, Holocaust denial—it thereafter became impossible for them to regain lost professional ground. Nor would the broadsides necessarily stop after they had been fired from a conservative magazine, dismissed from a GOP foundation, or removed from the board of self-described traditionalist or libertarian institutes. At most, these targets might hope that their enemies would forget about them. In some cases, however, those thrown off the bus were subject to at least intermittent abuse intended to justify their fall. This happened in a particularly bizarre way to Murray Rothbard, in the form of an obituary that Buckley inserted into *National Review* shortly after Rothbard's death.[21] Here Buckley offered a comparison between Rothbard and cult leader David Koresh. Neither apparently had more than a handful of followers: Rothbard had "as many disciples as David Koresh had in his redoubt in Waco." "Yes, Rothbard believed in freedom; David Koresh believed in God." It had not been enough for *National Review*'s founder to scold Rothbard during his lifetime.

Purges over the past thirty years have reflected the leftist course of the conservative movement and, more generally, the Republican Party. Avowed positions of anti-racism, anti-anti-Semitism, moderate feminism, and, for the younger generation of neoconservatives, enthusiasm for gay rights, including gay marriage, have all become characteristic of a transformed conservative movement. Conservatism, Inc., has moved in exactly the same direction as the Center Left, albeit more slowly, and it has made critical decisions about what counts as permanent concerns and what may be changed. Clearly, support for the Israeli Right, liberal internationalism, as a foreign policy, and improving the tax and trade situation for large corporations are more important to the movement than whether an editor at *National Review* endorses gay marriage as a human right. Social issues get billing in such circles mostly as a parenthetical activity, intended to jolly along the GOP's evangelical base and to appease certain subscribers and donors.

Rupert Murdoch, Paul Singer, and Sheldon Adelson, who keep the conservative movement well financed, stand on the left on most social issues but are also fervent Zionists. These benefactors put up with what are to them uncongenial social positions because they are mindful of the pro-Israel position taken by evangelical Christians. Their media beneficiaries, moreover, can distinguish between profitable and nonprofitable issues. The decidedly leftist positions on social issues once taken by Rudy Giuliani and Joe Lieberman did not keep either from enjoying the favor of the conservative media—for example, when their names came up in connection with a presidential nomination. In 2008 and even earlier, William Bennett was pushing Joe Lieberman for president. Despite the fact that the Connecticut senator took social and economic stands that closely coincided with those of Barack Obama, he was a hawk on foreign policy, which is all that mattered to Heritage, and the rest of Lieberman's fan base.

Equally relevant, the effect of the leftist shifts of the conservative movement, punctuated by widely publicized purges, has resulted in pushing permissible political discussion in the same direction. It is naive to believe that their movement has veered toward the left only in response to where "the culture" has drifted. The conservative movement, no less than its Center Right counterparts in Canada and Western Europe, has contributed to where our political culture has moved.

The establishment opposition on the right has absorbed many of the ideological positions previously or still held by its opponents. The conservative movement's younger representatives often sound like the opposition, and for a transparent reason: they have been educated in the same institutions, have picked up the same ideas, and inhabit the same social world. What is more, they encounter only feeble resistance on their side of an exaggerated political divide. Because of neoconservative-GOP media outreach and the lack of a visible alternative on the right, rank-and-file Republicans assume that the anti-Democratic side must be conservative.

Beyond ideological change, certain unacknowledged connections have contributed to the purges under consideration. The conservative movement acts and speaks as part of a larger media enterprise. As Jack Kerwick underscores in his chapter, the authorized conservative movement works to accommodate the Center Left, plays by its rules, and pursues many of the same interests. The conservative movement seeks to be "inclusive," but not by embracing those on its Right.

All members of what Jack Kerwick calls the "Big Con" share certain beliefs, however much they may bicker over elections and hot-button issues. They each accept a vast welfare state, opportunistically invoke the spirit of the civil rights era, accuse the other side of "racism," and celebrate the advance of feminist and gay rights. These discussants define for the rest of us what is allowable political discourse. Even if these authorized members of the public conversation disagree on the achievements of President Donald Trump, a cleavage that divides official conservatives from each other as well as from official liberals, they agree about who on the right should be treated as nonpersons. Those who suffer expulsion with all its consequences have been guilty of interfering in some way with business as usual. They raise unwanted questions or are trying to reintroduce ideas that the media class no longer cares to entertain. Unlike the long-vilified "paleoconservatives" or the younger and more obstreperous racialists and "altrightists," the Murdoch empire enjoys the status of a respectable adversary. Integral to this honor, as Samuel Francis observed in the 1980s, is a willingness to purge and humiliate right-wing dissenters.

Aside from the Birchers, who constituted a mass movement that was independent of Buckley, most of the objects of purges posed no real threat to official conservatism. Those who fell into outer darkness became for their critics a social embarrassment and/or, in the early days of Buckley's career, a diversion from the central theme of anti-Communism. Such considerations already affected the purges that took place in the decades of conservatism's ascendancy. Looking back on the Birchers of 2008, Buckley claimed to be isolating a lunatic fringe that would damage the courteous Right. At the time of the purge, however (October 1965), James Burnham provided a very different explanation as to why his fellow editors were reacting against the John Birch Society. They were opposing the Birchers because of their "unpatriotic" opposition to America's latest foreign intervention. The leader of this society, Robert Welch, had "given up on the Vietnam War," and he and his members were accused of representing "the isolationist tradition that survives in many parts of the country, though it no longer gets much recognition, even from many of those who still share it."[22] Virtually every conservative purge since the 1960s has been subject to the same process, namely, a calculated reconstruction of the circumstances intended to make the expulsion fit public relations needs. Whether or not the Birchers pushed bizarre conspiratorial views (which in fact they did), it is unlikely that Buckley and his circle would have moved against them were it not for the Society's isolationist foreign policy.

The purges were not a passing ancillary aspect of conservatism; they were a *defining* characteristic of a movement, whose modus operandi was to take up stands where the Left had been the moment before. "Conservatism" turned by design into a "harmless persuasion" (Samuel Francis's memorable term) vis-á-vis the progress of liberalism, including Cultural Marxism. Through its alliance with corporate interests and ethnic lobbies and through a carefully limited (and thus easily abandoned) opposition to such initiatives from the Left as the Voting Rights Act and the feminist revolution, Conservatism, Inc., has been able to survive and grow as a media power. It has also depicted the welfare society in which we live, for better or worse, as a product of "free-market capitalism." For decades, conservative power brokers have been blacklisting original and independent minds. What has been lost from the public debate is a generation of serious critical thinkers on what is now the nonaligned Right. The calls by the conservative movement for "tolerance" in universities and the media ring hollow, given their tainted source.

Notes

INTRODUCTION

1. Ali A. Rizvi, "What Ilhan Omar Needs to Learn from London's Muslim Mayor," *New York Post*, May 4, 2019, https://nypost.com/2019/05/04/what-ilhan-omar-needs-to-learn -from-londons-muslim-mayor/.

2. Gary Dorrien, *The Neoconservative Mind: Politics, Culture, and the War of Ideology* (Philadelphia: Temple University Press, 1993), 180–82; Norman Podhoretz, "The Culture of Appeasement," *Harper's* 255, no. 1529 (October 1977): 32.

3. On the extent of this remarkable about-face driven by Buchanan's presidential bid, see my book *Conservatism in America: Making Sense of the American Right* (New York: Palgrave MacMillan, 2007), 47–50, 128–31.

4. Dorrien, *Neoconservative Mind*, 369.

5. Rich Lowry, "Mothball the Confederate Monuments," *National Review*, August 15, 2017, https://www.nationalreview.com/2017/08/charlottesville-virignia-robert-e-lee-statue -remove-right-decision-confederate-monuments-museums/.

6. Kyle Smith, "Destroying Symbols: Where Does It End?," *National Review*, August 16, 2017, https://www.nationalreview.com/2017/08/destroying-confederate-statues-whats-end -point-washington-monument/.

1. BIG CONSERVATISM AND AMERICAN EXCEPTIONALISM

1. Michael Oakeshott, "Rationalism in Politics," in *Rationalism in Politics and Other Essays* (Indianapolis: Liberty Fund, 1962), 8.

2. Edmund Burke, *Reflections on the Revolution in France*, in *The Portable Edmund Burke*, ed. Isaac Kramnick (New York: Penguin Books, 1999), 451.

3. Ibid., 419.

4. Ibid., 424.

5. Ibid., 431.

6. Ibid., 433.

7. Ibid., 438.

8. Ibid., 448.

9. Ibid., 447.

10. Oakeshott, "Rationalism in Politics," 6.

11. Ibid., 8.

12. Burke, *Reflections on the Revolution*, 436.

13. Ibid., 440.

14. David Hume, "Of the Original Contract," in *Essays: Moral, Political, and Literary*, rev. ed., ed. Eugene F. Miller (Indianapolis: Liberty Classics, 1987), 477.

15. Burke, *Reflections on the Revolution*, 431.

16. Ibid., 423.

17. Ibid., 440.

18. Hume, "Of the Original Contract," 470.

19. Ibid., 39.

20. Burke, *Reflections on the Revolution*, 451.

21. Ibid., 428 (emphasis original).

22. Russell Kirk, *The Conservative Mind: From Burke to Eliot,* 7th ed. (Washington, DC: Regnery, 1985), xv.

23. Ibid., xv (emphasis original).

24. Ibid., xvi.

25. Ibid., xv.

26. Ibid., xvi.

27. Ibid., 8.

28. Ibid., 9.

29. Ibid., 42

30. Oakeshott, "Rationalism in Politics," 40.

31. David Hume, *Enquiries Concerning the Principles of the Understanding and the Principles of Morality,* 3rd ed., ed. P. H. Nidditch (Oxford: Oxford University Press, 1990), 172.

32. Robert P. George, *The Clash of Orthodoxies: Law, Religion, and Morality in Crisis* (Wilmington, DE: ISI Books, 2001, 142.

33. Ibid., 128.

34. Ibid., 142

35. Allan Bloom, *The Closing of the American Mind: How Higher Education Has Failed Democracy and Impoverished the Souls of Today's Students* (New York: Simon and Schuster, 1987), 39.

36. Ibid., 27.

37. Ibid., 259.

38. Irving Kristol, *The Neoconservative Persuasion: Selected Essays, 1942–2009* (New York: Basic Books, 2011), 182.

39. Ibid., 227.

40. Ibid., 229.

41. Ibid., 150.

42. Ibid., 227.

43. William J. Bennett, ed., *The Spirit of America* (New York: Touchstone, 1997), 26.

44. Dennis Prager, "Who Believes in American Exceptionalism? Judeo-Christian Values Part XXIV," Townhall, November 2005, http://townhall.com/columnists/dennisprager/2005/11/01/who_believes_in_american_exceptionalismnbsp;_judeo-christian_values_part_xxiv.

45. Dennis Prager, "Why America Is Still the Best Hope," Townhall, April 2012, http://townhall.com/columnists/dennisprager/2012/04/24/why_america_is_still_the_best_hope.

46. Charles Krauthammer, "Democratic Realism," in *Things That Matter* (New York: Random House, 2013), 346.

47. Wilson, "Irish U2 Frontman Bono Perfectly Sums Up the American Ideal," Glenn Beck, February 13, 2015, https://www.glennbeck.com/2015/02/13/watch-irish-u2-frontman-bono-may-have-perfectly-summed-up-the-american-idea/.

48. Paul Bond, "Why Dinesh D'Souza's 'America' Features Clips of Matt Damon, Woody Harrelson," Hollywood Reporter, July 5, 2014, https://www.hollywoodreporter.com/news/why-dinesh-dsouzas-america-features-716708.

49. Mark J. Perry, "Bono: America Is 'an Idea.' That's How We See You around the World, as One of the Greatest Ideas in Human History," American Enterprise Institute, July 6, 2014, http://www.aei.org/publication/bono-america-is-an-idea-thats-how-we-see-you-around-the-world-as-one-of-the-greatest-ideas-in-human-history/.

50. Jonah Goldberg, "When Would You Stop Loving America?," *National Review,* July 5, 2017, https://www.nationalreview.com/2017/07/america-can-you-stop-loving-her-if-she-changes/.

51. David Adesnik, "Still Exceptional," *National Review,* February 12, 2014, https://www.nationalreview.com/2014/02/still-exceptional-david-adesnik/.

52. Matt Franck, "A Lincoln for Our Times." Review of *Lincoln Unbound: How an Ambitious Young Railsplitter Saved the American Dream—and How We Can Do it Again,* by Rich Lowry, *National Review,* July 19, 2013, https://www.nationalreview.com/bench-memos/rich-lowrys-lincoln-unbound-matthew-j-franck/.

53. Francis Fukuyama, "Immigrants and Family Values," *Commentary,* May 1, 1993, https://www.commentarymagazine.com/articles/immigrants-and-family-values/.

54. Douglas Murray, *Neoconservatism: Why We Need It* (New York: Encounter Books, 2006), 73.

55. Quoted in C. Bradley Thompson, with Yaron Brook, *Neoconservatism: An Obituary for an Idea* (Boulder, CO: Paradigm Books, 2010), 47.

56. Kristol, *Neoconservative Persuasion,* 191.

57. Ibid., 149.

58. Ibid., 182.

59. Ibid., 229.

60. Ibid., 150.

61. Ibid., 227.

62. Krauthammer, "Democratic Realism," 347.

63. Ben Shapiro, "Why War in Iraq Is Right for America," Townhall, August 10, 2005, https://townhall.com/columnists/benshapiro/2005/08/10/why-war-in-iraq-is-right-for-america-n1216871.

64. Ibid.

65. Larisa Epatko, "How the World Is Reacting to Trump's Use of S***hole," PBS News Hour, January 12, 2018, https://www.pbs.org/newshour/world/how-the-world-is-reacting-to-trumps-use-of-shole.

66. Julie Hirschfeld Davis, "A Senior Republican Senator Admonishes Trump: 'America Is an Idea, Not a Race,'" *New York Times,* January 12, 2018, https://www.nytimes.com/2018/01/12/us/politics/trump-immigration-congress.html.

67. Julia Hahn, "Paul Ryan's Open Borders Push with Luis Gutierrez Exposed in 2013 Video," Breitbart, October 17, 2015, https://www.breitbart.com/big-government/2015/10/17/paul-ryans-open-borders-push-luis-gutierrez-exposed-2013-video/.

68. Paul Greenberg, "Real Hope and Change," Jewish World Review, November 25, 2014, http://www.jewishworldreview.com/cols/greenberg112514.php3.

69. William J. Bennett, Linda Chavez, Angelo M. Codevilla, Edward J. Erler, and Stanley Kurtz, "Immigration and American Exceptionalism," *Claremont Review of Books* 13 (Fall 2013), http://www.claremont.org/crb/article/immigration-and-american-exceptionalism/.

70. David Brooks, "The American Idea and Today's GOP," *New York Times,* September 25, 2015, https://www.nytimes.com/2015/09/25/opinion/david-brooks-the-american-idea-and-todays-gop.html.

2. THE SIGNIFICANCE OF THE M. E. BRADFORD AFFAIR

1. Paul Gottfried and Richard B. Spencer, eds., *The Great Purge: The Deformation of the Conservative Movement* (Washington, DC: Washington Summit Publishers, 2015).

2. William King, "Neoconservatives and 'Trotskyism,'" *American Communist History* 3, no. 2 (2004): 247–66.

3. Jack Ross, *The Socialist Party of America: A Complete History* (Lincoln: University of Nebraska Press, 2015).

4. Justin Vaisse, *Neoconservatism: The Biography of a Movement* (Cambridge, MA: Harvard University Press, 2010).

5. Ibid.

6. Chuck Hagel and Peter Kaminsky, *America: Our Next Chapter* (New York: Harper Collins, 2008), 50.

7. Paul Craig Roberts, "Neo-Jacobins Push for World War IV," LewRockwell.Com, September 20, 2003, https://www.lewrockwell.com/2003/09/paul-craig-roberts/neo-jacobins -push-for-world-war-iv/.

8. Claes G. Ryn, *The New Jacobin: America as a Revolutionary State* (Washington, DC: National Humanities Institute, 2011).

9. James Lehrberger, email to the author, March 12, 2018.

10. George Will, "A Shrill Assault on Mr. Lincoln," *Washington Post*, December 29, 1981, https://www.washingtonpost.com/archive/opinions/1981/11/29/a-shrill-assault-on -mr-lincoln/453b1986-761e-4a86-9b71-759ce0729f87/?utm_term=.9913973997b4.

11. Melvin E. Bradford, "It's George Will Who's Being Shrill," *Washington Post*, December 12, 1981, https://www.washingtonpost.com/archive/politics/1981/12/12/its-george -will-whos-being-shrill/414705c8-543a-4a0a-bc1b-48b070b942cc/?utm_term= .4cf02c89dfde.

12. Ibid.

13. Thomas H. Landess, "Mel Bradford, Old Indian Fighters, and the NEH," LewRockwell.com, April 25, 2003, https://www.lewrockwell.com/2003/04/thomas-h-landess/mel -bradford-old-indian-fighters-and-the-neh/.

14. Ibid.

15. David Gordon, "Southern Cross," *American Conservative*, April 1, 2010, http://www .theamericanconservative.com/articles/southern-cross/.

16. Landess, "Mel Bradford."

17. David Frum, "Unpatriotic Conservatives," *National Review*, March 25, 2003, https:// www.nationalreview.com/2003/03/unpatriotic-conservatives-david-frum/.

18. Ibid.

19. Norman Podhoretz, "My Negro Problem—and Ours," *Commentary*, February 1963, http://www.lukeford.net/Images/photos/out.pdf.

20. Ann Pettifer, "Zionism Unbound," CounterPunch, December 14, 2002, https://www .counterpunch.org/2002/12/14/zionism-unbound/.

21. Ibid.

22. Eric Foner, "Lincoln, Bradford, and the Conservatives," *New York Times*, February 13, 1982, https://www.nytimes.com/1982/02/13/opinion/lincoln-bradford-and-the -conservatives.html.

23. Ibid.

24. David von Drehle, "Bennett Reportedly High-Stakes Gambler—Former Education Secretary Lost $8 Million in Past Decade, Magazines Find," *Washington Post*, May 3, 2003; Joshua Green, "The Bookie of Virtue," *Washington Monthly*, June 2003, https:// washingtonmonthly.com/magazine/june-2003/the-bookie-of-virtue/.

3. THE TORY RIGHT AND THE AMERICAN CONSERVATIVE MOVEMENT

1. George Grant, *Lament for a Nation: The Defeat of Canadian Nationalism* (Ottawa: Carleton University Press, 1991), 68.

2. See Ron Dart, *The North American High Tory Tradition* (New York: American Anglican Press, 2016), 140–41, 155.

3. George Grant, "Conversation with George Grant: Canadian Politics," in *George Grant in Process: Essays and Conversations*, ed. Larry Schmidt (Toronto: House of Anansi Press, 1978), 21.

4. Grant, *Lament for a Nation*, 64–65.

5. Ibid., 8.

6. Ibid.

7. Louis Hartz, *The Founding of New Societies: Studies in the History of the United States, Latin America, South Africa, Canada, and Australia* (New York: Harcourt Brace Jovanovich, 1964), 34.

8. Gad Horowitz, "Conservatism, Liberalism, and Socialism in Canada: An Interpretation," *Canadian Journal of Economics and Political Science* 32, no. 2 (1966): 159. See also Dart, *North American High Tory Tradition*, 208–13.

9. Barry Cooper, "Did George Grant's Canada Ever Exist?," in *George Grant and the Future of Canada*, ed. Yusuf K. Umar with a foreword by Barry Cooper (Calgary: University of Calgary Press, 1992), 156–57, 163.

10. Grant, *Lament for a Nation*, 10.

11. Barry Cooper, *It's the Regime, Stupid! A Report from the Cowboy West on Why Stephen Harper Matters* (Toronto: Key Porter Books, 2009), 98–109. See also Janet Ajzenstat, *The Canadian Founding: John Locke and Parliament* (Montreal: McGill-Queen's University Press, 2007), 102–3, 174.

12. Cooper has pressed this point most forcefully. See his *It's the Regime*, 106, and "Did George Grant's Canada Ever Exist?," 154.

13. Thomas Hutchinson, "A Dialogue between an American and a European Englishman," ed. Bernard Bailyn, *Perspectives in American History* 11 (1975): 393–96.

14. Bernard Bailyn, "Introduction: A Dialogue by Thomas Hutchinson," *Perspectives in American History* 11 (1975): 360.

15. Cooper, "Did George Grant's Canada Ever Exist?," 163.

16. See Ajzenstat, *Canadian Founding*, 75–76, 103. For an identitarian critique of this interpretation, see Ricardo Duchesne, *Canada in Decay: Mass Immigration, Diversity, and the Ethnocide of Euro-Canadians* (London: Black House, 2017), 192–97.

17. Cooper, "Did George Grant's Canada Ever Exist?," 160.

18. George Grant, *Technology and Empire: Perspectives on North America* (Toronto: House of Anansi Press, 1969), 68.

19. Ibid.

20. Grant, *Lament for a Nation*, 70. See also pages 33 and 96 of this work, where Grant admits that this tradition of conservatism has rarely received a robust philosophical defense.

21. Ibid.

22. Ibid., 63.

23. Ibid.

24. Claude H. Van Tyne, *The Loyalists in the American Revolution* (Safety Harbor, FL: Simon Publications, 2001), 105–7.

25. Edmund Burke, *Reflections on the Revolution in France*, ed. Conor Cruise O'Brien (Harmondsworth: Penguin English Library, 1982), 170. Burke, of course, was a Rockingham Whig, not a Tory.

26. Ibid., 194.

27. Oswald Spengler, "Prussianism and Socialism," in *Selected Essays*, translated with an introduction by Donald O. White (Chicago: Gateway, 1967), 73. This essay was first published in German in 1920.

28. Russell Kirk, "Bolingbroke, Burke, and the Statesman," *Kenyon Review*, no. 28 (June 1966): 428.

29. E. P. Thompson, *The Making of the English Working Class* (Harmondsworth: Penguin Books, 1991), 594 (emphasis original).

30. Thompson, *Making*, 595. These radical changes (along with the decline of Toryism) spurred the rise of Luddism among the working class. See Thompson, *Making*, 591–94.

31. See Dart, *North American High Tory Tradition*, 215, 217.

32. See George Grant, *Philosophy in the Mass Age*, ed. with an introduction by William Christian (1959; Toronto: University of Toronto Press, 1995), 49–61. Although Grant doubted that a Marxian version of socialism could ever compete with the "more progressive" achievements of state capitalism (see *Lament for a Nation*, 58), he praised Marx as an astute critic whose concept of the good "is rooted in the teleological philosophy that predates the age of progress" (*Lament for a Nation*, 56). Marx and Engels, in *The Communist Manifesto*, constantly emphasize that capitalism is a threat to conservative tradition, an insight that impressed Grant.

33. George Grant, review of *Benjamin Disraeli: The Early Letters*, ed. J. A. W. Gunn et al., *Globe and Mail*, May 8, 1982. This piece is reprinted in *The George Grant Reader*, ed. William Christian and Sheila Grant (Toronto: University of Toronto Press, 1998), 139. Grant was not unequivocally a fan of Disraeli and his successors, who applied the term "conservative" in a manner that "was hardly more than a nationalist desire to take as much from the age of progress as they could." Grant, *Lament for a Nation*, 73.

34. Dart, *North American High Tory Tradition*, 145–46.

35. Nathan Coombs, "The Political Theology of Red Toryism," *Journal of Political Ideologies* 16, no. 1 (February 2011): 82–84. Gad Horowitz (see note 8) applied this term to Grant. For a discussion of Horowitz's interpretation of Grant, see Dart, *North American High Tory Tradition*, 207–13. However, as Dart notes, Grant was "somewhat wary of how such a term was applied to him" (208).

36. George Grant, "An Ethic of Community," in *The George Grant Reader*, 69.

37. Grant, review of *Benjamin Disraeli*, in *The George Grant Reader*, 139.

38. Grant, *Lament for a Nation*, 70.

39. Ibid., 57.

40. Ibid., 47.

41. Ibid., 65–66.

42. Ibid., 66.

43. Peter Kolozi, *Conservatives against Capitalism: From the Industrial Revolution to Globalization* (New York: Columbia University Press, 2017), 109.

44. James Burnham thought that "state capitalism" was an oxymoronic term, since he assumed that this system required the state to abolish private property while it ran industries for profit. In short, this system was statist, not capitalist. See *The Managerial Revolution* (1941; Harmondsworth: Penguin, 1962), 114–15. Burnham failed to understand, as Grant did, that state capitalism embodied the alliance of the state and big business while it kept separate the distinctive functions of each sphere of influence.

45. These policies or practices are what Marxists respectively call the coercive, accumulative, and legitimization functions that the state performs on behalf of capitalism. See Kai Nielsen, "On Marxist Theories of the State," *Indian Political Science Review* 19, nos. 1–2 (1985): 53–56. For an informative history of Marxian attempts to analyze state capitalism, see Michael Harrington, *The Twilight of Capitalism* (New York: Simon and Schuster, 1976), 208–35.

46. Grant, *Lament for a Nation*, 60.

47. William F. Buckley Jr., "Contemporary Challenges and the Social Order," in *American Conservative Thought in the Twentieth Century*, ed. William F. Buckley Jr. (New York: Bobbs-Merrill, 1970), 218.

48. Russell Kirk, *The Conservative Mind: From Burke to Eliot*, 7th rev. ed. (Washington, DC: Regnery, 2001), 5.

49. Ibid., 17.

50. Ibid., 22.

51. Ibid., 54. See also pp. 47–64.

52. Ibid., 64.

53. Paul Gottfried, *Conservatism in America: Making Sense of the American Right* (New York: Palgrave, 2007), 4–7. See also Louis Hartz, *The Liberal Tradition in America: An Interpretation of American Political Thought since the Revolution* (New York: Harcourt Brace, 1955).

54. Grant, *Lament for a Nation*, 73–74.

55. Gottfried, *Conservatism in America*, 22.

56. Ibid., 21.

57. Gertrude Himmelfarb, *The Roads to Modernity: The British, French, and American Enlightenments* (New York: Vintage Books, 2004), 227. See also pp. 229 and 232.

58. Kirk, *The Conservative Mind*, 9.

59. Quoted in John R. E. Bliese, "Richard M. Weaver, Russell Kirk, and the Environment," *Modern Age* 38, no. 2 (Winter 1996): 149.

60. Ibid., 156.

61. Kolozi, *Conservatives against Capitalism*, 129.

62. Ralph Nader, *Unstoppable: The Emerging Left-Right Alliance to Dismantle the Corporate State* (New York: Nation Books, 2014), 29, 112–13.

63. Russell Kirk, "Is Capitalism Still Viable?," *Journal of Business Ethics* 1 (1982): 278.

64. Ibid., 279.

65. Ibid., 278 (emphasis original).

66. Burnham, *Managerial Revolution*, 112–13; Samuel T. Francis, *Leviathan and Its Enemies: Mass Organization and Managerial Power in Twentieth-Century America* (Arlington, VA: Washington Summit Publishers, 2016), 36–40.

67. Kirk, "Is Capitalism Still Viable?," 278. As far back as the 1950s, Kirk associated state capitalism with socialism while downplaying the possibility of a "recrudescence" that this practice might experience in a prosperous economy. See his *Prospects for Conservatives* (New York: Gateway Editions, 1956), 137.

68. Kirk, "Is Capitalism Still Viable?," 278.

69. Grant, "Ethic of Community," 65.

70. Kirk, "Is Capitalism Still Viable?," 278.

71. Grant, "Ethic of Community," 66.

72. Kirk, "Is Capitalism Still Viable?," 279.

73. Grant, *Lament for a Nation*, 63.

74. Kirk, "Is Capitalism Still Viable?," 279. In *Prospects for Conservatives*, Kirk also warns: "As the consolidation of economic power progresses, the realm of personal freedom will diminish, whether the masters of the economy are state servants or the servants of private corporations" (134).

75. Kolozi, *Conservatives against Capitalism*, 133–34. For Kirk's praise of economic competition, see his *American Cause* (Wilmington, DE: ISI Books, 2004), 97–102.

76. Russell Kirk, "Will American Caesars Arise?," *Modern Age* 32, no. 3 (Summer 1989): 208–14. Grant similarly predicted that a "democratic Caesarism" coming from the Right may arise from the political and social instability that was engulfing the United States in the 1960s. See *Lament for a Nation*, 67.

77. Grant, *Lament for a Nation*, 93.

78. Kirk, "Will American Caesars Arise?," 212.

79. Grant at times uses this term to emphasize the need for a radical critique of power. See Grant, *Technology and Empire*, 31.

80. For an informative discussion of corporate support for LBJ, see Murray N. Rothbard, *Wall Street, Banks, and American Foreign Policy* (Auburn, AL: Ludwig von Mises Institute, 2011), 50–54.

81. Kolozi, *Conservatives against Capitalism*, 129. Kirk was also sympathetic to the program of decentralized and small-scale economic ownership that the economist Wilhelm

Roepke articulated. This program offered an alternative to both corporate capitalism and socialism. See Russell Kirk, *The Politics of Prudence* (Bryn Mawr, PA: Intercollegiate Studies Institute, 1993), 114–24.

82. Harrington makes exactly this point in response to Kirk in his essay "Is Capitalism Still Viable?" *Journal of Business Ethics* 1 (1982): 283–84.

83. Frank S. Meyer, *In Defense of Freedom and Related Essays* (Indianapolis: Liberty Fund, 1996), 161–62. This book was first published in 1962.

84. Ibid., 159–60.

85. Ibid., 92–94.

86. George Grant, *English-Speaking Justice* (Toronto: House of Anansi Press, 1985), 65. This book was first published in 1974.

87. For a critical discussion of Grant's association of liberalism with Protestantism, see my "Marshall McLuhan, George Grant, and the Ancient-Modern-Protestant Quarrel in Canada," in *Liberal Education, Civic Education, and the Canadian Regime*, ed. David Livingstone (Montreal: McGill-Queen's University Press, 2015), 152–60.

88. For Meyer's critique of Kirk, see *In Defense of Freedom*, 122–26. Like Grant, Meyer thought that Burke lacked a coherent political philosophy, or a "firm political position" (10). This fact threw into question the coherence of Kirk's own thought, according to Meyer. For a detailed discussion of the differences between Meyer and Kirk, see Kevin J. Smant, *Principles and Heresies: Frank S. Meyer and the Shaping of the American Conservative Movement* (Wilmington, DE: ISI Books, 2002), 32–33, 105–6.

89. Meyer, *In Defense of Freedom*, 107. This term is taken from William H. Whyte Jr.'s famous book, *The Organization Man* (New York: Anchor Books, 1957).

90. Meyer, *In Defense of Freedom*, 109.

91. Ibid.

92. Ibid., 107.

93. Grant, *Lament for a Nation*, 46.

94. Ibid., 17.

95. For an illuminating historical overview of the pros and cons of fusionism, see Samuel Goldman, "Fusionism Once and Future," *Modern Age* 59, no. 2 (Spring 2017): 65–74.

96. Grant, *Lament for a Nation*, 57.

97. See Marshall McLuhan, *The Mechanical Bride: Folklore of Industrial Man* (Boston: Vanguard Press, 1951).

98. Michael Novak, *The Spirit of Democratic Capitalism* (Lanham, MD: Madison Books, 1991), 111–12. This book was first published in 1982.

99. Grant, "Ethic of Community," 65. In *Lament*, Grant notes that "Roosevelt and Kennedy had found it useful to harness elements from the intellectual community to their administrations" (24). For Grant's views on the co-optation of the North American university, see *Technology and Empire*, 113–33.

100. Grant, "Ethic of Community," 65.

101. Irving Kristol, *Two Cheers for Capitalism* (New York: Basic Books, 1978), 18. See also pp. 140 and 147.

102. Ibid., 22.

103. Ibid., 19.

104. Ibid.

105. Ibid., 262 (emphasis original).

106. Ibid., 88.

107. Grant, *Lament for a Nation*, 59.

108. Kristol, *Two Cheers for Capitalism*, 20.

109. Ibid., 22.

110. Ibid., 7–8.

111. Ibid., 7.

112. Ibid., 22. See also Kolozi, *Conservatives against Capitalism*, 150.

113. Novak, *Spirit of Democratic Capitalism*, 178.

114. Ibid., 180. Novak is referring to Charles Lindblom's *Politics and Markets* (New York: Basic Books, 1977).

115. Kristol, *Two Cheers for Capitalism*, 269. For Kristol's disagreements with Michael Oakeshott on the meaning of conservatism, see Kristol's *Neoconservatism: The Autobiography of an Idea* (Chicago: Elephant Paperbacks, 1999), 373–86. In brief, Kristol insists that America's "exceptional" (capitalistic and populist) conservatism has nothing in common with Oakeshott's version.

116. Kristol, *Two Cheers for Capitalism*, 75. See also pp. 76–77, 92–95, and 100. Kristol warns that the "mirror-magic of 'public relations'" alone will not solve the corporation's image problem (118).

117. Ibid., 27–29, 183. The Serbian Communist Milovan Djilas coined this term in the late 1950s to describe the power of the bureaucratic elites in Communist regimes.

118. Ibid., 30.

119. See Rothbard, *Wall Street, Banks, and American Foreign Policy*.

120. Kristol, *Two Cheers for Capitalism*, 4.

121. Ibid., 8.

122. Ibid., 5.

123. Ibid., 9–10.

124. Grant, "Ethic of Community," 68.

125. Ibid., 73.

126. Kristol, *Two Cheers for Capitalism*, 28–29.

127. Grant, *Technology and Empire*, 30.

128. Ibid.

129. Grant, "A Critique of the New Left," in *The George Grant Reader*, 87–88. I refrain from discussing Richard Weaver and other Southern traditionalists whose ideas had some influence on the post–World War II conservative movement. The reason for this omission lies in my agreement with Grant that Southern traditionalism (which fueled the Goldwater campaign) represented the "last-ditch stand of a local culture." Grant, *Lament for a Nation*, 66. By the 1960s, they had lost whatever influence they had once enjoyed.

130. Grant, *Lament for a Nation*, 66.

131. Grant, "Critique of the New Left," 88.

132. Dart briefly draws this connection in *North American High Tory Tradition*, 115–16.

133. Francis, *Leviathan and Its Enemies*, 28–29.

134. Ibid., 37–40.

135. Ibid., 536–38.

136. Grant, *Technology and Empire*, 126.

137. Paul E. Gottfried, "Liberal Democracy as a God Term," in *Revisions and Dissents: Essays* (DeKalb: Northern Illinois University Press, 2017), 68.

138. Francis, *Leviathan and Its Enemies*, 538.

139. See Kristol, *Neoconservatism*, 234, 298–99, 309.

140. Grant, *Technology and Empire*, 39.

141. Kolozi, *Conservatives against Capitalism*, 150–52.

142. See Samuel Francis, "Neoconservatism and the Managerial Revolution," in *Beautiful Losers: Essays on the Failure of American Conservatism* (Columbia: University of Missouri Press, 1993), 95–117.

143. Francis, *Leviathan and Its Enemies*, 33.

144. Kolozi, *Conservatives against Capitalism*, 160–61.

145. James W. Ceaser, "The Great Divide: American Interventionism and Its Opponents," in *Present Dangers: Crisis and Opportunity in American Foreign and Defense Policy*, ed. Robert Kagan and William Kristol (San Francisco: Encounter Books, 2000), 29.

146. James W. Ceaser, "Foundational Concepts and American Political Development," in *Nature and History in American Political Development: A Debate*, ed. James W. Ceaser (Cambridge, MA: Harvard University Press, 2006), 22. For a critique of Ceaser, see Gottfried, *Revisions and Dissents*, 63–64.

147. Grant, *Lament for a Nation*, 43.

148. Ibid., 85.

149. Leo Strauss, *Natural Right and History* (Chicago: University of Chicago Press, 1953), 1–3.

150. Leo Strauss, "Progress or Return? The Contemporary Crisis in Western Civilization," in *Ten Essays by Leo Strauss: An Introduction to Political Philosophy*, ed. with an introduction by Hilail Gildin (Detroit: Wayne State University Press, 1989), 257

Leora Batnitzky quotes this passage in order to caution against associating Strauss with the neoconservative promotion of democracy on a global scale. See her *Leo Strauss and Emmanuel Levinas: Philosophy and the Politics of Revelation* (Cambridge: Cambridge University Press, 2006), 211. Nevertheless, others have drawn clear connections between Strauss and neoconservatism. See Paul E. Gottfried, *Leo Strauss and the Conservative Movement in America: A Critical Appraisal* (Cambridge: Cambridge University Press, 2012), 106–30; Claes Ryn, *America the Virtuous: The Crisis of Democracy and the Quest for Empire* (New Brunswick, NJ: Transaction, 2003), 31–34.

151. George Grant, "Letter of Resignation," in *The George Grant Reader*, 189.

152. I have written extensively on Grant's misreading of Strauss. See my "George Grant and Leo Strauss: Modernist and Postmodernist Conservatisms," *Topia* 8 (Fall 2002): 91–106; "Leo Strauss's Influence on George Grant," in *Athens and Jerusalem: George Grant's Theology, Philosophy, and Politics*, ed. Ian Angus, Ron Dart, and Peg Peters (Toronto: University of Toronto Press, 2006), 124–35; *Leo Strauss and Anglo-American Democracy: A Conservative Critique* (DeKalb: Northern Illinois University Press, 2013), 123–36.

153. See note 86.

154. Grant, *English-Speaking Justice*, 39.

155. Ibid., 40.

156. Ibid., 42.

157. Ibid.

158. Allan Bloom, "Justice: John Rawls versus the Tradition of Political Philosophy," in *Giants and Dwarfs: Essays 1960–1990* (New York: Simon and Schuster, 1990), 316.

159. Ibid., 318. See also Grant, *English-Speaking Justice*, 44–47.

160. Bloom, "Justice: John Rawls," 316. For Rawls's inattention to Marx, see Grant, *English-Speaking Justice*, 40.

161. Bloom, "Justice: John Rawls," 326–45.

162. Ibid., 322–26. See also John Rawls, *A Theory of Justice*, rev. ed. (1971; Cambridge, MA: Harvard University Press, 1999), 102–59.

163. Grant, *English-Speaking Justice*, 97.

164. Ibid., 24.

165. Ibid., 37.

166. Ibid., 33.

167. Brayton Polka has leveled this accusation against Rawls. See his "History between Biblical Religion and Modernity: Reflections on Rawls' *Lectures on the History of Moral Philosophy*," *European Legacy* 7, no. 4 (2002): 445–51.

168. Grant, "Ethic of Community," 69–70.

169. For a discussion of Grant's attitude toward Protestantism, see my "Marshall McLuhan, George Grant, and the Ancient-Modern-Protestant Quarrel in Canada," 152–60.

170. Grant, "Conversation with George Grant," 21.

171. Bloom, "Justice: John Rawls," 317.

172. Ibid., 327. See also page 337.

173. The challenge that revelation poses to philosophy is a recurrent theme in Strauss's writings. See, for example, *Natural Right and History*, 75; "Progress or Return?," 305.

174. Bloom, "Western Civ," in *Giants and Dwarfs*, 17.

175. Allan Bloom, *The Closing of the American Mind: How Higher Education Has Failed Democracy and Impoverished the Souls of Today's Students* (New York: Simon and Schuster, 1987), 161. Bloom also writes: "The essence of philosophy is the abandonment of all authority in favor of individual human reason" (253). Bloom is building on Strauss's idea of "unassisted reason." See Strauss, *Natural Right and History*, 75. Rawls similarly argues that human beings can employ their reason, independent of authority, tradition, and religion. See his *Political Liberalism*, expanded ed. (New York: Columbia University Press, 2005), xxvi–xxvii.

176. See Havers, *Leo Strauss and Anglo-American Democracy*, 133–36.

177. Ibid., 31–32.

178. Bloom, *Closing of the American Mind*, 152.

179. Ibid., 153.

180. Ibid., 152–53. See also Bloom, "Western Civ," 31.

181. Bloom, "Justice: John Rawls," 318.

182. As Kai Nielsen observes, Rawls's theory "works for Norway but not Cambodia." See his "Rawls and the Socratic Ideal," *Analyse & Kritik* 13 (1991): 82.

183. Grant, *Technology and Empire*, 65.

184. Ibid.

185. George Grant, "The Great Society 1967," in *The George Grant Reader*, 97.

186. See John von Heyking and Barry Cooper, "'A Cow Is Just a Cow': George Grant and Eric Voegelin on the United States," in Angus, Dart, and Peters, *Athens and Jerusalem*, 172–73.

187. Both of Grant's grandfathers, George Parkin and George Munro Grant, were staunch supporters of British imperialism during the Victorian era. See Carl Berger, *The Sense of Power: Studies in the Ideas of Canadian Imperialism 1867–1914* (Toronto: University of Toronto Press, 1970), 229–30.

188. Grant, *Lament for a Nation*, 73.

189. Grant, review of *Benjamin Disraeli*, in *The George Grant Reader*, 141.

190. Grant, *English-Speaking Justice*, 8–9.

191. Anthony J. Parel, "Multiculturalism and Nationhood," in *George Grant and the Future of Canada*, 148–150.

192. Duchesne, *Canada in Decay*, 235–68.

193. Grant, *Technology and Empire*, 49.

194. Ibid.

195. Ibid.

196. Ibid., 57.

197. Grant, *Lament for a Nation*, 42.

198. Walter Berns, *Making Patriots* (Chicago: University of Chicago Press, 2001), 32. For a refutation of this Straussian hermeneutic, see Barry Alan Shain, "Harry Jaffa and the Demise of the Old Republic," *Modern Age* 49, no. 4 (Fall 2007): 477–78.

199. Michael Ignatieff, "Human Rights: The Midlife Crisis," *New York Review of Books*, May 20, 1999, 58.

200. See Gottfried, "Liberal Democracy as a God Term," 70–72.

201. Grant, "Conversation with George Grant," 21.

4. WHO FUNDS CONSERVATISM, INC.?

1. C. K., "Why Think-Tanks Are Concerned about a Trump Administration," *The Economist*, November 17, 2016, https://www.economist.com/blogs/democracyinamerica/2016/11/worried-wonks.

2. Ibid.

3. Thomas Frank, "Thus Spake Zinsmeister," *New York Times*, August 25, 2006, http://www.nytimes.com/2006/08/25/opinion/25frank.html.

4. James McCartney and Molly Sinclair McCartney, "The Military-Industrial-Propaganda Complex: The Neo-Con Think-Tanks That Drive Policy and Send Us to War," *Salon*, November 2, 2015, https://www.salon.com/2015/11/02/the_military_industrial_propaganda_complex_the_neo_con_think_tanks_that_drive_policy_and_send_us_to_war/.

5. Ibid.

6. Rajiv Chandrasekaran, "Civilian Analysts Gained Petraeus's Ear While He Was Commander in Afghanistan," *Washington Post*, December 18, 2012, https://www.washingtonpost.com/world/national-security/civilian-analysts-gained-petrauss-ear-while-he-was-commander-in-afghanistan/2012/12/18/290c0b50-446a-11e2-8061-253bccfc7532_story.html?utm_term=.611be3fb3dcf.

7. Stephen M. Walt, "A Modest Proposal," *Foreign Policy*, November 20, 2009, http://foreignpolicy.com/2009/11/20/a-modest-proposal/.

8. Nathan Hodge, "How the Afghan Surge Was Sold," *WIRED*, December 3, 2009, https://www.wired.com/2009/12/how-the-afghan-surge-was-sold/.

9. Adam Johnson, "Lockheed Martin-Funded Experts Agree: South Korea Needs More Lockheed Martin Missiles," FAIR, May 8, 2017, https://fair.org/home/lockheed-martin-funded-experts-agree-south-korea-needs-more-lockheed-martin-missiles/.

10. Ibid.

11. Alex Shephard, "The D.C. Think Tank behind Donald Trump," *New Republic*, February 22, 2017, https://newrepublic.com/article/140271/dc-think-tank-behind-donald-trump.

12. *The Heritage Foundation and Affiliates Consolidated Financial Report*, Amazonnews, December 31, 2016, 6, http://thf-reports.s3.amazonaws.com/2017/Heritage%20Foundation_16FS_Final.pdf.

13. Alex Lee, "Emails Show Close Ties between Heritage Foundation and Lockheed Martin," The Intercept, September 15, 2015, https://theintercept.com/2015/09/15/heritage-foundation/.

14. Ibid.

15. Ibid.

16. Paul Gottfried, "Heritage Foundation + the War Industry: What a Pair," *American Conservative*, November 30, 2017, http://www.theamericanconservative.com/articles/heritage-foundation-the-war-industry-what-a-pair/.

5. IMAGINATION AND ITS FAILURES

1. James Burnham, "Communism: The Struggle for the World," in *American Conservative Thought in the Twentieth Century*, ed. William F. Buckley Jr. (Indianapolis: Bobbs-Merrill, 1970), 271.

2. It was first used by Dwight D. Eisenhower in his Farewell Address, in a warning against allowing this complex too much influence in the American government.

3. Originally a lecture delivered at Grinnell College in 1984.

4. George F. Kennan, "American Democracy and Foreign Policy," in *At a Century's Ending* (New York: Norton, 1996), 128.

5. Ibid., 133.

6. Ibid., 129–30.

7. Ibid., 130.

8. Ibid.

9. Ibid., 134.

10. Ibid., 135.

11. Ibid., 137.

12. See David Frum's "Unpatriotic Conservatives," *National Review*, March 25, 2003, https://www.nationalreview.com/2003/03/unpatriotic-conservatives-david-frum/.

13. Edward N. Luttwak, "The Strange Case of George F. Kennan," *Commentary*, November 1, 1977, https://www.commentarymagazine.com/articles/the-strange-case-of-george-f-kennan/.

14. George Kennan, "Letter to an American," *New Yorker*, September 24, 1984.

15. George Kennan, foreword to *The Pathology of Power*, by Norman Cousins (New York: Norton, 1987), 11–12.

16. Richard Brookhiser, "Waiting for Righty," *National Review*, January 20, 1992, 40–42.

17. The continuity between Buchanan and Trump extends even to the groups that hate them: former ACT-UP organizers, who once protested Buchanan, now train activists against Trump. See Eric Westervelt, "ACT UP at 30: Reinvigorated for Trump Fight," NPR, April 17, 2017, https://www.npr.org/2017/04/17/522726303/act-up-at-30-reinvigorated-for-trump-fight.

18. Patrick J. Buchanan, "A Crossroads in Our Country's History" (speech, New Hampshire State Legislative Office Building, December 10, 1991).

19. Ibid.

20. See Tom Bethell, "The Case for Buchanan," *National Review*, March 2, 1992, 34–38.

21. John O'Sullivan, "Mr. Buchanan and His Friends," *National Review*, March 16, 1992, 40.

22. James W. Ceaser and Andrew E. Busch, *Losing to Win: The 1996 Elections and American Politics* (Lanham, MD: Rowman and Littlefield, 1997), 84.

23. Robert D. Novack, "Pat Buchanan, Populist Republican," *National Review*, August 14, 1995, 40.

24. William F. Buckley, "Buchanan and the GOP," *National Review*, March 25, 1996, 67.

25. Virginia Postrel, "Standing Pat," *National Review*, March 11, 1996, 14.

26. Norman Podhoretz, "Anti-Semitism and a Presidential Candidacy," *Weekly Standard*, March 11, 1996, 21. It is worth noting that the *Weekly Standard* archives show that most of the letters written to and published by the magazine concerning Pat Buchanan's candidacy were sharply critical of the *Standard*'s partisanship against Buchanan.

27. David Tell, for the Editors, "The Buchanan Accident," *Weekly Standard*, March 11, 1996, 11.

28. Norman Ornstein, "Elite Men of the People," *Weekly Standard*, March 18, 1996, 16.

29. See Tom Squitieri, "A Look Back at Trump's First Run," The Hill, October 7, 2015, http://thehill.com/blogs/pundits-blog/presidential-campaign/256159-a-look-back-at-trumps-first-run; Ronald G. Shaefer, "Washington Wire," *Wall Street Journal*, September 17, 1999.

30. See Donald J. Trump, "What I Saw at the Revolution," *New York Times*, February 19, 2000, https://www.nytimes.com/2000/02/19/opinion/what-i-saw-at-the-revolution.html.

31. Patrick J. Buchanan, *A Republic, Not an Empire: Reclaiming America's Destiny* (Washington, DC: Regnery, 1999), xiii.

32. Ramesh Ponnuru, "A Conservative No More: The Tribal Politics of Pat Buchanan," *National Review*, October 11, 1999, 38.

33. Andrew J. Bacevich, "Nativist Son," *National Review*, October 11, 1999, 59.

34. Ibid. It could be argued that this is an unjust gloss on Buchanan's argument in the book itself.

35. Daniel J. Mahoney, "Conservatism, Democracy, and Foreign Policy," in *The Future of Conservatism*, ed. Charles W. Dunn (Wilmington, DE: ISI Books, 2007), 69.

36. See the home page for the Project for the New American Century, https://web .archive.org/web/20131006055540/http://www.newamericancentury.org/aboutpnac.htm, and the "Statement of Principles," archived, https://web.archive.org/web/20130922010137 /http://www.newamericancentury.org/statementofprinciples.htm.

37. Paul Reynolds, "End of the Neo-con Dream," BBC News, December 21, 2006.

38. William Kristol and Robert Kagan, "Toward a Neo-Reaganite Foreign Policy," *Foreign Affairs*, July 1, 1996, https://www.foreignaffairs.com/articles/1996-07-01/toward-neo -reaganite-foreign-policy.

39. William Kristol and Robert Kagan, "Bombing Iraq Isn't Enough," *New York Times*, January 30, 1998, https://www.nytimes.com/1998/01/30/opinion/bombing-iraq-isn-t -enough.html.

40. William Kristol et al., "Letter to George W. Bush," September 20, 2001. https://web .archive.org/web/20131018052135/http://www.newamericancentury.org/Bushletter.htm.

41. Frum, "Unpatriotic Conservatives."

42. Ibid.

43. David D. Kirkpatrick, "National Review Founder Says It's Time to Leave Stage," *New York Times*, June 29, 2004, https://www.nytimes.com/2004/06/29/us/national-review -founder-says-it-s-time-to-leave-stage.html.

44. See Patrick J. Buchanan, "But Who Was Right—Rudy or Ron?," Patrick J. Buchanan—Official Website, May 18, 2007, http://buchanan.org/blog/pjb-but-who-was -right-%E2%80%93-rudy-or-ron-759.

45. "Statement of Principles and Positions," Republican Liberty Caucus, accessed May 19, 2019, http://rlc.org/principles.

46. Charles Mahtesian, "Paul: I Don't Fully Endorse Romney," *Politico*, August 26, 2012, https://www.politico.com/blogs/charlie-mahtesian/2012/08/paul-i-dont-fully-endorse -romney-133239.

47. Charlie Spiering, "Full Text: Rand Paul's Speech on 'Containment and Radical Islam,'" *Washington Examiner*, February 6, 2013, https://www.washingtonexaminer.com/full -text-rand-pauls-speech-on-containment-and-radical-islam.

48. Rand Paul, "The Case for Conservative Realism," *National Interest*, October 23, 2014, https://nationalinterest.org/feature/rand-paul-the-case-conservative-realism-11544.

49. CBS News South Carolina Debate, https://www.youtube.com/watch?v=Un3OhYs -tCE.

50. Donald J. Trump, "Transcript: Donald Trump's Foreign Policy Speech," *New York Times*, April 27, 2016, https://www.nytimes.com/2016/04/28/us/politics/transcript-trump -foreign-policy.html

51. Ibid.

52. Publius Decius Mus [Michael Anton], "The Flight 93 Election," *Claremont Review of Books*, September 5, 2016, https://www.claremont.org/crb/basicpage/the-flight-93 -election/.

53. Tim Alberta, "The Ideas Made It, but I Didn't," *Politico*, May-June 2017, https:// www.politico.com/magazine/story/2017/04/22/pat-buchanan-trump-president-history -profile-215042.

54. This has been pointed out by Democratic candidate Tulsi Gabbard, who has expressed in tweets her fears that Trump's reaction to the Russian collusion narrative has been

to weaken diplomatic ties with Russia rather than improve them, as he promised to do during his first campaign.

55. Rand Paul, "Trump Is Right to Meet Putin," *Politico*, July 16, 2018, https://www.politico.com/magazine/story/2018/07/16/trump-is-right-to-meet-putin-219012.

56. This statement remains true as of March 2019. While Rand Paul is likely closer to Trump on foreign policy than to any other major GOP figure, Trump has the habit of preferring personal loyalty to shared policy concerns. This renders it unlikely that he will elevate Rand Paul to a high position in his administration.

57. Kenneth Waltz, "Structural Realism after the Cold War," *International Security* 25, no. 1 (Summer 2000): 19.

58. Ibid., 20–21.

59. Ibid., 22.

6. THE CONTRADICTIONS OF CATHOLIC NEOCONSERVATISM

1. In 1899 Pope Leo XIII wrote a letter to the archbishop of Baltimore, James Cardinal Gibbons, titled "Testem Benevolentiae Nostrae," in which the Holy Father had admonished American Catholics who believed that "the Church should shape her teachings more in accord with the spirit of the age and relax some of her ancient severity and make some concessions to new opinions." Leo XIII, "Testem Benevolentiae Nostrae," Papal Encyclicals Online, 1899, http://www.papalencyclicals.net/leo13/l13teste.htm. Later, the entire Catholic neoconservative movement would be dedicated to the effort of modernizing the church and grafting the American strand of liberal Enlightenment thought onto the Catholic tradition, a hybridization against which Leo and other nineteenth- and early twentieth-century popes specifically warned. The Catholic neocons themselves were well aware that their own breed of American liberalism had been condemned as a heresy by Pope Leo XIII. In "Catholic 'Americanism,'" George Weigel argues that Americanism was merely a "phantom heresy," and then switches gears to attack Catholic members of the Democratic Party as being the real Americanists due to their support of abortion. "Catholic 'Americanism,'" *National Review*, May 31, 2012, https://www.nationalreview.com/2012/05/catholic-americanism-george-weigel/.

2. Father Murray's quintessential text in which he attempts, with varying degrees of success, to root American political thought in strands of medieval Catholic thinking is *We Hold These Truths* (Lanham, MD: Sheed and Ward, 2005). The writings of Jacques Maritain, who originally began his Catholic intellectual career as a man of the Right associated with the controversial French monarchist group Action Française, are voluminous, but Maritain's most critical later works advocating a rapprochement between liberalism and the Catholic philosophical tradition, rooted in the High Scholastic writings of St. Thomas Aquinas, include *Man and the State* (Washington, DC: Catholic University of America Press, 1998) and his seminal *Integral Humanism: Temporal and Spiritual Problems of a New Christendom* (New York: Scribners, 1968), which, originally published in French as *Humanisme intégral* in 1936, like Father Murray's writings, had a tremendous influence on the liberal political documents of Vatican II. Yves Simon, a figure lesser known than Maritain, also sought to infuse Catholic political philosophy with liberalism in such works as *A General Theory of Authority* (Notre Dame, IN: University of Notre Dame Press, 1991) and *Philosophy of Democratic Government* (Notre Dame, IN: University of Notre Dame Press, 1993).

3. The quintessential Jewish neoconservative *Bildungsroman* is, of course, Norman Podhoretz's *Making It* (New York: New York Review of Books, 1967). The collected writings of Irving Kristol, himself hallowed as the godfather of neoconservativism, who tutored many of the Catholic neoconservatives, can be found in Irving Kristol's *Neoconservative*

Revolution: Selected Essays, 1942–2009 (New York: Basic Books, 2013). For scholarly work on the Jewish strand of the neoconservative movement and the American Jewish Committee's *Commentary Magazine*, which became the most powerful and articulate medium of neoconservative ideas, see Benjamin Balint's *Running Commentary: The Contentious Magazine That Transformed the Jewish Left into the Neoconservative Right* (New York: Public Affairs, 2010) as well as Murray Friedman, *The Neoconservative Revolution: Jewish Intellectuals and the Shaping of Public Policy* (Cambridge: Cambridge University Press, 2005).

4. For the Catholic migration from the Democratic to the Republican Party, see William Prendergast's *The Catholic Voter in American Politics: The Passing of the Democratic Monolith* (Washington, DC: Georgetown University Press, 1999).

5. Abraham J. Heschel, Michael Novak, and Robert McAfee, *Vietnam: Crisis of Conscience* (New York: New York Association Press, 1967).Novak left the Holy Cross Fathers months before his ordination to the priesthood, becoming a speechwriter for Democratic political candidates. He eventually penned two autobiographical works of fiction, *The Tiber Was Silver* (New York: Doubleday, 1961) and the erotic *Naked I Leave* (New York: Macmillan, 1970). Novak's first big break, however, came when he went to work as a journalist for the progressive Catholic journals *National Catholic Reporter, America, Commonweal,* and even, interestingly, *Time Magazine*, covering Vatican II, which ultimately culminated in *The Open Church* (New York: Macmillan, 1964).

6. Heschel, Novak, and McAfee, *Vietnam*, 46.

7. For a trenchant discussion of post–World War II American conservativism's roots in the thought of the German philosopher G. W. Hegel, see Paul Gottfried, *Search for Historical Meaning: Hegel and the Postwar American Right* (DeKalb: Northern Illinois University Press, 1987).

8. George Weigel, *Lessons in Hope: My Unexpected Life with St. John Paul II* (New York: Basic Books, 2017).

9. Weigel writes, "I saw the helicopters of Operation Frequent Wind lift off from the roof of the US embassy in Saigon, frantic refugees hanging onto the landing skids and even more desperate men and women abandoned on the roof below. Something, it seemed to me, was very, very wrong here." Weigel, *Lessons in Hope*, 15.

10. Michael Novak, "A Closet Capitalist Confesses," *Wall Street Journal*, April 20, 1976.

11. Michael Novak, "Needing Niebuhr Again," *Commentary*, September 1, 1972, https://www.commentarymagazine.com/articles/needing-niebuhr-again/.

12. Ibid.

13. Ibid.

14. Richard John Neuhaus, *In Defense of People: Ecology and the Seduction of Radicalism* (New York: Macmillan, 1971).

15. Paul R. Ehrlich, *The Population Bomb* (Cutchogue, NY: Buccaneer Books, 1968).

16. Neuhaus's professional and personal relationships with other neoconservatives would experience tremendous strain after the November 1996, "End of Democracy" issue of *First Things*, in which Neuhaus compared the American government's disregard of the value of human life to the policies of Nazi Germany, further suggesting that a revolution may be necessary in America. "The End of Democracy" controversy would even prompt a response from Norman Podhoretz in the February 1997 issue of *Commentary*.

17. United States Conference of Catholic Bishops, *The Challenge of Peace: God's Promise and Our Response*, May 3, 1983, http://www.usccb.org/upload/challenge-peace-gods -promise-our-response-1983.pdf.

18. United States Conference of Catholic Bishops, *Economic Justice for All: Pastoral Letter on Catholic Social Teaching and the U.S. Economy*, 1986, http://www.usccb.org/upload /economic_justice_for_all.pdf.

19. Patrick Allitt, *Catholic Intellectuals and Conservative Politics in America, 1950–1985* (Ithaca, NY: Cornell University Press, 1993).

20. Allitt's presentation of Catholic conservative and traditionalist thought is fair and scholarly; for a more polemical attack on the American Catholic Right, see Michael W. Cuneo's *The Smoke of Satan: Conservative and Traditionalist Dissent in Contemporary American Catholicism* (Baltimore: Johns Hopkins University Press, 1999). Cuneo, however, admits that Catholic neoconservatives are "considerably less antagonistic . . . toward the democratic and pluralistic ethos of American culture" than "traditional" Catholics (189).

21. While the term "neoconservative" can be used as an insult by those on both the left and the right, one of the principal Catholic neoconservatives, George Weigel, proudly appropriates the term for the movement in his essay "The Neoconservative Difference: A Proposal for Renewal of Church and Society," in *Being Right: Conservative Catholics in America*, ed. Mary Jo Weaver and R. Scott Appleby (Bloomington: Indiana University Press, 1995), 138–62. For Weigel, what distinguishes Catholic neoconservatives from those Catholics who identify as "traditionalists" is the neoconservatives' openness to those aspects of "modern intellectual life in which they have discerned openings to the transcendent" (139).

22. Michael Novak, *The Spirit of Democratic Capitalism* (Washington, DC: American Enterprise Institute, 1982).

23. Ibid., 39.

24. Ibid., 48.

25. Ibid., 68. For many of the neoconservatives, liberal democracy is a sacrosanct political form, and John Paul II is the saint of this system. In *The God That Did Not Fail* (New York: Encounter Books, 2006), Robert Royal pairs John Paul II with Margaret Thatcher, Ronald Reagan, and even Aleksandr Solzhenitsyn as being among "the main leaders" of the resistance to Soviet Communism "who had deep convictions about Christianity" (258). It is not as though Royal is wrong in his assessment of these men and women's faith or their noble resistance to Soviet Communism; it is that, in the writings of the Catholic neoconservatives, a specific form of liberal democracy becomes enshrined as the new official political system of Catholic Christianity. Robert George writes even more strongly of democracy in his work *In Defense of Natural Law* (Oxford: Oxford University Press, 2001).

26. During the presidency of George W. Bush and the height of neoconservative power, a number of works were published critiquing the Catholic neoconservatives, or "theocons" as they became known. Damon Linker, a former staff member of *First Things*, wrote the hysterically titled *The Theocons: Secular America under Siege* (New York: Anchor Books, 2007). See also Chris Hedges's *American Fascists: The Christian Right and the War on America* (New York: Free Press, 2006). While marketing itself as a "conspiracy" book released after fears of evangelical political power had crested during the presidency of George W. Bush, Jeff Sharlet's *The Family: The Secret Fundamentalism at the Heart of American Power* (New York: Harper Perennial, 2009) provides a rough but at times brilliantly detailed and narrated sketch of the rise of the conservative American evangelical political power in America that was so intimately intertwined with neoconservative thought.

27. Richard John Neuhaus, *The Naked Public Square: Religion and Democracy in America* (Grand Rapids, MI: Willian B. Eerdmans, 1988), 18.

28. Ibid., 35.

29. Ibid., 28.

30. Ibid., 39.

31. Ibid., 69. Neuhaus earlier had defined his revolutionary ethos in *Movement and Revolution* (New York: Doubleday, 1970), which he wrote with Peter Berger.

32. George Weigel, *Tranquillitas Ordinis: The Present Failure and Future Promise of American Catholic Thought on War and Peace* (Oxford: Oxford University Press, 1987).

33. Ibid., 147.

34. In *Lessons in Hope* Weigel lets the reader know that it was the Italian politician Rocco Buttiglione who pushed John Paul II to give *Centesimus* a seemingly pro-capitalist slant and to reject the draft of *Centesimus* that the Pontifical Council for Justice and the Peace composed, by informing the pope, "This is not the way the economy works today and it isn't the way it will work tomorrow" (42).

35. In *Lessons in Hope* Weigel reveals the person who gave the advance copy of the encyclical to him, Father Neuhaus, and Michael Novak: U.S. ambassador to the Holy See, Thomas Melady (42).

36. John Paul II, *Centesimus Annus*, May 1, 1991, The Holy See, https://w2.vatican.va /content/john-paul-ii/en/encyclicals/documents/hf_jp-ii_enc_01051991_centesimus -annus.html.

37. The most prolific and capable combatant of the Catholic neoconservatives' misreading of *Centesimus Annus* is David Schindler. See, for example, Schindler's *Heart of the World, Center of the Church: Communio Ecclesiology, Liberalism, and Liberation* (Grand Rapids, MI: W. B. Eerdmans, 1996).

38. Capitalizing on the success of the neoconservative appropriation of the American reception of John Paul II's complex and nuanced economic encyclical, Michael Novak's 1993 work, *The Catholic Ethic and the Spirit of Capitalism* (New York: Basic Books), is largely a meditation on John Paul's writings in which Novak attempts to recruit the Polish pontiff as a spokesperson for Novak's own personal economic policy. See a similar effort in Father Neuhaus's *Doing Well and Doing Good: The Challenge to the Christian Capitalist* (New York: Doubleday, 1992), and the collection of essays edited by George Weigel in *A New Worldly Order: John Paul II and Human Freedom* (Washington, DC: American Enterprise Institute, 1992).

39. In Paul Kengor's *A Pope and a President: John Paul II, Ronald Reagan, and the Extraordinary Untold Story of the 20th Century* (Wilmington, DE: ISI Books, 2017), the neoconservative thinker Paul Kengor uses John Paul II's alleged liberalism and image as the American pope to rework the traditional Catholic devotion to Our Lady of Fatima. Instead of the Virgin Mary's prophecies announcing an eventual victory of the Catholic Church over secularism, the prophecies of Our Lady of Fatima become, in Kengor's view, the story of the triumph of American liberalism under Ronald Reagan over Soviet Communism. Likewise, the neoconservative John O'Sullivan crafts an image of John Paul II, Margaret Thatcher, and Ronald Reagan as a triumvirate for liberal democratic capitalism in *The Pope, the President and the Prime Minister* (Washington, DC: Regnery History, 2006).

40. George Weigel, *The Final Revolution: The Resistance Church and the Collapse of Communism* (Oxford: Oxford University Press, 1992).

41. Tad Szulc, *John Paul II: The Biography* (New York: Scribner's, 2007).

42. George Weigel, *Witness to Hope: The Biography of John Paul II* (New York: Harper Collins, 1999).

43. George Weigel, *The End and the Beginning: Pope John Paul II: The Victory of Freedom, the Last Years, the Legacy* (New York: Image, 2010).

44. George Weigel, *God's Choice: Pope Benedict XVI and the Future of the Catholic Church* (New York: Harper, 2005).

45. In *God's Choice*, George Weigel uses Hegelian language to describe John Paul II's "world-historical" effect on spreading democracy and liberalism throughout the world; (35). Weigel uses "world-historical" again in *God's Choice*, describing John Paul's two addresses to the U.N. General Assembly, his encyclicals *Centesimus Annus*, *Evangelium Vitae*, and *Veritas Splendor*, "as well as his homilies in New York, Brooklyn, and Baltimore during his 1995 pastoral visit to the United States, all of which took up important questions of the relationship of public virtue to democratic self-governance." (48).

46. Robert P. George, *Making Men Moral: Civil Liberties and Public Morality* (Oxford: Clarendon Press, 1995).

47. Robert P. George, *The Clash of Orthodoxies: Law, Religion, and Morality in Crisis* (Wilmington, DE: ISI Press, 2001.

48. Robert P. George, *In Defense of Natural Law* (New York: Oxford University Press, 1999).

49. In *The Clash of Orthodoxies*, George explains that natural law theory is based in the notion that "humanly created 'positive' law is morally good or bad—just or unjust—depending on its conformity to the standards of a 'natural,' (viz., moral) law that is more human creation. The natural law is thus, a 'higher' law, albeit a law that is in principle accessible to human reason and not dependent on (though entirely compatible with and, indeed, illumined by) divine revelation" (169). Aquinas, however, argues in chapter 14 of *De Regno*, for example, that the Roman pontiff is he "to whom all kings over Christian people should be subject as to Christ himself," in *St. Thomas Aquinas: On Politics and Ethics*, trans. and ed. Paul E. Sigmund (New York: Norton, 1988), 28.

50. Clyde Haberman, "Pope Denounces the Gulf War as a 'Darkness,'" *New York Times*, April 1, 1990.

51. George Weigel and James Turner Johnson, *Just War and the Gulf War* (Washington, DC: Ethics and Public Policy Center, 1991).

52. In *Lessons in Hope*, Weigel describes an interesting conversation that he had with Charles Krauthammer after the fall of the Berlin Wall in December 1989, in which Weigel explained that the neocons would be very busy for the future: "I told him that I imagined there would be plenty to keep us occupied, as I didn't buy Francis Fukuyama's 'end of history' thesis and was confident that 'history' had a few surprises left in her pocket" (39).

53. Project for the New American Century, "Statement of Principles," June 3, 1997, https://web.archive.org/web/20050205041635/http://www.newamericancentury.org/statementofprinciples.htm.

54. Weigel, *Lessons in Hope*, 293.

55. Weigel, *God's Choice*, 70.

56. Michael Novak, *Writing Left to Right: My Journal from Liberal to Conservative* (New York: Image, 2013), 313. Novak further admits, "I hated to take a position different from that of the Pope, which might mean I would lose of his friendship, one of my most precious treasures" (313).

57. George Weigel, *The Cube and the Cathedral: Europe, America, and Politics without God* (New York: Basic Books, 2005).

58. Robert Kagan, *Of Paradise and Power: America and Europe in the New World Order* (New York: Vintage Books, 2004).

59. George Weigel, *Faith, Reason, and the War against Jihadism: A Call to Action* (New York: Image, 2007).

60. Norman Podhoretz, *World War IV: The Long Struggle against Islamofascism* (New York: Doubleday, 2007).

61. Weigel, *Faith, Reason, and the War against Jihadism*, 69.

62. Ibid., 63.

63. Benedict XVI, "Letter of His Holiness Benedict XVI to the Bishops on the Occasion of the Publication of the Apostolic Letter 'Motu Proprio Data' Summorum Pontificum on the Use of the Roman Liturgy Prior to the Reform of 1970," The Holy See, July 7, 2007, https://w2.vatican.va/content/benedict-xvi/en/letters/2007/documents/hf_ben-xvi_let_20070707_lettera-vescovi.html.

64. George Weigel, "Did the Pope Heal or Deepen a Catholic Schism?," *Newsweek*, January 25, 2009, http://www.newsweek.com/did-pope-heal-or-deepen-catholic-schism-78423.

65. Francis, *Evangelii Gaudium: Apostolic Exhortation on the Proclamation of the Gospel in Today's World*, The Holy See, November 24, 2013, https://w2.vatican.va/content/francesco/en/apost_exhortations/documents/papa-francesco_esortazione-ap_20131124_evangelii-gaudium.html.

66. Michael Novak, "Agreeing with Pope Francis," *National Review*, December 7, 2013, https://www.nationalreview.com/2013/12/agreeing-pope-francis-michael-novak/.

67. While he has made many gestures and statements in support of homosexuality, the most pronounced was his refusal to condemn homosexual priests encapsulated in the phrase "Who am I to judge?" made on a plane trip from Brazil at the beginning of his pontificate in 2013. See, for example, Rachel Donadio, "On Gay Priests, Pope Francis Asks, "Who Am I to Judge?," *New York Times*, July 29, 2013, https://www.nytimes.com/2013/07/30/world/europe/pope-francis-gay-priests.html.

68. Francis, *Amoris Laetitia*, The Holy See, March 19, 2016, https://w2.vatican.va/content/dam/francesco/pdf/apost_exhortations/documents/papa-francesco_esortazione-ap_20160319_amoris-laetitia_en.pdf.

69. John Paul II, *Evangelium Vitae*, The Holy See, March 25, 1995, http://w2.vatican.va/content/john-paul-ii/en/encyclicals/documents/hf_jp-ii_enc_25031995_evangelium-vitae.html.

70. David Bentley Hart, "Mammon Ascendant: Why Global Capitalism Is Inimical to Christianity," *First Things*, June 2016, https://www.firstthings.com/article/2016/06/mammon-ascendant. Samuel Gregg, an Acton Institute fellow, attacked Hart and *First Things* in "Global Capitalism versus Christianity? A Response to David Bentley Hart," *Public Discourse*, May 17, 2016, http://www.thepublicdiscourse.com/2016/05/16979/?utm_source=The+Witherspoon+Institute&utm_campaign=61c98bdade-RSS_EMAIL_CAMPAIGN&utm_medium=email&utm_term=0_15ce6af37b-61c98bdade-84111297. See also *First Things* editor R. R. Reno's defense of Hart's essay, "Capitalism beyond Caricature," *First Things*, May 18, 2016, https://www.firstthings.com/blogs/firstthoughts/2016/05/capitalism-beyond-caricatures.

71. See Robert T. Miller, "The Mortara Case and the Limits of State Power: *First Things* Should Disavow Fr. Cessario's Defense of Pius IX in the Mortara Case," Public Discourse, January 11, 2018, http://www.thepublicdiscourse.com/2018/01/20868/; as well as Charles Chaput's "The Mortara Affair, Redux," *Jewish Review of Books*, January 29, 2018, https://jewishreviewofbooks.com/articles/2979/mortara-affair-redux/.

72. The rightward drift of Catholic conservatives has been strangely matched by the leftward drift of the younger generation of Jewish neoconservative thinkers such as John Podhoretz, William "Bill" Kristol, and Jonah Goldberg.

73. Robert P. George and George Weigel, "An Appeal to Our Fellow Catholics," *National Review*, May 7, 2016, https://www.nationalreview.com/2016/03/donald-trump-catholic-opposition-statement/.

74. George and Weigel, "Appeal to Our Fellow Catholics."

75. Michael Novak, "Silver Linings for Never Trumpers," *First Things*, November 15, 2016, https://www.firstthings.com/blogs/firstthoughts/2016/11/silver-linings-for-never-trumpers.

76. Michael Novak, "What on Earth Happened on November 8?," *National Review*, November 22, 2016, https://www.nationalreview.com/2016/11/progressivism-rebuked-donald-trump-2016-presidential-election/. Novak, in fact, ends the piece with a surprising benediction for President Trump: "God bless the new president of the United States."

7. TRUMP, NEOCONSERVATIVES, AND THE MISREPRESENTATION OF THE AMERICAN FOUNDING

1. Donald J. Trump, "Remarks at the South Florida Fair Expo Center in West Palm Beach, Florida," American Presidency Project, October 13, 2016, http://www.presidency.ucsb.edu/ws/index.php?pid=119180.

2. Donald J. Trump, "President Donald J. Trump's State of the Union Address," The White House, January 30, 2018, https://www.whitehouse.gov/briefings-statements/president-donald-j-trumps-state-union-address.

3. For more on this topic, see Barry A. Shain, *The Myth of American Individualism* (Princeton, NJ: Princeton University Press, 1994); Barry A. Shain, review of *Vindicating the Founders*, by Thomas West, *Modern Age* 42, no. 1 (Winter 2000): 63–70; Paul Gottfried, *Leo Strauss and the Conservative Movement in America* (New York: Cambridge University Press, 2012); Grant N. Havers, *Leo Strauss and Anglo-American Democracy: A Conservative Critique* (DeKalb: Northern Illinois University Press, 2013).

4. See, for example, Thomas G. West, *Vindicating the Founders: Race, Sex, Class, and Justice in the Origins of America* (Lanham, MD: Rowman & Littlefield Publishers, 2000); Thomas G. West, *The Political Theory of the American Founding* (Cambridge: Cambridge University Press, 2017); Publius Decius Mus [Michael Anton], "Toward a Sensible, Coherent Trumpism," UNZ Review, March 10, 2016, http://www.unz.com/article/toward-a-sensible-coherent-trumpism; Publius Decius Mus [Michael Anton], "The Flight 93 Election," *Claremont Review of Books*, September 5, 2016, http://www.claremont.org/crb/basicpage/the-flight-93-election.

5. The Zuckerts have dubbed a third camp the "Midwest Straussians." See Catherine H. Zuckert and Michael P. Zuckert, *The Truth about Leo Strauss: Political Philosophy and American Democracy* (Chicago: University of Chicago Press, 2008), 22. For more on the topic of Straussian divisions, see Thomas G. West, "Jaffa versus Mansfield: Does America Have a Constitutional or a 'Declaration of Independence' Soul?" *Perspective on Political Science* 31, no. 4 (2002) 235–46; Jet Heer, "The Failure of Pro-Trump Intellectualism," *New Republic*, February 28, 2017, https://newrepublic.com/article/140933/failure-pro-trump-intellectualism; Mike Sabo, "Rod Dreher, Meet Leo Strauss and Friends," American Greatness, April 8, 2017, https://amgreatness.com/2017/04/08/rod-dreher-meet-leo-strauss-friends.

6. Allan Bloom, *The Closing of the American Mind: How Higher Education Has Failed Democracy and Impoverished the Souls of Today's Students* (New York: Simon and Schuster, 2012), 167. Bloom attributes this quote to his teacher Strauss. See also Martin Diamond, "The Federalist," in *History of Political Philosophy*, ed. Leo Strauss and Joseph Crospey (Chicago: Rand McNally, 1972), 648–50; Thomas Pangle, *The Spirit of Modern Republicanism* (Chicago: University of Chicago Press, 1988), 92, 94–98. Straussian analysis of the Founding should not always be understood as a full endorsement. For example, Bloom bemoans the fact that "civil societies dedicated to the end of self-preservation cannot be expected to provide fertile soil for the heroic or the inspired. They do not require or encourage the noble." Allan Bloom, *Giants and Dwarfs* (New York: Simon & Schuster, 1990), 285.

7. Bloom, *Closing of the American Mind*, 27–28, 31, 33. Mansfield says the Constitution supplants the Declaration and ultimately rejects Locke because of its replacement of revolution with the amendment process. Harvey Mansfield, "Unfinished Revolution," in *Legacy of the French Revolution*, ed. Ralph C. Hancock and L. Gary Lambert (Lanham, MD: Rowman & Littlefield, 1996), 7.

8. Bloom, *Closing of the American Mind*, 27, 31. Bloom also contends that America's universalistic founding mandates the use of military force to impose democracy and human rights on the world (153).

9. Harry V. Jaffa, "Aristotle and Locke in the American Founding," *Claremont Review of Books* 1, no. 2 (Winter 2001). http://www.claremont.org/crb/article/aristotle-and-locke -in-the-american-founding/ See also Harry V. Jaffa, *A New Birth of Freedom* (Lanham, MD: Rowman & Littlefield, 2000); West, *Political Theory of the American Founding*, 188–214; Thomas G. West, review of *A New Birth of Freedom*, by Harry V. Jaffa, October 31, 2001, http://www.csub.edu/~mault/jaffa1.htm.

10. Abraham Lincoln, "Gettysburg Address," Avalon Project, accessed April 9, 2018, http://avalon.law.yale.edu/19th_ century/gettyb.asp. Another key Lincoln text emphasized by the West Coast Straussians is his "electric cord" speech. See Abraham Lincoln, "Electric Cord," Vindicating the Founders, July 10, 1858, http://www.vindicatingthefounders .com/library/electric-cord-speech.html.

11. See, for example, West, *Political Theory of the American Founding*, chaps. 8–13.

12. Harry V. Jaffa, *Crisis of the House Divided* (Chicago: University of Chicago Press, 1982),345. See also pages 359–61.

13. For more on the relationship between the neoconservatives and the Straussians, see Gottfried, *Leo Strauss*, 122–30; Daniel J. Mahoney, *Conservative Foundations of the Liberal Order* (Wilmington, DE: ISI Books, 2011), 107–19. For a view that downplays this relationship, see Tony Burns and James Connelly, eds., *The Legacy of Leo Strauss* (Charlottesville, VA: Imprint Academic, 2016), 197–276.

14. For an especially vivid example of this approach, see Max Boot, "We Didn't Kick Britain's Ass to Be This Kind of Country," *Foreign Policy*, July 3, 2017, http://foreignpolicy .com/2017/07/03/we-didnt-kick-britains-ass-to-be-this-kind-of-country.

15. Leo Strauss, *Persecution and the Art of Writing* (Chicago: University of Chicago Press, 1988), 17. The "godfather" of neoconservatism himself wrote a thoughtful review of this work. See William Kristol, review of *Persecution and the Art of Writing*, by Leo Strauss, *Commentary*, October 1, 1952, https://www.commentarymagazine.com/articles/persecution -and-the-art-of-writing-by-leo-strauss.

16. See, for example, Francis Fukuyama, *America at the Crossroads: Democracy, Power, and the Neoconservative Legacy* (New Haven, CT: Yale University Press, 2007); Jon Utley, "Iraq, Syria, Iran . . . Are We to Destroy Iran Next?," *American Conservative*, December 14, 2017, http://www.theamericanconservative.com/articles/iraq-syria-iran-are-we-to-destroy -iran-next.

17. Ross Barkan, "The Blood on George W Bush's Hands Will Never Dry. Don't Glorify This Man," *The Guardian*, October 20, 2017, https://www.theguardian.com /commentisfree/2017/oct/20/george-w-bush-donald-trump-speech-blood-hands. See also Larry Elder, "Democrats and the Nazi Card," RealClear Politics, November 24, 2016, https://www.realclearpolitics.com/articles/2016/11/24/democrats_and_the_nazi_card _132428. html; Michael Janofsky, "The 2004 Campaign: Advertising; Bush-Hitler Ads Draw Criticism," *New York Times*, January 6, 2004, https://www.nytimes.com/2004/01/06/us/the -2004-campaign-advertising-bush-hitler-ads-draw-criticism.html.

18. Trevor Timm, "Is Hillary Clinton a Neocon?," *The Guardian*, June 27, 2016, https://www.theguardian.com/commentisfree/2016/jun/27/hillary-clinton-necono -republican-endorsements-donald-trump-policy-issues; Sam Levine, "Paul Wolfowitz Is So concerned with Trump He May Vote for Clinton," *Huffington Post*, August 27, 2016, https://www.huffingtonpost.com/entry/paul-wolfowitz-donald-trump_us_57 c1b121e4b 04193420f69b9.

19. Bret Stephens, "The Donald and the Demagogues," *Wall Street Journal*, August 31, 2015, https://www.wsj.com/articles/the-donald-and-the-demagogues-1441064072; Andrea

Mammone, "Trump and the Demagogues of Modern Nationalism," *Huffington Post*, December 6, 2017, https://www.huffingtonpost.com/andrea-mammone/trump-in-the-west_b_9991262.html.

20. Irving Kristol, "The Neoconservative Persuasion," *Weekly Standard*, August 25, 2003, https://www.weeklystandard.com/the-neoconservative-persuasion/article/4246.

21. Ibid. See also George Hawley, *Right-Wing Critics of American Conservatism* (Lawrence: University Press of Kansas, 2016), 50–51.

22. "What Does Entryism Mean?," *New Statesman*, August 10, 2016, https://www.newstatesman.com/politics/staggers/2016/08/what-does-entryism-mean.

23. Irving Kristol, "Memoirs of a Trotskyist," *New York Times* archives, January 23, 1977, https://www.nytimes.com/1977/01/23/archives/memoirs-of-a-trotskyist-memoirs.html.

24. Ibid.

25. Hawley, *Right-Wing Critics*, 28; Bret Stephens, "Hands Up, Straussians! If All Values Are Relative, Then Cannibalism Is a Matter of Taste," *Jerusalem Post*, June 5, 2003, http://www.freerepublic.com/focus/f-news /9245 58/posts; Gerhard Spörl and Br/Der Spiegel, "The Leo-conservatives," *New York Times*, August 4, 2003, https://www.nytimes.com /2003/08/04/international/europe/the-leoconservatives.html.

26. Danny Cooper, *Neoconservatism and American Foreign Policy: A Critical Analysis* (Abingdon: Routledge, 2010), 30. For examples of the appearance of Straussian themes, see Robert Kagan, "Neocon Nation: Neoconservatism, c. 1776," World Affairs, accessed May 20, 2018, http://www.worldaffairsjournal.org/article/neocon-nation-neoconservatism -c-1776; Robert Kagan, "Our 'Messianic Impulse,'" December 10, 2006, *Washington Post*, http://www.washingtonpost.com/wp-dyn/content/article/2006/12/08/AR2006120801516 .html; Jim Garamone, "West Must Encourage Moderate Voices of Islam, Wolfowitz Says," DOD News, May 6, 2002, http://archive.defense.gov/news/newsarticle.aspx?id=44093.

27. Bret Stephens, "Four Questions about American Greatness," *New York Times*, December 17, 2017, https://www.nytimes.com/2017/12/07/opinion/four-questions-american -greatness.html; Stephens, "Donald and the Demagogues."

28. Jennifer Rubin, "Trump's State of the Union: A Diatribe against Immigrants," *Washington Post*, January 30, 2018, https://www.washingtonpost.com/blogs/right-turn/wp /2018/01/30/trumps-state-of-the-union-a-diatribe-against-immigrants.

29. Jennifer Rubin, "Jennifer Rubin: Republicans Wear the Ugly Face of Ethnonationalists," *Salt Lake Tribune*, January 22, 2018, https://www.sltrib.com/opinion /commentary/2018/01/22/jennifer-rubin-republicans-wear-the-ugly-face-of-ethno -nationalists/.

30. George W. Bush, "Full Text: George W. Bush Speech on Trumpism," *Politico*, October 19, 2017, https://www.politico.com/story/2017/10/19/full-text-george-w-bush -speech-trump-243947.

31. Ibid.

32. See, for example, Christianna Silva, "Trump's Full List of 'Racist' Comments about Immigrants, Muslims and Others," *Newsweek*, January 11, 2018, http://www.newsweek .com/trumps-full-list-racist-comments-about-immigrants-muslims-and-others-779061.

33. *The Federalist Papers* (New York: Signet Classic, 2003), no. 2 (John Jay).

34. See, for example, Sanford Levinson, *An Argument Open to All: Reading The Federalist in the 21st Century* (New Haven, CT: Yale University Press, 2015), 12–14; Charles Murray, "The United States of Diversity," *Commentary*, June 2015, https://www.commentarymagazine.com/articles/the-united-states-of-diversity. Incidentally, the progressive thinker Levinson is more sympathetic to Jay's concerns about "a requisite degree of homogeneity" than is the neoconservative Murray. Levinson also offers a more qualified measurement of early America's citizenry in his book *Framed*. See Levinson, *Argument*

Open to All, 14; Sanford Levinson, *Framed: America's 51 Constitutions and the Crisis of Governance* (New York: Oxford University, 2002), 95. For an evenhanded assessment of America's diversity during this period, see Richard B. Morris, *The Forging of the Union 1781–1789* (New York: Harper and Row, 1987), 10–30.

35. Murray makes this argument, but to his credit he also emphasizes important cultural and political divisions in America stemming from variances in population density. Murray, "United States of Diversity."

36. Thomas L. Purvis, "The European Ancestry of the United States Population, 1790: A Symposium," *William and Mary Quarterly* 41, no. 1 (January 1984): 85–101.

37. These numbers have been adjusted to reflect a correction I made in the census report's miscounting of Delaware's total population. Because I am using the correct number of 59,096 (rather than 59,094), the total population of the United States (excluding the territories) was 3,893,637. See "1790 Census: Return of the Whole Number of Persons within the Several Districts of the United States," United States Census Bureau, accessed February 2, 2019, https://www.census.gov/library/publications/1793/dec/number-of-persons.html.

38. *Federalist*, no. 2 (Jay). For more on the similarities and differences of early American culture, see David H. Fischer, *Albion's Seed: Four British Folkways in America* (New York: Oxford University Press, 1989); Shain, *Myth of American Individualism*; Roger Finke and Rodney Stark, *The Churching of America 1776–2005* (New Brunswick, NJ: Rutgers University, 2014), 22–35.

39. *Federalist*, no. 14 (James Madison); James Madison to Jacob De La Motta, August 1820, in *The Papers of James Madison Retirement Series*, ed. David B. Mattern et al. (Charlottesville: University of Virginia Press, 2013), II, 81–82 (hereafter cited as *PJMRS*); James Madison, Naturalization, January 1, 1795, in *The Papers of James Madison*, ed. Thomas A. Mason et al. (Charlottesville: University Press of Virginia, 1985), XV, 432–33 (hereafter cited as *PJM*); George Washington to Roman Catholics in America, March 15, 1790, in *The Papers of George Washington, Presidential Series*, ed. Dorothy Twohig et al. (Charlottesville: University Press of Virginia, 1996), V, 299–301; George Washington to the Hebrew Congregation in Newport, Rhode Island, August 18, 1790, in *Papers of George Washington, Presidential Series*, VI, 284–86.

40. *Federalist*, no. 14 (James Madison).

41. James Madison, "Foreign Influence," January 23, 1799, *PJM*, XVII, 217.

42. Alexander Hamilton, "Conversation with George Beckwith," October 1789, in *The Papers of Alexander Hamilton*, ed. Harold C. Syrett (New York: Columbia University, 1961–79), V, 482 (hereafter cited as *PAH*); Alexander Hamilton, New York Ratifying Convention, Third Speech of June 21 (Francis Childs's Version), June 21, 1788, *PAH*, X, 57–58.

43. Hamilton, "The Examination Number VIII," January 12, 1802, *PAH*, XXV, 496. See also Hamilton, "The Examination Number VII," 491–92.

44. See, for example, Glenn Weaver, "Benjamin Franklin and the Pennsylvania Germans," *William and Mary Quarterly*, 3rd ser., 14, no. 4 (October 1957): 536–59; Agrippa, December 28, 1787, in *The Complete Anti-Federalist*, ed. Herbert Storing (Chicago: University of Chicago Press, 1981), 4.6.34 (hereafter cited as Storing); Thomas Jefferson, *Notes on the State of Virginia* (New York: W. W. Norton, 1982), no. 8, 84–85. Jefferson's hardline views on immigration would soften, perhaps because newly arrived immigrants favored his political party. See Hamilton, "Examination Number VII," *PAH*, XXV, 493.

45. James Madison, Naturalization, February 3, 1790, *PJM*, XIII, 17.

46. Ibid.

47. Ibid. See also Naturalization Act, in *The Documentary History of the First Federal Congress of the United States of America, March 4, 1789–March 3, 1791*, ed. Charlene Bangs Bickford and Helen E. Veit (Baltimore: Johns Hopkins University, 1986), 1516. Madison

would support a similar law in 1795. James Madison to Thomas Jefferson, January 11, 1795, *PJM*, XV, 440.

48. James Madison to Lecomte de Lafayette, November 25, 1820, *PJMRS*, II, 158–60. See also James Madison, "Memorandum on an African Colony for Freed Slaves," October 20, 1789, *PJM*, XII, 437–38.

49. Jefferson, *Notes*, no. 14; Phillip W. Magness and Sebastian N. Page, *Colonization after Emancipation: Lincoln and the Movement for Black Resettlement* (Columbia: University of Missouri, 2011).

50. Madison, "Memorandum," *PJM*, XII, 437–38; James Madison, For the National Gazette, ca. December 12, 1791, *PJM*, XVII, 560; James Madison to Lafayette, ca. October 7, 1821, *PJMRS*, II, 405–7; Jefferson, *Notes*, no. 14.

51. James Madison to Thomas L. McKenney, February 10, 1826, *PJMRS*, III, 685–86. Madison considered the option of resettling freed slaves on the western frontier, but he concluded that such a settlement "would be destroyed by the Savages who have a peculiar antipathy to the blacks." Madison, "Memorandum," 438.

52. West, *Political Theory of the American Founding*, 147–48, 265–67; Thomas West, "Immigration: The Founders' View and Today's Challenge," in *The Founders on Citizenship and Immigration* (Lanham, MD: Rowman & Littlefield, 2007), 75–113.

53. West, "Immigration," 98. Other West Coast Straussians such as Kesler and John Marini share this concern and see the Trump presidency as a potential solution. See Charles Kesler, "The Promise of President Trump," *Wall Street Journal*, January 19, 2017, https://www. wsj.com/articles/the-promise-of-president-trump-charles-kesler-1484868295; John Marini, "Donald Trump and the American Crisis," *Claremont Review of Books*, July 22, 2016, http://www.claremont.org/crb/basicpage/donald-trump-and-the-american -crisis. See also Jon Baskin, "The Academic Home of Trumpism," *Chronicle Review*, March 17, 2017, https://www.chronicle.com/article/The-Academic-Home-of-Trumpism /239495.

54. West, "Immigration," 107.

55. Ibid., 110. For a similar perspective, see Arthur M. Schlesinger, *The Disuniting of America: Reflections on a Multicultural Society* (New York: W. W. Norton, 1998); Carol Iannone, "One Nation Divisible," *American Conservative*, May 21, 2007, 25–28.

56. West, "Immigration," 113.

57. Ibid., 79; "Declaration of Independence," National Archive, accessed April 10, 2018, https://www.archives.gov/founding-docs/declaration (emphasis mine).

58. Publius Decius Mus [Anton], "Toward a Sensible, Coherent Trumpism"; Publius Decius Mus [Anton], "The Flight 93 Election."

59. Publius Decius Mus [Anton], "Toward a Sensible, Coherent Trumpism."

60. Ibid (emphasis added). See also West, "Immigration," 80; Jacob Pramuk, "Sen. Lindsey Graham: 'I Said My Piece' to Trump following His Immigration Comments," CNBC, January 12, 2018, https://www.cnbc.com/2018/01/12/sen-lindsey-graham-i-said-my-piece -to-trump-during-immigration-meeting.html; Rosalind S. Helderman, "McCain Praises Obama's Immigration Speech," *Washington Post*, January 29, 2013, https://www.washington post.com/news/post-politics/wp/2013/01/29/mccain-offers-general-praise-for-obamas -immigration-speech.

61. Publius Decius Mus [Anton], "Toward a Sensible, Coherent Trumpism."

62. *Federalist*, no. 34 (Alexander Hamilton); Thomas Jefferson to the Mayor of Alexandria, March 11, 1790, in *The Papers of Thomas Jefferson*, ed. Julian P. Boyd (Princeton, NJ: Princeton University Press, 1961), XVI, 225.

63. "To John Adams from John C. Herbert, 10 June 1798," Founders Online, National Archives, June 10, 1798, https://founders.archives.gov/documents/Adams/99-02-02-2566; George Washington to Joseph Hopkinson, May 27, 1798, in *The Papers of George Washington*,

Retirement Series, ed. W. W. Abbot (Charlottesville: University Press of Virginia, 1998), II, 301; *Federalist*, no. 14 (Madison).

64. James Madison, Presidential Proclamation, June 19, 1812, in *The Papers of James Madison, Presidential Series*, ed. Angela Kreider (Charlottesville: University Press of Virginia, 2008), IV, 489–90; James Madison to Congress, *Papers of James Madison, Presidential Series*, May 25, 1813, VI, 339–43. The importance of intergenerational duty for Madison has also been noted by other scholars. See Drew R. McCoy, *The Last of the Fathers: James Madison and the Republican Legacy* (Cambridge: Cambridge University Press, 1991), 59–60; Lance Banning, *Jefferson and Madison: Three Conversations from the Founding* (Madison: Madison House, 1995), 31–35; Mark E. Kann, *A Republic of Men: The American Founders, Gendered Language, and Patriarchal Politics* (New York: NYU Press, 1998), 91–96.

65. Alexander Hamilton to Marquis de Lafayette, October 6, 1789, *PAH*, V, 425.

66. James Madison to Thomas Jefferson, February 4, 1790, *PJM*, XIII, 18.

67. See, for example, *Federalist*, no. 9 (Hamilton); *Federalist*, no. 47 (Madison).

68. For more on this topic, see Mark C. Henrie, "Thomas Pangle and the Problems of a Straussian Founding," *Modern Age* 28, no. 1 (Winter 1994): 129–30; Daniel P. Moynihan, "The 'New Science of Politics' and the Old Art of Government," *National Affairs* (Winter 1987); Austin Ranney, "'The Divine Science': Political Engineering in American Culture," *American Political Science Review* 70, no. 1 (1976): 140–48; Darren Staloff, *Hamilton, Adams, Jefferson: The Politics of Enlightenment and the American Founding* (New York: Hill and Wang, 2005), 78; Donald S. Lutz, "The Relative Influence of European Writers on Late Eighteenth-Century American Political Thought," *American Political Science Review* 78, no. 1 (1984): 189 97.

69. See, for example, *Federalist*, nos. 1, 9 (Hamilton); *Federalist*, no. 39 (Madison).

70. See, for example, Brutus, October 18, 1787, Storing, 2.9.12; Old Whig, October 27, 1787, Storing, 3.3.20.

71. Baron de Montesquieu, *The Spirit of the Laws*, trans. and ed. Anne M. Cohler et al. (New York: Cambridge University Press, 1989), IV.6, 7, VII.2, VIII.16. See also Baron de Montesquieu, *Considerations on the Causes of the Greatness of the Romans and Their Decline* (Indianapolis: Hackett Publishing, 1999), VIII, IX.

72. Montesquieu, *Spirit of the Laws*, VIII.2, VIII.16. See also Montesquieu, *Considerations*, VIII, IX, XI, XIII.

73. Montesquieu, *Spirit of the Laws*, IX.1–3, XI.6, XIX.27.

74. *Federalist*, nos. 9, 23, 33, 78 (Hamilton); *Federalist*, no. 44 (Madison).

75. *Federalist*, nos. 10, 51 (Madison).

76. See, for example, Brutus, October 18, 1787, Storing, 2.9.4–21; Centinel, October 5, 1787, Storing, 2.7.17–19; Centinel, "The Address and Reasons of Dissent of the Minority of the Convention of Pennsylvania to Their Constituents," December 18, 1787, Storing, 3.11.16–17, 20–31; Federal Farmer, October 8, 1787, Storing, 2.8.14; Old Whig, October 27, 1787, Storing, 3.3.20, 24.

77. James Madison, "Vices of the Political System of the United States," April 1787, *PJM*, IX, 357. See also *Federalist*, nos. 10, 51 (Madison).

78. *Federalist*, no. 10 (Madison).

79. James Madison to Thomas Jefferson, October 24, 1787, *PJM*, X.

80. James Madison, "A Candid State of Parties," September 22, 1792, *PJM*, XIV, 371–72. See also James Madison, "Who Are the Best Keepers of the People's Liberties?" December 22, 1792, *PJM*, XIV, 426–27; James Madison, "The Union: Who Are Its Real Friends?" March 31, 1792, *PJM*, XIV, 274; James Madison, "Spirit of Governments," February 18, 1792, *PJM*, XIV, 233–34; James Madison, "Property," March 27, 1792, *PJM*, XIV, 267.

81. *Federalist*, no. 51 (Madison).

82. *Federalist*, no. 14 (Madison). See also Ibid., nos. 55, 57; James Madison, Virginia Ratifying Convention, June 20, 1788, *PJM*, XI; James Madison, "Charters," January 18, 1792, *PJM*, XIV; James Madison, "Political Reflections," February 23, 1799, *PJM*, vol. 14, 238–39; James Madison, "Government of the United States," February 6, 1792, *PJM*, vol. 14.

83. Madison, "Consolidation," December 3, 1791, *PJM*, XIV.

84. Madison to Jefferson, October 24, 1787. Madison also used the terms "practicable sphere" and "practical sphere." See *Federalist*, no. 51 (Madison). For more on the topic of Madison's "practical sphere," see Tiffany Jones Miller, "James Madison's Republic of 'Mean Extent' Theory: Avoiding the Scylla and Charybdis of Republican Government," *Polity* 39, no. 4 (2007): 545–69; Teena Gabrielson, "James Madison's Psychology of Public Opinion," *Political Research Quarterly* 62, no. 3 (2009): 434.

85. *Federalist*, no. 10 (Madison). For more on this topic, see Douglas W. Jaenicke, "Madison v. Madison: The Party Essays v. Federalist Papers," in *Reflections on the Constitution*, ed. Richard Maidment and John Zvesper (Manchester: Manchester University Press, 1989), 118–30; Colleen Sheehan, *James Madison and the Spirit of Republican Self-Government* (New York: Cambridge University Press, 2009), 80–81, 103–6, 167, 170; West, *Political Theory of the American Founding*, chaps. 8–13.

86. *Federalist*, no. 51 (Madison); James Madison, Import Duties, April 17, 1789, *PJM*, XII, 85–87; James Madison, "Parties," January 23, 1792, *PJM*, XIV, 197; Madison, "A Candid State of Parties"; Madison, "Consolidation"; James Madison, "Public Opinion," December 19, 1791, *PJM*, XIV, 170; James Madison to Samuel H. Smith, November 4, 1826, in *Letters and Other Writings of James Madison* (Philadelphia: Lippincott, 1867), III, 533; James Madison et al., "Report of the Board of Commissioners for the University of Virginia to the Virginia General Assembly, [4 August] 1818," *PJMRS*, I, 326–40.

87. Montesquieu, *Spirit of the Laws*, VIII.2; Montesquieu, *Considerations*, IX, XI; *Federalist*, no. 10 (Madison); *Federalist*, nos. 1, 68, 85 (Hamilton). For more on this topic, see Nicholas W. Drummond, "Plutocrats and Demagogues," *Starting Points Journal*, June 26, 2017, http://startingpointsjournal.com/plutocrats-and-demagogues-the-prophetic-warning-of -montesquieu.

88. For more on plutocracy, see Martin Gilens and Benjamin I. Page, "Testing Theories of American Politics: Elites, Interest Groups, and Average Citizens," *Perspectives on Politics* 12, no. 3 (2014): 565; Jacob S. Hacker and Paul Pierson, *Winner-Take-All Politics: How Washington Made the Rich Richer—and Turned Its Back on the Middle Class* (New York: Simon and Schuster, 2010). For more on divide-and-rule politics, see David Rieff, "Multiculturalism's Silent Partner: It's the Newly Globalized Consumer Economy, Stupid," *Harper's*, August 1993, 62–72; Berndt Ostendorff, *Multiculturalism in Transit: A German-American Exchange* (New York: Berghahn Books, 1998), 62; Todd Gitlin, *The Twilight of Common Dreams: Why America Is Wracked by Culture Wars* (New York: Metropolitan Books, 1995).

89. See, for example, "The Partisan Divide on Political Values Grows Even Wider," Pew Research Center, October 5, 2017, www.people-press.org/2017/10/05/the-partisan-divide -on-political-values-grows-even-wider; David Wasserman, "Purple America Has All but Disappeared," FiveThirtyEight, March 8, 2017, https://fivethirtyeight.com/features/purple -america-has-all-but-disappeared.

90. See, for example, Agrippa, November 23, 1787, Storing, 4.6.5; Agrippa, November 27, 1787, Storing, 4.6.16–17; Agrippa, January 11, 1788, Storing, 4.6.48; Brutus, October 18, 1787, Storing, 2.9.14–16, 19; Cato, October 25, 1787, Storing, 2.6.16–20; Centinel, October 5, 1787, Storing, 2.7.17–19, 22.

91. See, for example, A Farmer, March 7, 1788, in *The Essential Antifederalist*, ed. William B. Allen and Gordon Lloyd (Lanham, MD: Rowman & Littlefield Publishers, 2001), 127.

8. WHY THE ALT RIGHT IS NOT GOING ANYWHERE (REGARDLESS OF WHAT WE CALL IT)

1. Steven Pinker, "Political Correctness Is Redpilling America," excerpted from Spiked Magazine's "Unsafe Space Tour" panel discussion at Harvard University, YouTube, January 2, 2018, video, 8:07, https://www.youtube.com/watch?v=kTiRnbNT5uE; Joe Rogan and Steven Pinker, "The Intelligence of the Alt-Right," YouTube, February 5, 2018, video, 6:58, https://www.youtube.com/watch?v=HXATSgZuMS4.

2. Jesse Singal, "Social Media Is Making Us Dumber. Here's Exhibit A," *New York Times*, January 11, 2018, https://www.nytimes.com/2018/01/11/opinion/social-media-dumber-steven-pinker.html.

3. Angela Nagle, *Kill All Normies: Online Culture Wars from 4Chan and Tumblr to Trump and the Alt-Right* (Winchester, UK: Zero Books, 2017).

4. "It's Okay to Be White," Know Your Meme, 2019, https://knowyourmeme.com/memes/its-okay-to-be-white. There is evidence that some outlets are becoming more strategically savvy in their response to some of these initiatives; for example, an anti–pit bull campaign that linked pit bull incidents with racial differences was not picked up and spread widely by the media. "AntiPit: Addressing the Pit Bull Question - Wild Goose," YouTube, May 18, 2018, video, 34:44, https://www.youtube.com/watch?v=GM9eUpDG9h4.

5. The Streisand effect refers to a process whereby "an attempt to hide, remove, or censor a piece of information has the unintended consequence of publicizing the information more widely, usually facilitated by the Internet." Wikipedia, s.v. "Streisand effect," last modified August 28, 2019, https://en.wikipedia.org/wiki/Streisand_effect.

6. See Jonathan Bowden, "Stewart Home: Communism, Nihilism, Neoism, and Decadence," Counter-Currents Publishing, February 13, 2010, https://www.counter-currents.com/2014/08/stewart-home/.

7. Nagle, *Kill All Normies*, 52.

8. Bowden, "Stewart Home."

9. See "The White Nationalist Manifesto," Counter-Currents Publishing, accessed May 19, 2019, https://www.counter-currents.com/the-white-nationalist-manifesto/.

10. Stewart Home, *The Assault on Culture: Utopian Currents from Lettrisme to Class War* (London: Aporia Press and Unpopular Books, 1988); Jan Zielonka, *Counter-Revolution: Liberal Europe in Retreat* (Oxford: Oxford University Press, 2018).

11. Andrew Hussey, *The Game of War: The Life and Death of Guy Debord* (London: Random House, 2001); Vincent Kaufmann, *Guy Debord: Revolution in the Service of Poetry* (Minneapolis: University of Minneapolis Press, 2006); Andy Merrifield, *Guy Debord* (London: Reaktion Books, 2005).

12. Richard T. Marcy, "Breaking Mental Models as a Form of Creative Destruction: The Role of Leader Cognition in Radical Social Innovations," *Leadership Quarterly* 26, no. 3 (2015): 370–85.

13. Simon Chapman, *Public Health Advocacy and Tobacco Control: Making Smoking History* (London: Wiley-Blackwell, 2017), 276–77.

14. Marcy, "Breaking Mental Models."

15. Jared Taylor, *Paved with Good Intentions: The Failure of Race Relations in Contemporary America* (New York: Carroll & Graf Publishers, 1992); Jared Taylor, *White Identity: Racial Consciousness in the 21st Century* (Oakton, VA: New Century Books, 2011); Greg Johnson, *North American New Right*, vol. 2 (San Francisco: Counter-Currents Publishing, 2018); Kevin B. MacDonald, *The Culture of Critique: An Evolutionary Analysis of Jewish Involvement in Twentieth-Century Intellectual and Political Movements* (Bloomington: 1st Books Library, 2002).

16. See the YouTube channel of Walt Bismarck, https://www.youtube.com/channel /UCLziPZRfH3CZEozrVBo7BKw/videos.

17. Richard T. Marcy and Valerie J. D'Erman, "The European 'New Right' as Radical Social Innovation," *Journal for the Study of Radicalism* 13, no. 2 (2019): 65–90.

18. It is clear that some members of the Alt Right espouse white supremacist views, but there appear to be others that do not, with both groups often employing very different strategies to effect political influence. While a more in-depth analysis of the varying political beliefs of Alt Right members is beyond the scope of this chapter (the focus here being more on tactical and psychological concerns), an excellent review of the Alt Right can be found in George Hawley, *Making Sense of the Alt Right* (New York: Columbia University Press, 2017).

19. Kevin Lewin, "Frontiers in Group Dynamics: Concept, Method and Reality in Social Science; Social Equilibria and Social Change," *Human Relations* 1, no. 1 (1947): 5–41. https://doi.org/10.1177/001872674700100103.

20. Marcy, "Breaking Mental Models."

21. Ibid.

22. Examples here include (but are not limited to) public disagreements between Richard Spencer and Patrick Casey of *Identity Evropa*, Greg Johnson and Richard Spencer, and *Arktos* and Greg Johnson.

23. Marcy defined détournement as "appropriating everyday cultural materials (for example, magazines, cartoons, and films) and then reworking them to expose the spectacular nature of them (spectacular here used in the sense of being a part of the Spectacle) as well as have them serve a more Situationist purpose. This was often accomplished through different techniques such as collage (juxtaposing various sensational images) and editing (such as changing the word balloons of characters within cartoons and comic books, or the use of dubbing in films, to reflect Situationist positions)." Marcy, "Breaking Mental Models," 380.

24. Home, *Assault on Culture*, 37.

25. Marcy "Breaking Mental Models."

26. *Can Dialectics Break Bricks? (La dialectique peut-elle casser des briques?)*, directed by René Viénet (France, 1973), film.

27. Erica Gabrielle Foldy, Laurie Goldman, and Sonia Ospina, "Sensegiving and the Role of Cognitive Shifts in the Work of Leadership," *Leadership Quarterly* 19, no. 5 (2008): 514–29.

28. Robert Maranto and Patrick J. Wolf, "Cops, Teachers, and the Art of the Impossible: Explaining the Lack of Diffusion of Innovations That Make Impossible Jobs Possible," *Public Administration Review* 73, no. 2 (2013): 230–40.

29. See "Paul Nehlen and the Red Pill," YouTube, December 31, 2017, video, 11:55 mins, https://www.youtube.com/watch?v=3MU7LEXBzoM.

30. Two relevant Millennial Woes vlog examples are "Alt-Right: Identity, Community, Ideology," YouTube, September 13, 2017, video, https://www.youtube.com/watch?v =jACJ0ycUlZk (beginning at 19:00 minutes); and "Urban Progressive Hatred of the Local and Innocent (I)," YouTube, September 11, 2017, video, 14:40, https://www.youtube.com /watch?v=WBYuGJkEvV0.

31. Dennis Roddy, "Jared Taylor, a Racist in the Guise of 'Expert,'" *Pittsburgh Post-Gazette*, January 23, 2005, http://www.post-gazette.com/life/dennis-roddy/2005/01/23 /Jared-Taylor-a-racist-in-the-guise-of-expert/stories/200501230176; quotes in this sentence are from the Southern Poverty Law Center (SPLC), "Jared Taylor," August 17, 2018, https://www.splcenter.org/fighting-hate/extremist-files/individual/jared-taylor.

32. Gary A. Yukl, *Leadership in Organizations*, 7th ed. (Englewood Cliffs, NJ: Prentice Hall, 2009).

33. As seen in Leighton Woodhouse's "Trumpland: Kill All Normies" video at the 37:12 minute mark, https://vimeo.com/263452186.

34. For example, the *New York Times* published an article on the dark web that featured a number of intellectuals frequently associated with the Alt Lite brand and was immediately roundly criticized. See Bari Weiss, "Meet the Renegades of the Intellectual Dark Web," *New York Times*, May 8, 2018, https://www.nytimes.com/2018/05/08/opinion/intellectual -dark-web.html; and John Bonazzo, "NY Times 'Intellectual Dark Web' Story Savaged on Twitter—Even by Paper's Staffers," Observer, May 8, 2018, http://observer.com/2018/05 /new-york-times-bari-weiss-intellectual-dark-web-twitter/.

35. Some prominent examples include "Richard Spencer, Styx and Sargon Have a Chat - Andy and JF moderate," YouTube, January 4, 2018, video, 4:38, https://www.youtube .com/watch?v=UiUH-tWHbr8; "Extended Interview: Jorge Ramos Talks Race with Jared Taylor," on the American Renaissance YouTube channel, October 31, 2016, video, 22:21, https://www.youtube.com/watch?v=0T4jssO9t-0.

36. U.N.E.F. Strasbourg, "On the Poverty of Student Life," Nothingness.org, accessed May 19, 2019, http://library.nothingness.org/articles/SI/en/display/4.

37. George Hawley, "The Alt-Right Is Not Who You Think They Are," *American Conservative*, August 25, 2017, http://theamericanconservative.com/articles/the-alt-right-is-not -who-you-think-it-is/.

38. De Dreu, Carsten K. W., and Michael A. West, "Minority Dissent and Team Innovation: The Importance of Participation in Decision Making," *Journal of Applied Psychology* 86, no. 6 (2001): 1191–201; Antonis Gardikiotis, "Minority Influence," *Social and Personality Psychology Compass* 5, no. 9 (2011): 679–93, doi:10.1111/j.1751-9004.2011.00377; Serge Moscovici, "Toward a Theory of Conversion Behavior," *Advances in Experimental Social Psychology* 13 (1980): 209–39, https://doi.org/10.1016/S0065-2601(08)60133-1.

39. Jonathan Capehart, "A New Survey Shows White Millennials Think a Lot More Like Whites Than Millennials," *Washington Post*, October 31, 2017, https://www.washingtonpost. com/blogs/post-partisan/wp/2017/10/31/a-new-survey-shows-white-millennials -think-a-lot-more-like-whites-than-millennials/?noredirect=on&utm_term=.e7c17b3914cb.

40. Damon Centola, Joshua Becker, Devon Brackbill, and Andrea Baronchelli, "Experimental Evidence for Tipping Points in Social Convention," *Science* 360, no. 6393 (2018): 1116–119, doi:10.1126/science.aas8827.

41. Patrick S. Forscher and Nour Kteily, "A Psychological Profile of the Alt-Right," January 23, 2018, doi:10.31234/osf.io/c9uvw.

42. Michael Edison Hayden, "Great White Nope," *PocketMags*, March 30, 2018.

9. THE UNWANTED SOUTHERN CONSERVATIVES

1. David Gordon, "Southern Cross: The Meaning of the Mel Bradford Moment," *American Conservative*, April 1, 2010, http://www.theamericanconservative.com/articles /southern-cross/.

2. David Frum, "Culture Clash on the Right," *Wall Street Journal*, June 2, 1989; and Gordon, "Southern Cross: The Meaning of the Mel Bradford Moment." Although George Wallace ran for president on four occasions, 1964–1976, most prominent old-line Southern conservatives in the Democratic Party did not publicly support his candidacy. Bradford was one of the few academics who supported Wallace.

3. Elliott Johnson, David Walker, and Daniel Gray, *Historical Dictionary of Marxism. Historical Dictionaries of Religions, Philosophies, and Movements*, 2nd ed. (Lanham, MD: Rowman & Littlefield, 2014), 294; and also generally, Leon Trotsky, *The Permanent Revolution: Results and Prospects* (New York: Pathfinder Press, 1974).

4. Paul Buhle, "Lovestone's Thin Red Line," *The Nation*, May 6, 1999, https://www.thenation.com/article/lovestones-thin-red-line/.

5. Ted Morgan, *A Covert Life: Jay Lovestone: Communist, Anti-Communist, and Spymaster* (New York: Random House, 1999), 4–6.

6. Quoted by Paul Gottfried, "Dancing on a Hero's Grave," Takimag.com, May 29, 2007. http://ww.takimag/contributor/Gottfried/8/.

7. See Irving Kristol, "American Conservatism, 1945–1995," *Public Interest*, Fall 1995.

8. Russell Kirk, "The Neoconservatives: An Endangered Species," Heritage Foundation, December 15, 1988, https://www.heritage.org/political-process/report/the-neoconservatives-endangered-species. In response to Kirk's comments, Midge Decter, wife of Norman Podhoretz and director of the neoconservative-oriented Committee for the Free World, denounced his remark as "a bloody piece of anti-Semitism." See John Judis, "The Conservative Crackup," *American Prospect*, Fall 1990, http://prospect.org/article/conservative-crackup.

9. Albert Fried, *Communism in America: A History in Documents* (New York: Columbia University Press, 1997), 7.

10. Allan Bloom, quoted in Paul Gottfried, *War and Democracy: Selected Essays, 1975–2012* (London: Arktos Media, 2012), 110.

11. See, for example, Jonah Goldberg, "America Is Not as Intolerant as We Make It Out to Be," *National Review*, April 20, 2018, https://www.nationalreview.com/2018/04/america-not-most-racist-sexist-nation-progress-made/#slide-1; Seth Stevenson, "The Many Faces of Ben Shapiro," Slate, January 24, 2018, https://slate.com/news-and-politics/2018/01/is-ben-shapiro-a-conservative-liberals-can-count-on.html; and Guy Benson, "SCOTUS Rules 7–2 against Anti-religious Bullying, but Punts on Key Legal Question," Townhall, June 4, 2018, https://townhall.com/tipsheet/guybenson/2018/06/04/scotus-sides-with-christian-baker-72-what-the-ruling-does-and-doesnt-mean-n2487144?utm_source=thdailypm&utm_medium=email&utm_campaign=nl_pm&newsletterad.While Benson defends the Supreme Court decision supporting the Christian bakers' refusal to bake an individualized cake for a gay wedding, he also declares "some of us [conservatives] support LGBT rights," an increasing number within the conservative movement. Benson is openly gay.

12. M. E. Bradford, "The Heresy of Equality: Bradford Replies to Jaffa," *Modern Age* 20 (Winter 1976): 62–77, https://www.unz.com/print/ModernAge-1976q1-00062.

13. Richard Weaver, "Two Types of American Individualism," reprinted in *The Southern Essays of Richard M. Weaver*, ed. George M. Curtis III and James J. Thompson Jr. (Indianapolis: Liberty Press, 1987), 82, 102. See also, generally, Weaver, *The Southern Tradition at Bay: A History of Post-Bellum Thought* (New Rochelle, NY: Arlington House, 1968).

14. Peter d'Abrosca, "Daily Wire Tries to Coerce Jerry Falwell Jr. to Drop Corey Stewart Endorsement," Big League Politics, June 6, 2018, https://bigleaguepolitics.com/texts-daily-wire-tries-to-coerce-jerry-falwell-jr-to-drop-corey-stewart-endorsement/.

15. Victor Davis Hanson, "The Confederate Mind," *National Review*, March 20, 2018, https://www.nationalreview.com/2018/03/progressives-elizabeth-warren-hillary-clinton-race-based-worldview/.

16. See Gary Dorrien, *The Neoconservative Mind: Politics, Culture, and the War of Ideology* (Philadelphia: Temple University Press, 1993), 150–55, for a discussion of Podhoretz's controversial essay, "My Negro Problem—and Ours," *Commentary* 35, no. 2 (February 1963).

17. See Boyd Cathey, "Rejecting Progressivism by Recovering the Fullness of the American Past: Senator Sam Ervin," *My Corner by Boyd Cathey* (blog), October 23, 2017, http://boydcatheyreviewofbooks.blogspot.com/2017/10/october-23-2017-my-corner-by-boyd.html.

18. Stassa Edwards, "Lindsey Graham: GOP Should Change Its Position on Gay Marriage," Jezebel, June 28, 2015, https://jezebel.com/lindsey-graham-gop-should-change-its -position-on-gay-m-1714496783.

19. Eugene Scott, "Graham: 'Flag Had to Come Down. And Thank God That It Has,'" CNN, July 9, 2015, https://www.cnn.com/2015/07/09/politics/confederate-flag-2016 -south-carolina-lindsey-graham/index.html.

20. "Pastor John C. Hagee," Christians United for Israel, accessed May 19, 2019, https:// www.cufi.org/impact/leadership/executive-board/pastor-john-hagee/.

21. See Boyd Cathey, "Thoughts on Charlottesville and What It Means for Us," Unz Review, August 15, 2017, http://www.unz.com/article/thoughts-on-charlottesville-and -what-it-means-for-us/. Among neoconservative pundits Ben Shapiro has been consistent in his attacks on President Trump's response to the Charlottesville incident, accusing the president of turning a blind eye to what he called "increasingly reactionary racial polarization" by not forcefully singling out for condemnation the Alt Right and what he terms white nationalism. Ben Shapiro, "Left Tries to Blame Trump for Charlottesville. Here's Why They're Wrong," Daily Wire, August 14, 2017, https://www.dailywire.com/news/19676/left -tries-blame-trump-charlottesville-terror-ben-shapiro.

22. "Southern Baptists, Others Release Letter on 'Alt-Right' to Trump," Christian Index, October 2, 2017, https://christianindex.org/southern-baptists-others-release-letter-on-alt -right-to-trump/.

23. Max Boot, "I Left the Republican Party. Now I Want Democrats to Take Over," Washington Post, July 4, 2018, https://www.washingtonpost.com/opinions/i-left-the -republican-party-now-i-want-democrats-to-take-over/2018/07/03/54a4007a-7e38-11e8 -b0cf-fffcabcff946_story.html?noredirect=on&utm_term=.99d9ea3eba6a.

24. John Savage, "Where the Confederacy Is Rising Again," Politico, August 10, 2016, https://www.politico.com/magazine/story/2016/08/texas-confederacy-rising -again-214159; Max Greenwood, "Trump on Removing Confederate Statues: They're Trying to Take Away Our Culture," The Hill, August 22, 2017, http://thehill.com/homenews /administration/347589-trump-on-removing-confederate-statues-theyre-trying-to-take -away-our. For a northern perspective, see Sarah McCamon, "Feeling Kinship with the South, Northerners Let Their Confederate Flags Fly," National Public Radio, May 4, 2017, https://www.npr.org/2017/05/04/526539906/feeling-kinship-with-the-south-northerners -let-their-confederate-flags-fly. For a fearful but revealing leftist view, see Mason Adams, "How the Rebel Flag Rose Again—and Is Helping Trump," Politico, June 16, 2016, https://www.politico.com/magazine/story/2016/06/2016-donald-trump-south-confe derate-flag-racism-charleston-shooting-213954.

25. See, for example, Jennifer Agiesta, "Poll: Majority See Confederate Flag as Southern Pride Symbol, Not Racist," CNN, July 2, 2015, https://www.cnn.com/2015/07/02 /politics/confederate-flag-poll-racism-southern-pride/index.html; also, Aaron Moody, "How Does NC Feel about NFL Kneeling, Taking Down Confederate Monuments?," News and Observer, October 3, 2017, http://www.newsobserver.com/news/politics -government/article176748721.html#storylink=cpy; Jeffrey C. Billman, "According to a New Poll, 61 Percent of North Carolina Voters Are Fine with Confederate Monuments," IndyWeek, October 11, 2017, https://www.indyweek.com/indyweek/according-to-a -new-poll-61-percent-of-north-carolina-voters-are-fine-with-confederate-monuments /Content?oid=8681113; and "NPR/PBS News Hour/Marist Poll Results on Charlottesville," August 17, 2017, Marist Poll, http://maristpoll.marist.edu/nprpbs-newshourmarist -poll-results-on-charlottesville/.

10. REPUBLICAN VOTERS AND CONSERVATIVE IDEOLOGY

1. Ben Shapiro, "Is Donald Trump Conservative? Here's the Rundown," Breitbart, January 24, 2016, http://www.breitbart.com/big-government/2016/01/24/is-donald-trump-conservative-heres-the-rundown/.

2. Steven Loeb, "Andrew Breitbart: Donald Trump Is Not a Conservative," Business Insider, April 23, 2011, http://www.businessinsider.com/bill-orielly-andrew-breitbart-donald-trump-video-2011-4.

3. "Latest Bets in the Candidate Casino," Special Report video, April 20, 2015, www.foxnews.com/transcript/2015/04/20/latest-bets-in-candidate-casino/.

4. Jonah Goldberg, "Donald Trump, Statesman," *National Review*, April 21, 2015, http://www.nationalreview.com/corner/417242/donald-trump-statesman-jonah-goldberg.

5. Kevin D. Williamson, "Witless Ape Rides Escalator," *National Review*, June 16, 2015, http://www.nationalreview.com/article/419853/witless-ape-rides-escalator-kevin-d-williamson.

6. Al Weaver, "Glenn Beck: Trump Is 'Not a Conservative. He Is a Progressive,'" Daily Caller, June 17, 2015, http://dailycaller.com/2015/06/17/glenn-beck-trump-is-a-progressive-not-a-conservative-audio/.

7. John Fund, "Is Trump a Double Agent for the Left?" *National Review*, June 21, 2016, http://www.nationalreview.com/article/420093/presidential-candidate-donald-trump-double-agent-for-left.

8. Michael Reagan, "Donald Trump, Fake Conservative," Townhall, July 17, 2015, http://townhall.com/columnists/michaelreagan/2015/07/17/donald-trump-fake-conservative-n2026802.

9. Conor Friedersdorf, "Donald Trump Is No Conservative," *The Atlantic*, July 13, 2015, http://www.theatlantic.com/politics/archive/2015/07/donald-trump-running-for-president/398345/.

10. Matt Walsh, "To Trump Disciples: You're Embarrassing Conservatism and Yourselves," The Blaze, July 20, 2015, http://www.theblaze.com/contributions/to-trump-disciples-youre-embarrassing-conservatism-and-yourselves/.

11. "Against Trump," *National Review*, January 21, 2016, http://www.nationalreview.com/article/430137/donald-trump-conservative-movement-menace.

12. Ibid.

13. National Review Symposium, "Conservatives against Trump," *National Review*, January 21, 2016, http://c7.nrostatic.com/article/430126/donald-trump-conservatives-oppose-nomination.

14. Ibid.

15. Ibid.

16. Ibid.

17. For just one example of this, we can point to Rush Limbaugh's remarks after a Republican-dominated Congress approved a spending bill that funded many programs that conservatives opposed, rather than risk a government shutdown. According to Limbaugh, "This was out-and-out, in-our-face lying, from the campaigns to individual statements made about the philosophical approach Republicans had to all this spending. There is no Republican Party! You know, we don't even need a Republican Party if they're gonna do this. You know, just elect Democrats, disband the Republican Party, and let the Democrats run it, because that's what's happening anyway." Rush Limbaugh, "GOP Sells America down the River," RushLimbaugh.com, December 17, 2015, http://www.rushlimbaugh.com/daily/2015/12/17/gop_sells_america_down_the_river.

18. "Republicans Again Desire a Conservative Presidential Nominee," Gallup, December 21, 2015, http://www.gallup.com/poll/187901/republicans-again-desire-conservative-presidential-nominee.aspx.

19. Philip E. Converse, "The Nature of Belief Systems in Mass Publics (1964)," *Critical Review* 18 (2006): 3.

20. Donald R. Kinder, "Opinion and Action in the Realm of Politics," in *Handbook of Social Psychology*, eds. Gardner Lindzey, Daniel Gilbert, and Susan T. Fisk (Oxford: Oxford University Press, 1998), 778–867.

21. V. O. Key, *The Responsible Electorate: Rationality in Presidential Voting, 1936–1960* (Cambridge, MA: Harvard University Press).

22. Norman H. Nie and Kristi Andersen, "Mass Belief Systems Revisited: Political Change and Attitude Structure," *Journal of Politics* 36 (1974): 540–91.

23. Matthew Levendusky, *The Partisan Sort: How Liberals Became Democrats and Conservatives Became Republicans* (Chicago: University of Chicago Press, 2009).

24. Shawn Treier and D. Sunshine Hillygus, "The Nature of Political Ideology in the Contemporary Electorate," *Public Opinion Quarterly* 73 (2009): 679–703.

25. Edward G. Carmines, Michael J. Ensley, and Michael W. Wagner, "Political Ideology in American Politics: One, Two, or None?" *The Forum* 10, no. 3 (2012): 1–18.

26. Stephen Ansolabehere, Jonathan Rodden, and James M. Snyder Jr., "The Strength of Issues: Using Multiple Measures to Gauge Preference Stability, Ideological Constraint, and Issue Voting," *American Political Science Review* 102 (2008): 215–32.

27. Alan I. Abramowitz and Kyle L. Saunders, "Exploring the Bases of Partisanship in the American Electorate: Social Identity vs. Ideology," *Political Science Quarterly* 59, no. 2 (2006): 175–87.

28. Delia Baldassarri and Andrew Gelman, "Partisans without Constraint: Political Polarization and Trends in American Public Opinion," *American Journal of Sociology* 114, no. 2 (2008): 408–46.

29. Michael S. Lewis-Beck, Helmut Norpoth, William G. Jacoby, and Herbert F. Weisberg, *The American Voter Revisited* (Ann Arbor: University of Michigan Press, 2008).

30. Christopher H. Achen, "Mass Political Attitudes and the Survey Response," *American Political Science Review* 69, no. 4 (1975): 1218–31.

31. David E. RePass, "Searching for Voters along the Liberal-Conservative Continuum: The Infrequent Ideologue and the Missing Middle," *The Forum* 6, no. 2 (2008): 1–49.

32. D. Sunshine Hillygus and Todd G. Shields, *The Persuadable Voter: Wedge Issues in Presidential Campaigns* (Princeton, NJ: Princeton University Press, 2008), 59.

33. Donald R. Kinder and Nathan P. Kalmoe, *Neither Liberal nor Conservative: Ideological Innocence in the American Public* (Chicago: University of Chicago Press, 2017).

34. Geoffrey L. Cohen, "Party over Policy: The Dominating Impact of Group Influence on Political Beliefs," *Journal of Personality and Social Psychology* 85, no. 5 (2003), 808–22.

35. Benjamin Highton and Cindy D. Kam, "The Long-Term Dynamics of Partisanship and Issue Orientations," *Journal of Politics* 73, no. 1 (2011): 202–15.

36. Bruce E. Keith, David B. Magleby, Candice J. Nelson, Elizabeth Orr, Mark C. Westlye, and Raymond E. Wolfinger, *The Myth of the Independent Voter* (Berkeley: University of California Press, 1992).

37. Morris Fiorina, Samuel J. Abrams, and Jeremy C. Pope. *Culture War? The Myth of a Polarized America* (New York: Pearson Longman, 2005).

38. Christopher Ellis and James A. Stimson, *Ideology in America* (Cambridge, UK: Cambridge University Press, 2012).

39. Stephen Miller, "Conservatives and Liberals on Economics: Expected Differences, Surprising Similarities," *Critical Review* 19, no. 1 (2007): 47–64.

40. Lily Rothman, "The Conservative Case for Legalizing Marijuana," *Time*, February 26, 2015, http://time.com/3724131/conservatives-marijuana-buckley/.

41. Pew Research Center, "Contrasting Partisan Perspectives on Campaign 2016," October 2015, http://www.people-press.org/files/2015/10/10-02-2015-2016-release1.pdf.

42. Morris P. Fiorina, Samuel J. Abrams, and Jeremy C. Pope, *Culture War? The Myth of a Polarized America* (New York: Pearson Longman, 2005).

43. For example, Donald Green, Bradley Palmquist, and Eric Schickler, *Partisan Hearts and Minds: Political Parties and the Social Identities of Voters* (New Haven, CT: Yale University Press, 2002).

44. Lilliana Mason, "'I Disrespectfully Agree': The Differential Effects of Partisan Sorting on Social and Issue Polarization," *American Journal of Political Science* 59 (2015): 128–45.

45. Josh Feldman, "Limbaugh: Republicans Overestimated the Importance of Conservative Values to Trump Backers," Mediaite, January 21, 2016, http://www.mediaite.com/online/limbaugh-the-degree-of-conservatism-in-the-republican-party-has-been-overestimated/.

46. Ibid.

AFTERWORD: THE NEVER-ENDING PURGES

1. Michael M. Grynbaum, "The Atlantic Cuts Ties with Conservative Writer Kevin Williamson," *New York Times*, April 5, 2018, https://www.nytimes.com/2018/04/05/business/media/kevin-williamson-atlantic.html.

2. Rich Lowry, "Parting Ways," *National Review*, April 7, 2012, https://www.nationalreview.com/corner/parting-ways-rich-lowry.

3. John Derbyshire, "Radio Derb: Demographic Conservatism, the Pervnado Cultural Revolution, and Black Privilege, Etc.," Vdare, December 15, 2017, https://www.vdare.com/radio-derb/radio-derb-demographic-conservatism-the-pervnado-cultural-revolution-and-black-privilege-etc.

4. Jonah Goldberg, "Golden Days: Standing with Buckley & Co. & at 50 Years Young," *National Review*, October 27, 2005, http://www.nationalreview.com/articles/215784/golden-days/jonah-goldberg. An earlier, far less developed draft of this essay was published in *Radix Journal* (vol. II, 2015) as "The Logic of the Conservative Purges," 3–32; see also John Derbyshire's "Unperson: A Report from the Conservative Movement's Dustbin," ibid., 57–78.

5. E. J. Dionne, "Buckley: The Right's Practical Intellectual," *Washington Post*, October 11, 2005, http://www.washingtonpost.com/wp-dyn/content/article/2005/10/10/AR2005101001204.html.

6. See William F. Buckley Jr., "Goldwater, the John Birch Society, and Me," *Commentary*, March 1, 2008, http://www/commentarymagazine.com/article/goldwater-the-john-birch-society-and-me/.

7. Oliver wrote frequently for both *National Review* and the publications of the John Birch Society but had broken with both organizations by the mid-1960s. See Revilo P. Oliver, *America's Decline: The Education of a Conservative* (London: Londinium, 1981); Nesta Bevan, "The Forgotten Conservative," *Taki's Magazine*, September 22, 2009, http://www.takimag.com/article/the-forgotten-conservative; Dinesh D'Souza, *The End of Racism: Principles for a Multiracial Society* (New York: Free Press, 1995); Jared Taylor, "The 'Tainted' Sources of The End of Racism," American Renaissance, November 1995, http://www.amren.com/archives/back-issues/november-1995/#article2.

8. See Murray Rothbard, *The Betrayal of the American Right* (Auburn, AL: Ludwig von Mises Institute, 2007).

9. William F. Buckley Jr., *In Search of Anti-Semitism* (New York: Continuum, 1992).

10. See Paul E. Gottfried, "When Will Intercollegiate Studies Institute Disassociate Itself from Notorious Racist Russell Kirk?," Vdare, August 29, 2014, http://www.vdare.com /articles/when-will-intercollegiate-studies-institute-disassociate-itself-from-nototrious -racist-russell-kirk; Paul E. Gottfried, "Why I Was Dumped by Conservatism, Inc.," Unz Review, August 20, 2014, https://www.unz.com/pgottfried/why-i-was-dumped-by -conservativism-inc/.

11. David Frum, "Unpatriotic Conservatives," *National Review*, March 25, 2003, http:// archive.frontpagemag.com/readArticle.aspx?ARTID=19130.

12. See Paul E. Gottfried, "A Paleo Epitaph," *Taki's Magazine*, April 7, 2008, http:// takimag.com/article/apaleoepitaph/print#axzz37HaJQ1ll.

13. See Samuel T. Francis, *Essential Writings on Race*, ed. Jared Taylor (Oakton, VA: New Century Foundation, 2008).

14. D'Souza, *End of Racism*; Taylor, "'Tainted' Sources of The End of Racism."

15. Jason Richwine, "IQ and Immigration Policy" (PhD diss., Harvard Graduate School of Art & Sciences, 2009), accessed January 15, 2015, http://www.scribd.com/doc /140239668/IQ-and-Immigration-Policy-Jason-Richwine; "A Talk with Jason Richwine," Washington Examiner, May13, 2013,https://www.washingtonexaminer.com/a-talk-with -jason-richwine-i-do-not-apologize-for-any-of-my-work; Michael Barone, "In Defense of Jason Richwine and Charles Murray," May 16, 2013, https://www.washingtonexaminer.com/michael-barone-in-defense-of-jason-richwine-and-charles-murray.

16. Gary Dorrien, *The Neoconservative Mind: Politics, Culture, and the War of Ideology (Mapping Racism)* (Philadelphia: Temple University Press, 1993).

17. Jeane Kirkpatrick, "Blame America First," speech to Republican National Convention, August 20, 1984, http://www.cnn.com/ALLPOLITICS/1996/conventions/san.diego /facts/GOP.speeches.past/84.kirkpatrick.shtml.

18. M. E. Bradford, *A Better Guide Than Reason: Studies in the American Revolution* (Peru, IL: Sherwood Sugden, 1979).

19. Norman Podhoretz, "My Negro Problem—and Ours," *Commentary*, February 1, 1963, http://www.commentarymagazine.com/article/my-negro-problem-and-ours/.

20. Paul Gottfried, *The Conservative Movement*, rev. ed. (Woodbridge, CT: Twayne Publishers, 1992); Gottfried, "Conservatives: Another Guise of the Right Wing's Counterestablishment," *In These Times*, November 5, 1986, 13; Gottfried, "A Sensitized World Order," *Telos* (Fall 1999): 43–59; Gottfried, "Up from McCarthyism," *Telos* (Fall 1993): 105–8.

21. William F. Buckley Jr., "Murray Rothbard, RIP," *National Review*, February 6, 1995.

22. James Burnham, "Get Us Out!," *National Review*, October 19, 1965, 925. Although this brief against the Birchers offers several reasons for driving the John Birch Society out of the conservative movement, opposition to the war in Vietnam, particularly as stated in Burnham's attacks (925-27) and toward the end of Frank Meyer's comments (918-19), seems to have been the overriding cause. The Society's fixations about an internal Communist conspiracy certainly caused irritation on the establishment Right but never led to a break until its noninterventionist foreign policy became an intolerable point of difference.

Bibliography

Abramowitz, Alan I., and Kyle L. Saunders. "Exploring the Bases of Partisanship in the American Electorate: Social Identity vs. Ideology." *Political Research Quarterly* 59, no. 2 (2006): 175–87. doi:10.1177/106591290605900201.

Achen, Christopher H. "Mass Political Attitudes and the Survey Response." *American Political Science Review* 69, no. 4 (1975): 1218–231. doi:10.2307/1955282.

Adams, Mason. "How the Rebel Flag Rose Again—and Is Helping Trump." *Politico*, June 16, 2016. https://www.politico.com/magazine/story/2016/06/2016-donald-trump-south-confederate-flag-racism-charleston-shooting-213954.

Adesnik, David. "Still Exceptional." *National Review*, February 12, 2014. https://www.nationalreview.com/2014/02/still-exceptional-david-adesnik/.

"Against Trump." *National Review*, January 23, 2016. http://www.nationalreview.com/article/430137/donald-trump-conservative-movement-menace.

Agiesta, Jennifer. "Poll: Majority See Confederate Flag as Southern Pride Symbol, Not Racist." CNN. July 2, 2015. https://www.cnn.com/2015/07/02/politics/confederate-flag-poll-racism-southern-pride/index.html.

Ajzenstat, Janet. *The Canadian Founding: John Locke and Parliament*. Montreal: McGill-Queen's University Press, 2007.

Alberta, Tim. "The Ideas Made It, but I Didn't." *Politico*, May-June 2017. https://www.politico.com/magazine/story/2017/04/22/pat-buchanan-trump-president-history-profile-215042.

Allitt, Patrick. *Catholic Intellectuals and Conservative Politics in America, 1950–1985*. Ithaca, NY: Cornell University Press, 1993.

"Alt-Right: Identity, Community, Ideology." YouTube. September 13, 2017. Video. https://www.youtube.com/watch?v=jACJ0ycUlZk. 29:32 minutes.

Ansolabehere, Stephen, Jonathan Rodden, and James M. Snyder Jr. "The Strength of Issues: Using Multiple Measures to Gauge Preference Stability, Ideological Constraint, and Issue Voting." *American Political Science Review* 102, no. 2 (2008): 215–32. doi:10.1017/s0003055408080210.

"AntiPit: Addressing the Pit Bull Question—Wild Goose." YouTube, May 18, 2018. Video, 34:44. https://www.youtube.com/watch?v=GM9eUpDG9h4.

Bacevich, Andrew J. "Nativist Son." *National Review*, October 11, 1999.

Bailyn, Bernard. "Introduction: A Dialogue by Thomas Hutchinson." *Perspectives in American History* 11 (1975): 343–.

Baldassarri, Delia, and Andrew Gelman. "Partisans without Constraint: Political Polarization and Trends in American Public Opinion." *American Journal of Sociology* 114, no. 2 (2008): 408–46.

Balint, Benjamin. *Running Commentary: The Contentious Magazine That Transformed the Jewish Left into the Neoconservative Right*. New York: PublicAffairs, 2010.

Banning, Lance. *Jefferson and Madison: Three Conversations from the Founding*. Madison: Madison House, 1995.

Barkan, Ross. "The Blood on George W Bush's Hands Will Never Dry. Don't Glorify This Man." *The Guardian*, October 20, 2017. https://www.theguardian.com/commentisfree/2017/oct/20/george-w-bush-donald-trump-speech-blood-hands.

Barone, Michael. "In Defense of Jason Richwine and Charles Murray." May 16, 2013. https://www.washingtonexaminer.com/michael-barone-in-defense-of-jason -richwine-and-charles-murray.

Baskin, Jon. "The Academic Home of Trumpism." *Chronicle Review*, March 17, 2017. https://www.chronicle.com/article/The-Academic-Home-of-Trumpism/239495.

Batnitzky, Leora. *Leo Strauss and Emmanuel Levinas: Philosophy and the Politics of Revelation*. Cambridge: Cambridge University Press, 2006.

Benedict XVI. "Letter of His Holiness Benedict XVI to the Bishops on the Occasion of the Publication of the Apostolic Letter 'Motu Proprio Data' Summorum Pontificum on the Use of the Roman Liturgy prior to the Reform of 1970." The Holy See. July 7, 2007. https://w2.vatican.va/content/benedict-xvi/en/letters/2007/documents/hf_ben-xvi _let_20070707_lettera-vescovi.html.

Bennett, William J., ed. *The Spirit of America*. New York: Touchstone, 1997.

Bennett, William J., Linda Chavez, Angelo M. Codevilla, Edward J. Erler, and Stanley Kurtz. "Immigration and American Exceptionalism." *Claremont Review of Books*. 2013. Accessed May 17, 2019. http://www.claremont.org/crb/article/immigration -and-american-exceptionalism/.

Benson, Guy. "SCOTUS Rules 7–2 against Anti-religious Bullying, but Punts on Key Legal Question." Townhall. June 4, 2018. https://townhall.com/tipsheet/guybenson /2018/06/04/scotus-sides-with-christian-baker-72-what-the-ruling-does-and -doesnt-mean-n2487144?utm_source=thdailypm&utm_medium=email&utm _campaign=nl_pm&newsletterad.

Berger, Carl. *The Sense of Power: Studies in the Ideas of Canadian Imperialism, 1867–1914*. Toronto: University of Toronto Press, 1970.

Berger, Peter, and Richard John Neuhaus. *Movement and Revolution*. New York: Doubleday, 1970.

Berns, Walter. *Making Patriots*. Chicago: University of Chicago Press, 2001.

Bethell, Tom. "The Case for Buchanan." *National Review*, March 2, 1992.

Bevan, Nesta. "The Forgotten Conservative." *Taki's Magazine*, September 22, 2009. http:// www.takimag.com/article/the-forgotten-conservative.

"Beyond the Reach of Majorities: Closed Questions in the Open Society." WorldCat. March 1, 2019. https://www.worldcat.org/title/beyond-the-reach-of-majorities -closed-questions-in-the-open-society/oclc/14643887.

Billman, Jeffrey C. "According to a New Poll, 61 Percent of North Carolina Voters Are Fine with Confederate Monuments." *IndyWeek*, October 11, 2017. https://www .indyweek.com/indyweek/according-to-a-new-poll-61-percent-of-north-carolina -voters-are-fine-with-confederate-monuments/Content?oid=8681113.

Bliese, John R. E. "Richard M. Weaver, Russell Kirk, and the Environment." *Modern Age* 38, no. 2 (Winter 1996): 148–58.

Bloom, Allan. *The Closing of the American Mind: How Higher Education Has Failed Democracy and Impoverished the Souls of Today's Students*. New York: Simon and Schuster Paperbacks, 2012.

——. "Justice: John Rawls versus the Tradition of Political Philosophy." In *Giants and Dwarfs*. New York: Simon and Schuster, 1990.

Bonazzo, John. "NY Times 'Intellectual Dark Web' Story Savaged on Twitter—Even by Paper's Staffers." Observer. May 8, 2018. http://observer.com/2018/05/new-york -times-bari-weiss-intellectual-dark-web-twitter/.

Bond, Paul. "Why Dinesh D'Souza's 'America' Features Clips of Matt Damon, Woody Harrelson." Hollywood Reporter. July 5, 2014. https://www.hollywoodreporter .com/news/why-dinesh-dsouzas-america-features-716708.

Boot, Max. "I Left the Republican Party. Now I Want Democrats to Take Over." *Washington Post*, July 4, 2018. https://www.washingtonpost.com/opinions/i-left-the -republican-party-now-i-want-democrats-to-take-over/2018/07/03/54a4007a-7e38 -11e8-b0ef-fffcabeff946_story.html?noredirect=on&utm_term=.99d9ea3eba6a.

——. "We Didn't Kick Britain's Ass to Be This Kind of Country." *Foreign Policy*, July 3, 2017. http://foreignpolicy.com/2017/07/03/we-didnt-kick-britains-ass-to-be-this -kind-of-country.

Bowden, Jonathan. "Stewart Home: Communism, Nihilism, Neoism, and Decadence." Counter-Currents Publishing. February 13, 2010. https://www.counter-currents .com/2014/08/stewart-home/.

Bradford, M. E. *A Better Guide Than Reason: Studies in the American Revolution.* La Salle, IL: S. Sugden, 1979.

——. "The Heresy of Equality: Bradford Replies to Jaffa." *Modern Age*, Winter 1967, 62–77. https://www.unz.com/print/ModernAge-1976q1-00062.

——. "It's George Will Who's Being Shrill." *Washington Post*, December 12, 1981. https:// www.washingtonpost.com/archive/politics/1981/12/12/its-george-will-whos -being-shrill/414705c8-543a-4a0a-bc1b-48b070b942cc/?utm_term=.4cf02c89dfde.

——. "Publication." Unz Review. 1967. Accessed May 19, 2019. https://www.unz.com /print/ModernAge-1976q1-00062.

Brands, H. W. *The Strange Death of American Liberalism.* New Haven, CT: Yale University Press, 2010.

Brookhiser, Richard. "Waiting for Righty." *National Review*, January 20, 1992.

Brooks, David. "The American Idea and Today's GOP." *New York Times*, September 25, 2015. https://www.nytimes.com/2015/09/25/opinion/david-brooks-the-american -idea and-todays-gop.html.

Buchanan, Patrick J. "But Who Was Right—Rudy or Ron?" Patrick J. Buchanan—Official Website. May 18, 2007. http://buchanan.org/blog/pjb-but-who-was-right-—rudy -or-ron-759.

——. "A Crossroads in Our Country's History." Speech, New Hampshire State Legislative Office Building, December 10, 1991.

——. *A Republic, Not an Empire: Reclaiming America's Destiny.* Washington, DC: Regnery Pub., 2002.

Buckley, William F., Jr. "Buchanan and the GOP." *National Review*, March 25, 1996.

——. "Contemporary Challenges and the Social Order." In *American Conservative Thought in the Twentieth Century.* New York: Bobbs-Merrill, 1970.

——. "Goldwater, the John Birch Society, and Me." *Commentary*, March 1, 2008. http:// www/commentarymagazine.com/article/goldwater-the-john-birch-society-and -me/.

——. "Murray Rothbard, RIP." *National Review*, February 6, 1995.

——. *In Search of Anti-Semitism.* New York: Continuum, 1992.

Buhle, Paul. "Lovestone's Thin Red Line." *The Nation*, May 6, 1999. https://www.thenation .com/article/lovestones-thin-red-line/.

Burke, Edmund. *Reflections on the Revolution in France.* Edited by Conor Cruise O'Brien. Hammondsworth: Penguin, 1982.

——. *Reflections on the Revolution in France.* In *The Portable Edmund Burke,* ed. Isaac Kramnick. New York: Penguin Books, 1999.

Burnham, James. "Get Us Out!" *National Review*, October 19, 1965.

——. *The Managerial Revolution.* Harmondsworth: Penguin, 1962. First published 1941.

——. "The Struggle for the World." In *American Conservative Thought in the Twentieth Century.* Edited by William F. Buckley Jr. Indianapolis: Bobbs-Merrill, 1970.

Burns, Tony, and James Connelly, eds. *The Legacy of Leo Strauss*. Charlottesville, VA: Imprint Academic, 2016.

Bush, George W. "Full Text: George W. Bush Speech on Trumpism." *Politico*, October 19, 2017. https://www.politico.com/story/2017/10/19/full-text-george-w-bush-speech-trump-243947.

Can Dialectics Break Bricks? (La dialectique peut-elle casser des briques?). Directed by René Viénet. France, 1973. Film.

Capehart, Jonathan. "A New Survey Shows White Millennials Think a Lot More Like Whites Than Millennials." *Washington Post*, October 31, 2017. https://www.washingtonpost.com/blogs/post-partisan/wp/2017/10/31/a-new-survey-shows-white-millennials-think-a-lot-more-like-whites-than-millennials/?noredirect=on&utm_term=.e7c17b3914cb.

Carmines, Edward G., Michael J. Ensley, and Michael W. Wagner. "Political Ideology in American Politics: One, Two, or None?" *The Forum* 10, no. 3 (2012): 1–18. doi:10.1515/1540-8884.1526.

Cathey, Boyd. "Thoughts on Charlottesville and What It Means for Us." Unz Review. August 15, 2017. http://www.unz.com/article/thoughts-on-charlottesville-and-what-it-means-for-us/.

Ceaser, James W. "Foundational Concepts and American Political Development." In *Nature and History in American Political Development: A Debate*, edited by James W. Ceaser and Robert A. Kagan, 3–89. Cambridge, MA: Harvard University Press, 2006.

——. "The Great Divide: American Internationalism and its Opponents." In *Present Dangers: Crisis and Opportunity in American Foreign and Defense Policy*, edited by Robert Kagan and William Kristol, 25–43. San Francisco: Encounter Books, 2000.

Ceaser, James W., and Andrew Busch. *Losing to Win: The 1996 Elections and American Politics*. Lanham: Rowman & Littlefield, 1997.

Centola, Damon, Joshua Becker, Devon Brackbill, and Andrea Baronchelli. "Experimental Evidence for Tipping Points in Social Convention." *Science* 360, no. 6393 (2018): 1116–119. doi:10.1126/science.aas8827.

Chandrasekaran, Rajiv. "Civilian Analysts Gained Petraeus's Ear While He Was Commander in Afghanistan." *Washington Post*, December 18, 2012. https://www.washingtonpost.com/world/national-security/civilian-analysts-gained-petraeuss-ear-while-he-was-commander-in-afghanistan/2012/12/18/290c0b50-446a-11e2-8061-253bccfc7532_story.html?utm_term=.611be3fb3dcf.

Chapman, Simon. *Public Health Advocacy and Tobacco Control: Making Smoking History*. London: Wiley-Blackwell, 2017.

Chaput, Charles. "The Mortara Affair, Redux." *Jewish Review of Books*, January 29, 2018. https://jewishreviewofbooks.com/articles/2979/mortara-affair-redux/.

C.K. "Why Think-Tanks Are Concerned about a Trump Administration." *The Economist*, November 17, 2016. https://www.economist.com/blogs/democracyinamerica/2016/11/worried-wonks.

Cohen, Geoffrey L. "Party over Policy: The Dominating Impact of Group Influence on Political Beliefs." *Journal of Personality and Social Psychology* 85, no. 5 (2003): 808–22. doi:10.1037/0022-3514.85.5.808.

The Complete Anti-Federalist. Edited by Herbert Storing. Chicago: University of Chicago Press, 1981.

Converse, Philip E. "The Nature of Belief Systems in Mass Publics (1964)." *Critical Review* 18 (2006): 1–75.

Coombs, Nathan. "The Political Theology of Red Toryism." *Journal of Political Ideologies* 16, no. 1 (February 2011): 79–96.

Cooper, Barry. "Did George Grant's Canada Ever Exist?" In *George Grant and the Future of Canada*, edited by Yusuf K. Umar, with foreword by Barry Cooper, 151–64. Calgary: University of Calgary Press, 1992.

——. *It's the Regime, Stupid! A Report from the Cowboy West on Why Stephen Harper Matters*. Toronto: Key Porter Books, 2009.

Cooper, Danny. *Neoconservatism and American Foreign Policy: A Critical Analysis*. Abingdon: Routledge, 2010.

Cuneo, Michael W. *The Smoke of Satan: Conservative and Traditionalist Dissent in Contemporary American Catholicism*. Baltimore: Johns Hopkins University Press, 1999.

D'Abrosca, Peter. "Daily Wire Tries to Coerce Jerry Falwell Jr. to Drop Corey Stewart Endorsement." Big League Politics. June 6, 2018. https://bigleaguepolitics.com/texts -daily-wire-tries-to-coerce-jerry-falwell-jr-to-drop-corey-stewart-endorsement/.

Dart, Ron. *The North American High Tory Tradition*. New York: American Anglican Press, 2016.

Davis, Julie Hirschfeld. "A Senior Republican Senator Admonishes Trump: 'America Is an Idea, Not a Race.'" *New York Times*, January 12, 2018. https://www.nytimes .com/2018/01/12/us/politics/trump-immigration-congress.html.

"Declaration of Independence." National Archive. Accessed April 10, 2018. https://www .archives.gov/founding-docs/declaration.

De Dreu, Carsten K. W., and Michael A. West. "Minority Dissent and Team Innovation: The Importance of Participation in Decision Making." *Journal of Applied Psychology* 86, no. 6 (2001): 1191–201. doi:10.1037//0021-9010.86.6.1191.

Derbyshire, John. "Radio Derb: Demographic Conservatism, the Pervnado Cultural Revolution, and Black Privilege, Etc." Vdare.com. December 15, 2017. https://www .vdare.com/radio-derb/radio-derb-demographic-conservatism-the-pervnado -cultural-revolution-and-black-privilege-etc.

——. "Will National Review Derbyshire Victor Davis Hanson?" Vdare.com. July 23, 2013. http://www.vdare.com/articles/john-derbyshire-wonders-will-national-review -derbyshire-victor-davis-hanson.

Devlin, Roger F. "The Case of Victor Davis Hanson: Farmer, Scholar, Warmonger." http://www.toqonline.com/archives/v3n4/TOQv3n4Devlin.pdf.

Diamond, Martin. "The Federalist." In *History of Political Philosophy*, 2nd ed., edited by Leo Strauss and Joseph Crospey, 631–51. Chicago: Rand McNally, 1972.

Dionne, E. J. "Buckley: The Right's Practical Intellectual." *Washington Post*, October 11, 2005. http://www.washingtonpost.com/wp-dyn/content/article/2005/10/10 /AR2005101001204.html.

The Documentary History of the First Federal Congress of the United States of America, March 4, 1789–March 3, 1791. Edited by Charlene Bangs Bickford and Helen E. Veit. Baltimore: Johns Hopkins University, 1986.

Donadio, Rachel. "On Gay Priests, Pope Francis Asks, 'Who Am I to Judge?'" *New York Times*, July 29, 2013. https://www.nytimes.com/2013/07/30/world/europe/pope -francis-gay-priests.html.

Dorrien, Gary. *The Neoconservative Mind: Politics, Culture, and the War of Ideology*. Philadelphia: Temple University Press, 1993.

Drehle, David Von. "Bennett Reportedly High-Stakes Gambler—Former Education Secretary Lost $8 Million in Past Decade, Magazines Find." *Washington Post*, May 3, 2003.

Drummond, Nicholas W. "Plutocrats and Demagogues," *Starting Points Journal*, June 26, 2017, http://startingpointsjournal.com/plutocrats-and-demagogues-the-prophetic -warning-of-montesquieu.

D'Souza, Dinesh. *The End of Racism: Principles for a Multiracial Society.* New York: Free Press, 1995.

Duchesne, Ricardo. *Canada in Decay: Mass Immigration, Diversity, and the Ethnocide of Euro-Canadians.* London: Black House, 2017.

Edwards, Stassa. "Lindsey Graham: GOP Should Change Its Position on Gay Marriage." *Jezebel.* June 28, 2015. https://jezebel.com/lindsey-graham-gop-should-change-its -position-on-gay-m-1714496783.

Ehrlich, Paul R. *The Population Bomb.* Cutchogue, NY: Buccaneer Books, 1968.

Elder, Larry. "Democrats and the Nazi Card." *RealClear Politics.* November 24, 2016. https://www.realclearpolitics.com/articles/2016/11/24/democrats_and_the_nazi _card_132428. html.

Ellis, Christopher, and James A. Stimson. *Ideology in America.* Cambridge: Cambridge University Press, 2012.

Epatko, Larisa. "How the World Is Reacting to Trump's Use of S***hole." *PBS News Hour.* January 12, 2018. https://www.pbs.org/newshour/world/how-the-world-is-reacting -to-trumps-use-of-shole.

The Essential Antifederalist, ed. William B. Allen and Gordon Lloyd. Lanham, MD: Rowman & Littlefield Publishers, 2001.

"Extended Interview: Jorge Ramos Talks Race with Jared Taylor." American Renaissance YouTube channel, October 31, 2016. Video, 22:21. https://www.youtube.com /watch?v=0T4jssO9t-0.

The Federalist Papers. New York: Signet Classic, 2003.

Feldman, Josh. "Limbaugh: Republicans Overestimated the Importance of Conservative Values to Trump Backers." *Mediaite.* January 21, 2016. http://www.mediaite.com /online/limbaugh-the-degree-of-conservatism-in-the-republican-party-has-been -overestimated/.

Finke, Roger, and Rodney Stark. *The Churching of America 1776–2005.* New Brunswick, NJ: Rutgers University, 2014.

Fiorina, Morris P., Samuel J. Abrams, and Jeremy C. Pope. *Culture War? The Myth of a Polarized America.* Boston: Pearson Longman, 2011.

Fischer, David H. *Albion's Seed: Four British Folkways in America.* New York: Oxford University Press, 1989.

Foldy, Erica Gabrielle, Laurie Goldman, and Sonia Ospina. "Sensegiving and the Role of Cognitive Shifts in the Work of Leadership." *Leadership Quarterly* 19, no. 5 (2008): 514–29. doi:10.1016/j.leaqua.2008.07.004.

Foner, Eric. "Lincoln, Bradford, and the Conservatives." *New York Times,* February 13, 1982. https://www.nytimes.com/1982/02/13/opinion/lincoln-bradford-and-the -conservatives.html.

Forscher, Patrick S., and Nour Kteily. *A Psychological Profile of the Alt-right.* PsyARXiv Preprints, 2018. Retrieved from http://psyarxiv.com/c9uvw

Francis (pope). *Amoris Laetitia.* The Holy See. March 19, 2016. https://w2.vatican.va /content/dam/francesco/pdf/apost_exhortations/documents/papa-francesco _esortazione-ap_20160319_amoris-laetitia_en.pdf.

———. *Evangelii Gaudium: Apostolic Exhortation on the Proclamation of the Gospel in Today's World.* The Holy See. November 24, 2013. https://w2.vatican.va/content /francesco/en/apost_exhortations/documents/papa-francesco_esortazione-ap _20131124_evangelii-gaudium.html.

Francis, Samuel T. *Beautiful Losers: Essays on the Failure of American Conservatism.* Columbia: University of Missouri Press, 1993.

———. *Essential Writings on Race.* Edited by Jared Taylor. Oakton, VA: New Century Foundation, 2008.

——. *Leviathan and Its Enemies: Mass Organization and Managerial Power in Twentieth-Century America.* Arlington, VA: Washington Summit Publishers, 2016.

Franck, Matthew J. "A Lincoln for Our Times." *National Review,* July 19, 2013. https:// www.nationalreview.com/bench-memos/rich-lowrys-lincoln-unbound-matthew -j-franck/.

Frank, Thomas. "Thus Spake Zinsmeister." *New York Times,* August 25, 2006. http://www .nytimes.com/2006/08/25/opinion/25frank.html.

Fried, Albert. *Communism in America: A History in Documents.* New York: Columbia University Press, 1997.

Friedersdorf, Conor. "Donald Trump Is No Conservative." *The Atlantic,* July 13, 2015. http://www.theatlantic.com/politics/archive/2015/07/donald-trump-running-for -president/398345/.

Friedman, Murray. *The Neoconservative Revolution: Jewish Intellectuals and the Shaping of Public Policy.* Cambridge: Cambridge University Press, 2005.

Frum, David. "Culture Clash on the Right." *Wall Street Journal,* June 2, 1989.

——. "Unpatriotic Conservatives." *National Review,* March 25, 2003. https://www .nationalreview.com/2003/03/unpatriotic-conservatives-david-frum/.

Fukuyama, Francis. *America at the Crossroads: Democracy, Power, and the Neoconservative Legacy.* New Haven, CT: Yale University Press, 2007.

——. "Immigrants and Family Values." *Commentary,* May 1, 1993. https://www .commentarymagazine.com/articles/immigrants-and-family-values/.

Fund, John. "Is Trump a Double Agent for the Left?" *National Review,* June 21, 2016. http://www.nationalreview.com/article/420093/presidential-candidate-donald -trump-double-agent-for-left.

Gabrielson, Teena. "James Madison's Psychology of Public Opinion." *Political Research Quarterly* 62, no. 3 (2009): 431–44.

Garamone, Jim. "West Must Encourage Moderate Voices of Islam, Wolfowitz Says." *DOD News.* May 6, 2002. http://archive.defense.gov/news/newsarticle.aspx?id =44093.

Gardikiotis, Antonis. "Minority Influence." *Social and Personality Psychology Compass* 5, no. 9 (2011): 679–93. doi:10.1111/j.1751-9004.2011.00377.

George, Robert P. *The Clash of Orthodoxies: Law, Religion, and Morality in Crisis.* Wilmington, DE: ISI Books, 2001.

——. *In Defense of Natural Law.* New York: Oxford University Press, 1999.

——. *Making Men Moral: Civil Liberties and Public Morality.* Oxford: Clarendon Press, 1995.

George, Robert P., and George Weigel. "An Appeal to Our Fellow Catholics." *National Review,* May 7, 2016. https://www.nationalreview.com/2016/03/donald-trump -catholic-opposition-statement/.

Gilens, Martin, and Benjamin I. Page. "Testing Theories of American Politics: Elites, Interest Groups, and Average Citizens." *Perspectives on Politics* 12, no. 3 (2014): 564–81.

Gitlin, Todd. *The Twilight of Common Dreams: Why America Is Wracked by Culture Wars.* New York: Metropolitan Books, 1995.

Goldberg, Jonah. "America Is Not as Intolerant as We Make It Out to Be." *National Review,* April 20, 2018. https://www.nationalreview.com/2018/04/america-not-most -racist-sexist-nation-progress-made/#slide-1.

——. "Donald Trump, Statesman." *National Review,* April 21, 2015. http://www .nationalreview.com/corner/417242/donald-trump-statesman-jonah-goldberg.

——. "Golden Days: Standing with Buckley & Co. & at 50 Years Young." *National Review,* October 27, 2005. http://www/nationalreview.com/articles/215784/golden-days /jonah-goldberg.

——. "Kevin Williamson, Thought Criminal." *National Review*, April 6, 2018. https://www.nationalreview.com/g-file/kevin-williamson-thought-criminal/.

——. "When Would You Stop Loving America?" *National Review*, July 5, 2017. https://www.nationalreview.com/2017/07/america-can-you-stop-loving-her-if-she-changes/.

Goldman, Samuel. "Fusionism Once and Future." *Modern Age* 59, no. 2 (Spring 2017): 65–74.

Gordon, David. "Southern Cross." *American Conservative*, April 1, 2010. http://www.theamericanconservative.com/articles/southern-cross/.

Gottfried, Paul. *Conservatism in America: Making Sense of the American Right*. New York: Palgrave, 2007.

——. *The Conservative Movement*. Rev. ed. Woodbridge, CT: Twayne Publishers, 1992.

——. "Conservatives: Another Guise of the Right Wing's Counterestablishment." *In These Times*, November 5, 1986.

——. "Dancing on a Hero's Grave." Takimag.com. May 29, 2007. http://ww.takimag/contributor/Gottfried/8/.

April 17, 2007. https://www.unz.com/pgottfried/dancing-on-a-heros-grave/.

——. "Heritage Foundation + the War Industry: What a Pair." *American Conservative*, November 30, 2017. http://www.theamericanconservative.com/articles/heritage-foundation-the-war-industry-what-a-pair/.

——. *Leo Strauss and the Conservative Movement in America: A Critical Appraisal*. New York: Cambridge University Press, 2012.

——. "A Paleo Epitaph." *Taki's Magazine*, March 25, 2003. http://takimag.com/article/apaleoepitaph/print#axzz37HaJQ11l.

——. *Revisions and Dissents: Essays*. DeKalb: Northern Illinois University Press, 2017.

——. *Search for Historical Meaning: Hegel and the Postwar American Right*. Dekalb: Northern Illinois University Press, 1987.

——. "A Sensitized World Order." *Telos* (Fall 1999): 43–59.

——. "Up from McCarthyism." *Telos* (Fall 1993): 105–8.

——. *War and Democracy: Selected Essays, 1975–2012*. London: Arktos Press, 2012.

——. "When Will Intercollegiate Studies Institute Disassociate Itself from Notorious Racist Russell Kirk?" Vdare.com. August 29, 2014. http://www.vdare.com/articles/when-will-intercollegiate-studies-institute-disassociate-itself-from-nototrious-racist-russell-kir.

——. "Why I Was Dumped by Conservatism, Inc." Unz Review, August 20, 2014. https://www.unz.com/pgottfried/why-i-was-dumped-by-conservativism-inc/.

Gottfried, Paul, and Richard B. Spencer. *The Great Purge: The Deformation of the Conservative Movement*. Washington, DC: Washington Summit Publishers, 2015.

Grant, George. "Conversation with George Grant: Canadian Politics." In *George Grant in Process: Essays and Conversations*, edited by Larry Schmidt, 13–21. Toronto: House of Anansi Press, 1978.

——. "A Critique of the New Left." In *The George Grant Reader*, edited by William Christian and Sheila Grant, 84–90. Toronto: University of Toronto Press, 1998.

——. *English-Speaking Justice*. Toronto: House of Anansi Press, 1985.

——. *The George Grant Reader*. Edited by William Christian and Sheila Grant. Toronto: University of Toronto Press, 1998.

——. *Lament for a Nation: The Defeat of Canadian Nationalism*. Ottawa: Carleton University Press, 1991.

——. *Philosophy in the Mass Age*, edited with an introduction by William Christian. Toronto: University of Toronto Press, 1995. First published 1959.

——. *Technology and Empire: Perspectives on North America*. Toronto: House of Anansi Press, 1969.

Green, Donald, Bradley Palmquist, and Eric Schickler. *Partisan Hearts and Minds: Political Parties and the Social Identities of Voters*. New Haven, CT: Yale University Press, 2002.

Green, Joshua. "The Bookie of Virtue." *Washington Monthly*, June 2003. https://washingtonmonthly.com/magazine/june-2003/the-bookie-of-virtue/.

Greenberg, Paul. "Paul Greenberg—Real Hope and Change." Jewish World Review. November 25, 2015. http://www.jewishworldreview.com/cols/greenberg112514.php3.

Greenwood, Max. "Trump on Removing Confederate Statues: They're Trying to Take Away Our Culture." The Hill. August 22, 2017. http://thehill.com/homenews/administration/347589-trump-on-removing-confederate-statues-theyre-trying-to-take-away-our.

Gregg, Samuel. "Global Capitalism versus Christianity? A Response to David Bentley Hart." Public Discourse. May 17, 2016. http://www.thepublicdiscourse.com/2016/05/16979/?utm_source=The Witherspoon Institute&utm_campaign=61c98bdade-RSS_EMAIL_CAMPAIGN&utm_medium=email&utm_term=0_15ce6af37b-61c98bdade-84111297.

Grynbaum, Michael M. "The Atlantic Cuts Ties with Conservative Writer Kevin Williamson." *New York Times*, April 5, 2018. https://www.nytimes.com/2018/04/05/business/media/kevin-williamson-atlantic.html.

Haberman, Clyde. "Pope Denounces the Gulf War as 'Darkness.'" *New York Times*, April 1, 1990.

Hacker, Jacob S., and Paul Pierson. *Winner-Take-All Politics: How Washington Made the Rich Richer—and Turned Its Back on the Middle Class*. New York: Simon and Schuster, 2010.

Hagel, Chuck, and Peter Kaminsky. *America: Our Next Chapter*. New York: Harper Collins, 2008.

Hahn, Julia. "Paul Ryan's Open Borders Push with Luis Gutierrez Exposed in 2013 Video." Breitbart. October 17, 2015. https://www.breitbart.com/big-government/2015/10/17/paul-ryans-open-borders-push-luis-gutierrez-exposed-2013-video/.

Hamilton, Alexander. "Conversation with George Beckwith," October 1789. In *The Papers of Alexander Hamilton*, ed. Harold C. Syrett. New York: Columbia University, 1961–79.

Hanson, Victor Davis. "The Confederate Mind." *National Review*, March 20, 2018. https://www.nationalreview.com/2018/03/progressives-elizabeth-warren-hillary-clinton-race-based-worldview/.

——. "Facing Facts about Race: Young Black Males Are at Greater Risk from Their Peers Than from the Police or White Civilians." *National Review*, July 23, 2013. https://www.nationalreview.com/2013/07/facing-facts-about-race-victor-davis-hanson/.

Harrington, Michael. "Is Capitalism Still Viable?" *Journal of Business Ethics* 1 (1982): 281–84.

——. *The Twilight of Capitalism*. New York: Simon and Schuster, 1976.

Hart, David Bentley. "Mammon Ascendant: Why Global Capitalism Is Inimical to Christianity." First Things. June 1, 2016. https://www.firstthings.com/article/2016/06/mammon-ascendant.

Hartz, Louis. *The Founding of New Societies: Studies in the History of the United States, Latin America, South Africa, Canada, and Australia*. New York: Harcourt Brace Jovanovich, 1964.

The Liberal Tradition in America: An Interpretation of American Political Thought since the Revolution. New York: Harcourt Brace, 1955.

Havers, Grant N. "George Grant and Leo Strauss: Modernist and Postmodernist Conservatisms." *Topia* 8 (Fall 2002): 91–106.

——. *Leo Strauss and Anglo-American Democracy: A Conservative Critique.* DeKalb: Northern Illinois University Press, 2013.

——. "Leo Strauss's Influence on George Grant." In *Athens and Jerusalem: George Grant's Theology, Philosophy, and Politics*, ed. Ian Angus, Ron Dart, and Peg Peters, 124–35. Toronto: University of Toronto Press, 2006.

——. "Marshall McLuhan, George Grant, and the Ancient-Modern-Protestant Quarrel in Canada." In *Liberal Education, Civic Education, and the Canadian Regime*, edited by David Livingstone, 152–60. Montreal: McGill-Queen's University Press, 2015.

Hawley, George. "The Alt-Right Is Not Who You Think They Are." *American Conservative*, August 25, 2017. http://theamericanconservative.com/articles/the-alt-right-is-not-who-you-think-it-is/.

——. *Making Sense of the Alt Right.* New York: Columbia University Press, 2017.

——. *Right-Wing Critics of American Conservatism.* Lawrence: University Press of Kansas, 2016.

Hayden, Michael E. "Great White Nope." *PocketMags*, March 30, 2018.

Hedges, Chris. *American Fascists: The Christian Right and the War on America.* New York: Free Press, 2006.

Heer, Jet. "The Failure of Pro-Trump Intellectualism," *New Republic*, February 28, 2017, https://newrepublic.com/article/140933/failure-pro-trump-intellectualism.

Helderman, Rosalind S. "McCain Praises Obama's Immigration Speech." *Washington Post*, January 29, 2013. https://www.washingtonpost.com/news/post-politics/wp/2013/01/29/mccain-offers-general-praise-for-obamas-immigration-speech.

Henrie, Mark C. "Thomas Pangle and the Problems of a Straussian Founding." *Modern Age* 36.2(Winter 1994): 1: 128–38.

The Heritage Foundation and Affiliates Consolidated Financial Report. Amazonnews.com. December 31, 2016. http://thf-reports.s3.amazonaws.com/2017/Heritage Foundation_16FS_Final.pdf.

Heschel, Abraham J. , Michael Novak, and Robert McAfee. *Vietnam: Crisis of Conscience.* New York: New York Association Press, 1967.

Highton, Benjamin, and Cindy D. Kam. "The Long-Term Dynamics of Partisanship and Issue Orientations." *Journal of Politics* 73, no. 1 (2011): 202–15. doi:10.1017/s0022381610000964.

Hillygus, D. Sunshine, and Todd G. Shields. *The Persuadable Voter: Wedge Issues in Presidential Campaigns.* Princeton, NJ: Princeton University Press, 2009.

Himmelfarb, Gertrude. *The Roads to Modernity: The British, French and American Enlightenments.* New York: Vintage Books, 2004.

Hodge, Nathan. "How the Afghan Surge Was Sold." *WIRED*, December 3, 2009. https://www.wired.com/2009/12/how-the-afghan-surge-was-sold/.

Home, Stewart. *The Assault on Culture: Utopian Currents from Lettrisme to Class War.* London: Aporia Press, 1988.

Horowitz, Gad. "Conservatism, Liberalism, and Socialism in Canada: An Interpretation." *Canadian Journal of Economics and Political Science* 32, no. 2 (1966): 143–71.

Hume, David. *Enquiries Concerning the Principles of the Understanding and the Principles of Morality*, 3rd ed., edited by P.H. Nidditch. Oxford: Oxford University Press, 1987.

——. "Of the Original Contract." In *Essays: Moral, Political, and Literary*, rev. ed., edited by Eugene F. Miller. Indianapolis: Liberty Classics, 1987.

Hussey, Andrew. *The Game of War: The Life and Death of Guy Debord.* London: Random House, 2001.

Hutchinson, Thomas. "A Dialogue between an American and a European Englishman." Edited by Bernard Bailyn. *Perspectives in American History* 11 (1975): 369–410.

Iannone, Carol. "One Nation Divisible." *American Conservative*, May 21, 2007, 25–28.

Ignatieff, Michael. "Human Rights: The Midlife Crisis." *New York Review of Books*, May 20, 1999.

"It's Okay to Be White." Know Your Meme. April 27, 2019. https://knowyourmeme.com /memes/its-okay-to-be-white.

Jaenicke, Douglas W. "Madison v. Madison: The Party Essays v. Federalist Papers." In *Reflections on the Constitution*, edited by Richard Maidment and John Zvesper, 118–30. Manchester: Manchester University Press, 1989.

Jaffa, Harry V. "Aristotle and Locke in the American Founding." *Claremont Review of Books* 1, no. 2 (Winter 2001). https://www.claremont.org/crb/article/aristotle-and -locke-in-the-american-founding/.

——. *Crisis of the House Divided.* Chicago: University of Chicago Press, 1982.

——. *A New Birth of Freedom.* Lanham, MD: Rowman & Littlefield, 2000.

Janofsky, Michael. "The 2004 Campaign: Advertising; Bush-Hitler Ads Draw Criticism." *New York Times*, January 6, 2004, https://www.nytimes.com/2004/01/06/us/the -2004-campaign-advertising-bush-hitler-ads-draw-criticism.html.

Jefferson, Thomas. *Notes on the State of Virginia.* New York: W. W. Norton, 1982.

John Paul II (pope). *Centesimus Annus*, May 1, 1991. https://w2.vatican.va/content/john -paul-ii/en/encyclicals/documents/hf_jp-ii_enc_01051991_centesimus-annus .html.

——. *Evangelium Vitae.* March 25, 1995. http://w2.vatican.va/content/john-paul-ii/en /encyclicals/documents/hf_jp-ii_enc_25031995_evangelium-vitae.html.

Johnson, Adam. "Lockheed Martin-Funded Experts Agree: South Korea Needs More Lockheed Martin Missiles." FAIR. May 8, 2017. https://fair.org/home/lockheed -martin-funded-experts-agree-south-korea-needs-more-lockheed-martin -missiles/.

Johnson, Elliott, David Walker, and Daniel Gray. *Historical Dictionary of Marxism (Historical Dictionaries of Religions, Philosophies, and Movements).* Lanham, MD: Rowman & Littlefield, 2014.

Johnson, Greg. *North American New Right.* Vol. 2. San Francisco: Counter-Currents Publishing, 2018.

Johnson, James Turner, and George Weigel. *Just War and the Gulf War.* Washington, DC: Ethics and Public Policy Center, 1991.

Judis, John. "The Conservative Crackup." *American Prospect*, Fall 1990. http://prospect .org/article/conservative-crackup.

Kagan, Robert. "Neocon Nation: Neoconservatism, c. 1776." *World Affairs.* Accessed May 20, 2018. http://www.worldaffairsjournal.org/article/neocon-nation-neocon-servatism -c-1776.

——. *Of Paradise and Power: America and Europe in the New World Order.* New York: Vintage Books, 2004.

——. "Our 'Messianic Impulse.'" *Washington Post*, December 10, 2006. http://www .washingtonpost.com/wp-dyn/content/article/2006/12/08/AR2006120801516 .html.

Kann, Mark E. *A Republic of Men: The American Founders, Gendered Language, and Patriarchal Politics.* New York: NYU Press, 1998.

Kaufmann, Vincent. *Guy Debord: Revolution in the Service of Poetry.* Minneapolis: University of Minneapolis Press, 2006.

Keith, Bruce E., David B. Magleby, Candice J. Nelson, Elizabeth Orr, Mark C. Westlye, and Raymond E. Wolfinger. *The Myth of the Independent Voter*. Berkeley: University of California Press, 1992.

Kengor, Paul. *A Pope and a President: John Paul II, Ronald Reagan, and the Extraordinary Untold Story of the 20th Century*. Wilmington, DE: ISI Books, 2017.

Kennan, George F. "American Democracy and Foreign Policy." In *At a Century's Ending*, 127–38. New York: Norton, 1996.

——. Foreword to *The Pathology of Power*, by Norman Cousins, 11–12. New York: Norton, 1987.

——. "Letter to an American." *New Yorker*, September 24, 1984.

Kesler, Charles. "The Promise of President Trump." *Wall Street Journal*, January 19, 2017, https://www. wsj.com/articles/the-promise-of-president-trump-charles-kesler -1484868295.

Key, V. O. *The Responsible Electorate: Rationality in Presidential Voting. 1936–1960*. Foreword by Arthur Maass. Cambridge, MA: Belknap Press of Harvard University Press, 1968.

Kinder, Donald R. "Opinion and Action in the Realm of Politics." In *Handbook of Social Psychology*, eds. Gardner Lindzey, Daniel Gilbert, and Susan T. Fisk, 778–867. Oxford: Oxford University Press, 1998.

Kinder, Donald R., and Nathan P. Kalmoe. *Neither Liberal nor Conservative: Ideological Innocence in the American Public*. Chicago: University of Chicago Press, 2017.

King, William. "Neoconservatives and 'Trotskyism.'" *American Communist History* 3, no. 2 (2004): 247–66.

Kirk, Russell. *The American Cause*. Wilmington, DE: ISI Books, 2004.

——. "Bolingbroke, Burke, and the Statesman." *Kenyon Review*, no. 28 (June 1966): 426–32.

——. *The Conservative Mind: From Burke to Eliot*. 7th ed. Washington, DC: Regnery, 1985.

——. "Is Capitalism Still Viable?" *Journal of Business Ethics* 1 (1982): 277–80.

——. "The Neoconservatives: An Endangered Species." Heritage Foundation. December 15, 1988. https://www.heritage.org/political-process/report/the-neoconservatives -endangered-species.

——. *The Politics of Prudence*. Bryn Mawr, PA: Intercollegiate Studies Institute, 1993.

——. *Prospects for Conservatives*. New York: Gateway Editions, 1956.

——. "Will American Caesars Arise?" *Modern Age* 32, no. 3 (Summer 1989): 208–14.

Kirkpatrick, David. "National Review Founder Says It's Time to Leave Stage." *New York Times*, June 29, 2004. https://www.nytimes.com/2004/06/29/us/national-review -founder-says-it-s-time-to-leave-stage.html.

Kirkpatrick, Jeane. "Blame America First." Speech to Republican National Convention, August 20, 1984. http://www.cnn.com/ALLPOLITICS/1996/conventions/san .diego/facts/GOP.speeches.past/84.kirkpatrick.shtml.

Kolozi, Peter. *Conservatives against Capitalism: From the Industrial Revolution to Globalization*. New York: Columbia University Press, 2017.

Krauthammer, Charles. "Democratic Realism." In *Things that Matter*. New York: Random House, 2013.

Kristol, Irving. "American Conservatism, 1945–1995." *Public Interest*, Fall 1995.

——. "Memoirs of a Trotskyist." *New York Times* archives, January 23, 1977. https://www .nytimes.com/1977/01/23/archives/memoirs-of-a-trotskyist-memoirs.html.

——. *Neoconservatism: The Autobiography of an Idea*. Chicago: Elephant Paperbacks, 1999.

——. "The Neoconservative Persuasion." *Weekly Standard*, August 25, 2003. https://www .weeklystandard.com/the-neoconservative-persuasion/article/4246.

———. *The Neoconservative Persuasion: Selected Essays, 1942–2009.* New York: Basic Books, 2011.

———. *The Neoconservative Revolution: Selected Essays, 1942–2009.* New York: Basic Books, 2013.

———. *Two Cheers for Capitalism.* New York: Basic Books, 1978.

Kristol, William. "Letter to George W. Bush." Newsamericancentury.org, September 20, 2001. http://web.archive.org/web/20131018052135/http:/www.newamericancentury .org/Bushletter.htm.

———. Review of *Persecution and the Art of Writing*, by Leo Strauss, *Commentary*, October 1, 1952, https://www.commentarymagazine.com/articles/persecution-and-the -art-of-writing-by-leo-strauss.

Kristol, William, and Robert Kagan. "Bombing Iraq Isn't Enough." *New York Times*, January 30, 1998. https://www.nytimes.com/1998/01/30/opinion/bombing-iraq-isn-t -enough.html.

———. "Toward a Neo-Reaganite Foreign Policy." *Foreign Affairs*, July 1, 1996. https://www .foreignaffairs.com/articles/1996-07-01/toward-neo-reaganite-foreign-policy.

Landau, Diana. *Iowa: The Spirit of America.* New York: Touchstone, 1997.

Landess, Thomas H. "Mel Bradford, Old Indian Fighters, and the NEH." LewRockwell .com. April 25, 2003. https://www.lewrockwell.com/2003/04/thomas-h-landess /mel-bradford-old-indian-fighters-and-the-neh/.

"Latest Bets in the Candidate Casino." Special Report video, April 20, 2015. www.foxnews .com/transcript/2015/04/20/latest-bets-in-candidate-casino/.

Lee, Alex. "Emails Show Close Ties between Heritage Foundation and Lockheed Martin." The Intercept. September 15, 2015. https://theintercept.com/2015/09/15/heritage -foundation/.

Leo XIII (pope). "Testem Benevolentiae Nostrae." Papal Encyclicals Online. 1899. http:// www.papalencyclicals.net/leo13/l13teste.htm.

Letters and Other Writings of James Madison. Philadelphia: Lippincott, 1867.

Levendusky, Matthew. *The Partisan Sort: How Liberals Became Democrats and Conservatives Became Republicans.* Chicago: University of Chicago Press, 2009.

Levine, Sam. "Paul Wolfowitz Is So concerned with Trump He May Vote for Clinton." *Huffington Post*, August 27, 2016. https://www.huffingtonpost.com/entry/paul -wolfowitz-donald-trump_us_57 c1b121e4b 04193420f69b9.

Levinson, Sanford. *An Argument Open to All: Reading The Federalist in the 21st Century.* New Haven, CT: Yale University Press, 2015.

———. *Framed: America's 51 Constitutions and the Crisis of Governance.* New York: Oxford University, 2002.

Lewin, Kevin. "Frontiers in Group Dynamics: Concept, Method and Reality in Social Science; Social Equilibria and Social Change." *Human Relations* 1, no. 1 (1947): 5–41. doi:10.1177/001872674700100103.

Lewis-Beck, Michael S., Helmut Norpoth, William G. Jacoby, and Herbert F. Weisberg. *The American Voter Revisited.* Ann Arbor: University of Michigan Press, 2008.

Limbaugh, Rush. "GOP Sells America down the River." RushLimbaugh.com. December 17, 2015. http://www.rushlimbaugh.com/daily/2015/12/17/gop_sells_america _down_the_river.

Lincoln, Abraham. "Electric Cord." Vindicating the Founders, July 10, 1858. http://www .vindicatingthefounders.com/library/electric-cord-speech.html.

———. "Gettysburg Address." Avalon Project. Accessed April 9, 2018. http://avalon.law .yale.edu/19th_ century/gettyb.asp.

Lindblom, Charles. *Politics and Markets.* New York: Basic Books, 1977.

Linker, Damon. *The Theocons: Secular America under Siege.* New York: Anchor Books, 2007.

Loeb, Steven. "Andrew Breitbart: Donald Trump Is Not a Conservative." Business Insider. April 23, 2011. http://www.businessinsider.com/bill-orielly-andrew-breitbart-donald -trump-video-2011-4.

Lowry, Rich. "Mothball the Confederate Monuments." *National Review,* August 15, 2017. https://www.nationalreview.com/2017/08/charlottesville-virigina-robert-e-lee -statue-remove-right-decision-confederate-monuments-museums/.

———. "Parting Ways." *National Review,* April 7, 2012. http://www.nationalreview.com /corner/295514/parting-ways-rich-lowry.

Luttwak, Edward N. "The Strange Case of George F. Kennan." *Commentary,* November 1, 1977. https://www.commentarymagazine.com/articles/the-strange-case-of-george -f-kennan/.

Lutz, Donald S. "The Relative Influence of European Writers on Late Eighteenth-Century American Political Thought." *American Political Science Review* 78, no. 1 (1984): 189–97.

MacDonald, Kevin B. *The Culture of Critique: An Evolutionary Analysis of Jewish Involvement in Twentieth-Century Intellectual and Political Movements.* Bloomington: 1st Books Library, 2002.

Magness, Phillip W., and Sebastian N. Page. *Colonization after Emancipation: Lincoln and the Movement for Black Resettlement.* Columbia: University of Missouri, 2011.

Mahoney, Daniel J. "Conservatism, Democracy, and Foreign Policy. *The Intercollegiate Review* 41, no.2 (Fall 2006): 3–13.

———. *Conservative Foundations of the Liberal Order.* Wilmington, DE: ISI Books, 2011.

Mahtesian, Charles. "Paul: I Don't Fully Endorse Romney." *Politico,* August 26, 2012. https://www.politico.com/blogs/charlie-mahtesian/2012/08/paul-i-dont-fully -endorse-romney-133239.

Mammone, Andrea. "Trump and the Demagogues of Modern Nationalism." *Huffington Post,* December 6, 2017, https://www.huffingtonpost.com/andrea-mammone /trump-in-the-west_b_9991262.html.

Mansfield, Harvey. "Unfinished Revolution." In *Legacy of the French Revolution,* ed. Ralph C. Hancock and L. Gary Lambert, 19–41. Lanham, MD: Rowman & Littlefield, 1996.

Maranto, Robert, and Patrick J. Wolf. "Cops, Teachers, and the Art of the Impossible: Explaining the Lack of Diffusion of Innovations That Make Impossible Jobs Possible." *Public Administration Review* 73, no. 2 (2012): 230–40. doi:10.1111 /j.1540-6210.2012.02626.x.

Marcy, Richard T. "Breaking Mental Models as a Form of Creative Destruction: The Role of Leader Cognition in Radical Social Innovations." *Leadership Quarterly* 26, no. 3 (2015): 370–85. doi:10.1016/j.leaqua.2015.02.004.

Marcy, Richard T., and Valerie J. D'Erman. "The European 'New Right' as Radical Social Innovation." *Journal for the Study of Radicalism* 13, no. 2 (2019): 65–90.

Marini, John. "Donald Trump and the American Crisis." *Claremont Review of Books,* July 22, 2016. http://www.claremont.org/crb/basicpage/donald-trump-and-the -american-crisis.

Maritain, Jacques. *Integral Humanism: Temporal and Spiritual Problems of a New Christendom.* New York: Scribners, 1968.

———. *Man and the State.* Washington, DC: Catholic University of America Press, 1998.

Mason, Lilliana. "'I Disrespectfully Agree': The Differential Effects of Partisan Sorting on Social and Issue Polarization." *American Journal of Political Science* 59, no. 1 (2014): 128–45. doi:10.1111/ajps.12089.

McCammon, Sarah. "Feeling Kinship with the South, Northerners Let Their Confederate Flags Fly." National Public Radio. May 4, 2017. https://www.npr.org/2017/05/04/526539906/feeling-kinship-with-the-south-northerners-let-their-confederate-flags-fly.

McCartney, James, and Molly Sinclair McCartney. "The Military-Industrial-Propaganda Complex: The Neo-Con Think-Tanks That Drive Policy and Send Us to War." Salon. November 2, 2015. https://www.salon.com/2015/11/02/the_military_industrial_propaganda_complex_the_neo_con_think_tanks_that_drive_policy_and_send_us_to_war/.

McCoy, Drew R. *The Last of the Fathers: James Madison and the Republican Legacy.* Cambridge: Cambridge University Press, 1991.

McLuhan, Marshall. *The Mechanical Bride: Folklore of Industrial Man.* Boston: Vanguard Press, 1951.

Merrifield, Andy. *Guy Debord.* London: Reaktion Books, 2005.

Meyer, Frank S. *In Defense of Freedom and Related Essays.* Indianapolis: Liberty Fund, 1996.

Miller, Robert T. "The Mortara Case and the Limits of State Power: *First Things* Should Disavow Fr. Cessario's Defense of Pius IX in the Mortara Case." Public Discourse. January 11, 2018. http://www.thepublicdiscourse.com/2018/01/20868.

Miller, Stephen. "Conservatives and Liberals on Economics: Expected Differences, Surprising Similarities." *Critical Review* 19, no. 1 (2007): 47–64. doi:10.1080/08913810701499635.

Miller, Tiffany Jones. "James Madison's Republic of 'Mean Extent' Theory: Avoiding the Scylla and Charybdis of Republican Government." *Polity* 39, no. 4 (2007): 545–69.

Montesquieu, Baron de. *Considerations on the Causes of the Greatness of the Romans and Their Decline.* Indianapolis: Hackett Publishing, 1999.

——. *The Spirit of the Laws.* Translated and edited by Anne M. Cohler et al. New York: Cambridge University Press, 1989.

Moody, Aaron. "How Does NC Feel about NFL Kneeling, Taking Down Confederate Monuments?" *News and Observer,* October 3, 2017. http://www.newsobserver.com/news/politics-government/article176748721.html#storylink=cpy.

Morgan, Ted. *A Covert Life: Jay Lovestone, Communist, Anti-Communist, and Spymaster.* New York: Random House, 1999.

Morris, Richard B. *The Forging of the Union 1781–1789.* New York: Harper and Row, 1987.

Moscovici, Serge. "Toward a Theory of Conversion Behavior." *Advances in Experimental Social Psychology* 13 (1980): 209–39. https://doi.org/10.1016/S0065-2601(08)60133-1.

Moynihan, Daniel P. "The 'New Science of Politics' and the Old Art of Government." *National Affairs,* Winter 1987.

Murray, Charles. "The United States of Diversity." *Commentary,* June 2015. https://www.commentarymagazine.com/articles/the-united-states-of-diversity.

Murray, Douglas. *Neoconservatism: Why We Need It.* New York: Encounter Books, 2006.

Murray, John Courtney. *We Hold These Truths.* Lanham, MD: Sheed and Ward, 2005.

Nader, Ralph. *Unstoppable: The Emerging Left-Right Alliance to Dismantle the Corporate State.* New York: Nation Books, 2014.

Nagle, Angela. *Kill All Normies: Online Culture Wars from 4Chan and Tumblr to Trump and the Alt-Right.* Winchester, UK: Zero Books, 2017.

National Review Symposium. "Conservatives against Trump." *National Review,* January 21, 2016. http://c7.nrostatic.com/article/430126/donald-trump-conservatives-oppose-nomination.

Navasky, Victor S. *A Matter of Opinion.* New York: New Press, 2005.

———. "Protest and Survive." The Nation. June 29, 2015. http://www.thenation.com /article/protest-and-survive#.

Neuhaus, Richard. In Defense of People: Ecology and the Seduction of Radicalism. New York: Macmillan, 1971.

———. Doing Well and Doing Good: The Challenge to the Christian Capitalist. New York: Doubleday, 1992.

———. The Naked Public Square: Religion and Democracy in America. Grand Rapids, MI: William B. Eerdmans, 1988.

Nie, Norman H., and Kristi Andersen. "Mass Belief Systems Revisited: Political Change and Attitude Structure." Journal of Politics 36 (1974): 540–91.

Nielsen, Kai. "Marxist Theories of the State." Indian Political Science Review 19, nos. 1–2 (1985): 47–60.

———. "Rawls and the Socratic Ideal." Analyse & Kritik 13 (1991): 67–93.

Novack, Robert D. "Pat Buchanan, Populist Republican." National Review, August 14, 1995.

Novak, Michael. "Agreeing with Pope Francis." National Review, December 7, 2013. https://www.nationalreview.com/2013/12/agreeing-pope-francis-michael-novak/.

———. The Catholic Ethic and the Spirit of Capitalism. New York: Basic Books, 1993

———. "A Closet Capitalist Confesses." Wall Street Journal, April 20, 1976.

———. "Needing Niebuhr Again." Commentary, September 1, 1972. https://www .commentarymagazine.com/articles/needing-niebuhr-again/.

———. The Open Church. New York: Macmillan, 1964.

———. "Silver Linings for Never Trumpers." First Things, November 15, 2016. https://www .firstthings.com/blogs/firstthoughts/2016/11/silver-linings-for-never-trumpers.

———. The Spirit of Democratic Capitalism. Washington, DC: American Enterprise Institute, 1982.

———. The Spirit of Democratic Capitalism. Lanham, MD: Madison Books, 1991.

———. "What on Earth Happened on November 8?" National Review, November 22, 2016. https://www.nationalreview.com/2016/11/progressivism-rebuked-donald-trump -2016-presidential-election.

———. Writing Left to Right: My Journal from Liberal to Conservative. New York: Image, 2013.

"NPR/PBS News Hour/Marist Poll Results on Charlottesville." Marist Poll, August 17, 2017. http://maristpoll.marist.edu/nprpbs-newshourmarist-poll-results-on-charlottesville/.

Oakeshott, Michael. Rationalism in Politics and Other Essays. London: Methuen, 1984.

Oliver, Revilo P. America's Decline: The Education of a Conservative. London: Londinium, 1981.

Ornstein, Norman. "Elite Men of the People." Weekly Standard, March 18, 1996,

Ostendorff, Berndt. Multiculturalism in Transit: A German-American Exchange. New York: Berghahn Books, 1998.

O'Sullivan, John. "Mr. Buchanan and His Friends." National Review, March 16, 1992.

———. The Pope, the President and the Prime Minister. Washington, DC: Regnery History, 2006.

Pangle, Thomas. The Spirit of Modern Republicanism. Chicago: University of Chicago Press, 1988.

The Papers of George Washington, Presidential Series. Edited by Dorothy Twohig et al. Charlottesville: University Press of Virginia, 1987.

The Papers of George Washington, Retirement Series. Edited by W. W. Abbot. Charlottesville: University Press of Virginia, 1998.

The Papers of James Madison. Edited by William T. Hutchinson et al. Chicago and Charlottesville: University of Chicago Press and University of Virginia Press, 1962–91.

The Papers of James Madison, Presidential Series. Edited by Robert A. Rutland et al. Charlottesville: University Press of Virginia, 1984–.

The Papers of James Madison, Retirement Series. Edited by David B. Mattern et al. Charlottesville: University of Virginia Press, 2009–.

The Papers of Thomas Jefferson. Edited by Julian P. Boyd. Princeton, NJ: Princeton University Press, 1950–2014.

Parel, Anthony J. "Multiculturalism and Nationhood." In *George Grant and the Future of Canada*, edited by Yusuf K. Umar, with a foreword by Barry Cooper, 139–50. Calgary: University of Calgary Press, 1992.

"Pastor John C. Hagee." Christians United for Israel. Accessed May 19, 2019. https://www.cufi.org/impact/leadership/executive-board/pastor-john-hagee/.

Paul, Rand. "The Case for Conservative Realism." *National Interest*, October 23, 2014. https://nationalinterest.org/feature/rand-paul-the-case-conservative-realism-11544.

——. "Trump Is Right to Meet Putin." *Politico*, July 16, 2018. https://www.politico.com/magazine/story/2018/07/16/trump-is-right-to-meet-putin-219012.

"Paul Nehlen and the Red Pill." YouTube. December 31, 2017. Video, 11:55 min. https://www.youtube.com/watch?v=3MU7LEXBzoM.

Perry, Mark J. "Bono: America Is 'an Idea.' That's How We See You around the World, as One of the Greatest Ideas in Human History." AEIdeas. July 6, 2014. http://www.aei.org/publication/bono-america-is-an-idea-thats-how-we-see-you-around-the-world-as-one-of-the-greatest-ideas-in-human-history/.

Pettifer, Ann. "Zionism Unbound." CounterPunch.org. December 14, 2002. https://www.counterpunch.org/2002/12/14/zionism-unbound/.

Pew Research Center. "Contrasting Partisan Perspectives on Campaign 2016." October 2015. http://www.people-press.org/files/2015/10/10-02-2015-2016-release1.pdf.

——. "The Partisan Divide on Political Values Grows Even Wider." October 5, 2017. https://www.people-press.org/2017/10/05/the-partisan-divide-on-political-values-grows-even-wider.

Pinker, Steven. "Political Correctness Is Redpilling America." Excerpted from Spiked Magazine's "Unsafe Space Tour" panel discussion at Harvard University. YouTube. January 2, 2018. Video, 8:07. https://www.youtube.com/watch?v=kTiRnbNT5uE.

Podhoretz, Norman. "Anti-Semitism and a Presidential Candidacy." *Weekly Standard*, March 11, 1996.

——. "The Culture of Appeasement." *Harper's* 255, no. 1529 (October 1977): 32.

——. *Making It.* New York: New York Review of Books, 1967.

——. "My Negro Problem—and Ours." *Commentary*, February 1963. http://www.lukeford.net/Images/photos/out.pdf.

——. *World War IV: The Long Struggle against Islamofascism.* New York: Doubleday, 2007.

Polka, Brayton. "History between Biblical Religion and Modernity: Reflections on Rawls' *Lectures on the History of Moral Philosophy*." *European Legacy* 7, no. 4 (2002): 445–51.

Ponnuru, Ramesh. "A Conservative No More: The Tribal Politics of Pat Buchanan." *National Review*, October 11, 1999.

Postrel, Virginia. "Standing Pat." *National Review*, March 11, 1996.

Prager, Dennis. "Who Believes in American Exceptionalism? Judeo-Christian Values Part XXIV." Townhall. November 2005. https://www.dennisprager.com/who-believes-in-american-exceptionalism-judeo-christian-values-part-xxiv/.

——. "Why America Is Still the Best Hope." Townhall. April 2012. http://townhall.com/columnists/dennisprager/2012/04/24/why_america_is_still_the_best_hope.

Pramuk, Jacob. "Sen. Lindsey Graham: 'I Said My Piece' to Trump following His Immigration Comments." CNBC. January 12, 2018. https://www.cnbc.com/2018/01/12/sen-lindsey-graham-i-said-my-piece-to-trump-during-immigration-meeting.html.

Prendergast, William B. *The Catholic Voter in American Politics: The Passing of the Democratic Monolith*. Washington, DC: Georgetown University Press, 1999.

Project for the New American Century. "About PNAC." Accessed May 19, 2019. https://web.archive.org/web/20131006055540/http://www.newamericancentury.org/aboutpnac.htm.

———. "Statement of Principles." June 3, 1997. https://web.archive.org/web/20130922010137/http://www.newamericancentury.org/statementofprinciples.htm.

Publius Decius Mus [Michael Anton]. "The Flight 93 Election." *Claremont Review of Books*, September 5, 2016. https://www.claremont.org/crb/basicpage/the-flight-93-election/.

———. "Toward a Sensible, Coherent Trumpism." UNZ Review. March 10, 2016. http://www.unz.com/article/toward-a-sensible-coherent-trumpism.

Purvis, Thomas L. "The European Ancestry of the United States Population, 1790: A Symposium." *William and Mary Quarterly* 41, no. 1 (January 1984): 85–101. doi:10.2307/1919209.

Ranney, Austin, "'The Divine Science': Political Engineering in American Culture." *American Political Science Review* 70, no. 1 (1976): 140–48.

Rawls, John. *Political Liberalism*. Expanded ed. New York: Columbia University Press, 2005.

———. *A Theory of Justice*. Rev. ed. Cambridge, MA: Harvard University Press, 1999. First published 1971.

Reagan, Michael. "Donald Trump, Fake Conservative." Townhall. July 17, 2015. http://townhall.com/columnists/michaelreagan/2015/07/17/donald-trump-fake-conservative-n2026802.

Reno, R. R. "Capitalism beyond Caricatures." *First Things*, May 23, 2016. https://www.firstthings.com/blogs/firstthoughts/2016/05/capitalism-beyond-caricatures.

RePass, David E. "Searching for Voters along the Liberal-Conservative Continuum: The Infrequent Ideologue and the Missing Middle." *The Forum* 6, no. 2 (2008): 1–46. doi:10.2202/1540-8884.1220.

"Republicans Again Desire a Conservative Presidential Nominee." Gallup. December 21, 2015. http://www.gallup.com/poll/187901/republicans-again-desire-conservative-presidential-nominee.aspx.

Reynolds, Paul. "End of the Neo-con Dream." BBC News. December 21, 2006.

"Richard Spencer, Styx and Sargon Have a Chat—Andy and JF Moderate." YouTube, January 4, 2018. Video, 4:38. https://www.youtube.com/watch?v=UiUH-tWHbr8.

Richwine, Jason. "IQ and Immigration Policy." PhD diss., Harvard Graduate School of Art & Sciences, 2009. Accessed January 15, 2015. http://www.scribd.com/doc/140239668/IQ-and-Immigration-Policy-Jason-Richwine.

Rieff, David. "Multiculturalism's Silent Partner: It's the Newly Globalized Consumer Economy, Stupid." *Harper's*, August 1993, 62–72.

Rizvi, Ali A. "What Ilhan Omar Needs to Learn from London's Muslim Mayor." *New York Post*, May 4, 2019. https://nypost.com/2019/05/04/what-ilhan-omar-needs-to-learn-from-londons-muslim-mayor/.

Roberts, Paul Craig. "Neo-Jacobins Push for World War IV." LewRockwell.com. September 20, 2003. https://www.lewrockwell.com/2003/09/paul-craig-roberts/neo-jacobins-push-for-world-war-iv/.

Roddy, Dennis. "Jared Taylor, a Racist in the Guise of 'Expert.'" *Pittsburgh Post-Gazette*, January 23, 2005. http://www.post-gazette.com/life/dennis-roddy/2005/01/23/Jared-Taylor-a-racist-in-the-guise-of-expert/stories/200501230176.

Rogan, Joe, and Steven Pinker. "The Intelligence of the Alt-Right." YouTube. February 5, 2018. Video, 6:58. https://www.youtube.com/watch?v=HXATSgZuMS4.

Ross, Jack. *The Socialist Party of America: A Complete History*. Lincoln: University of Nebraska Press, 2015.

Rothbard, Murray. *The Betrayal of the American Right*. Auburn, AL: Ludwig Von Mises Institute, 2007.

———. *Wall Street, Banks, and American Foreign Policy*. Auburn, AL: Ludwig Von Mises Institute, 2011.

Rothman, Lily. "The Conservative Case for Legalizing Marijuana." *Time*, February 26, 2015. http://time.com/3724131/conservatives-marijuana-buckley/.

Royal, Robert. *The God That Did Not Fail*. New York: Encounter Books, 2006.

Rubin, Jennifer. "Jennifer Rubin: Republicans Wear the Ugly Face of Ethno-nationalists." *Salt Lake Tribune*, January 22, 2018. https://www.sltrib.com/opinion/commentary/2018/01/22/jennifer-rubin-republicans-wear-the-ugly-face-of-ethno-nationalists/.

———. "Trump's State of the Union: A Diatribe against Immigrants." *Washington Post*, January 30, 2018. https://www.washingtonpost.com/blogs/right-turn/wp/2018/01/30/trumps-state-of-the-union-a-diatribe-against-immigrants.

Ryn, Claes G. *America the Virtuous: The Crisis of Democracy and the Quest for Empire*. New Brunswick, NJ: Transaction, 2003.

———. *The New Jacobin: America as a Revolutionary State*. Washington, DC: National Humanities Institute, 2011.

Sabo, Mike. "Rod Dreher, Meet Leo Strauss and Friends." American Greatness. April 8, 2017, https://amgreatness.com/2017/04/08/rod-dreher-meet-leo-strauss-friends.

Savage, John. "Where the Confederacy Is Rising Again." *Politico*, August 10, 2016. https://www.politico.com/magazine/story/2016/08/texas-confederacy-rising-again-214159.

Schindler, David L. *Heart of the World, Center of the Church: Communio Ecclesiology, Liberalism, and Liberation*. Grand Rapids, MI: Eerdmans, 1996.

Schlesinger, Arthur M. *The Disuniting of America: Reflections on a Multicultural Society*. New York: W. W. Norton, 1998.

Scott, Eugene. "Graham: 'Flag Had to Come Down. And Thank God That It Has." CNN. July 9, 2015. https://www.cnn.com/2015/07/09/politics/confederate-flag-2016-south-carolina-lindsey-graham/index.html.

Seelye, Katharine Q. "Relentless Moral Crusader Is Relentless Gambler, Too." *New York Times*, May 3, 2003. http://www.nytimes.com/2003/05/03/national/03GAMB.html.

Shaefer, Ronald G. "Washington Wire." *Wall Street Journal*, September 17, 1999.

Shain, Barry A. "Harry Jaffa and the Demise of the Old Republic." *Modern Age* 49, no. 4 (Fall 2007): 476–89.

———. *The Myth of American Individualism*. Princeton, NJ: Princeton University Press, 1994.

———. Review of *Vindicating the Founders*, by Thomas West. *Modern Age* 42, no. 1 (Winter 2000): 63–70.

Shapiro, Ben. "Is Donald Trump Conservative? Here's the Rundown." Breitbart. January 24, 2016. http://www.breitbart.com/big-government/2016/01/24/is-donald-trump-conservative-heres-the-rundown/.

———. "Left Tries to Blame Trump for Charlottesville. Here's Why They're Wrong." *Daily Wire.* August 14, 2017. https://www.dailywire.com/news/19676/left-tries-blame-trump-charlottesville-terror-ben-shapiro.

———. "Why War in Iraq Is Right for America." *Townhall.* August 10, 2005. https://townhall.com/columnists/benshapiro/2005/08/10/why-war-in-iraq-is-right-for-america-n1216871.

Sharlet, Jeff. *The Family: The Secret Fundamentalism at the Heart of American Power.* New York: Harper Perennial, 2009.

Sheehan, Colleen. *James Madison and the Spirit of Republican Self-Government.* New York: Cambridge University Press, 2009.

Shephard, Alex. "The D.C. Think Tank behind Donald Trump." *New Republic,* February 22, 2017. https://newrepublic.com/article/140271/dc-think-tank-behind-donald-trump.

Silva, Christianna. "Trump's Full List of 'Racist' Comments about Immigrants, Muslims and Others." *Newsweek,* January 11, 2018. http://www.newsweek.com/trumps-full-list-racist-comments-about-immigrants-muslims-and-others-779061.

Simon, Yves R. *A General Theory of Authority.* Notre Dame, IN: University of Notre Dame Press, 1991.

———. *Philosophy of Democratic Government.* Notre Dame, IN: University of Notre Dame Press, 1993.

Singal, Jesse. "Social Media Is Making Us Dumber. Here's Exhibit A." *New York Times,* January 11, 2018. https://www.nytimes.com/2018/01/11/opinion/social-media-dumber-steven-pinker.html.

Smant, Kevin J. *Principles and Heresies: Frank S. Meyer and the Shaping of the American Conservative Movement.* Wilmington, DE: ISI Books, 2002.

Smith, Kyle. "Destroying Symbols: Where Does It End?" *National Review,* August 16, 2017. https://www.nationalreview.com/2017/08/destroying-confederate-statues-whats-end-point-washington-monument/.

"Southern Baptists, Others Release Letter on 'Alt-Right' to Trump." *Christian Index.* October 2, 2017. https://christianindex.org/southern-baptists-others-release-letter-on-alt-right-to-trump/.

Southern Poverty Law Center (SPLC). "Jared Taylor." August 17, 2018. https://www.splcenter.org/fighting-hate/extremist-files/individual/jared-taylor.

Spengler, Oswald. "Prussianism and Socialism." In *Selected Essays,* translated with an introduction by Donald O. White. Chicago: Gateway, 1967.

Spiering, Charlie. "Full Text: Rand Paul's Speech on 'Containment and Radical Islam.'" *Washington Examiner,* February 6, 2013. https://www.washingtonexaminer.com/full-text-rand-pauls-speech-on-containment-and-radical-islam.

Spörl, Gerhard, and Br/Der Spiegel. "The Leo-conservatives." *New York Times,* August 4, 2003. https://www.nytimes.com/2003/08/04/international/europe/the-leocon servatives.html.

Squitieri, Tom. "A Look Back at Trump's First Run." The Hill. October 7, 2015. http://thehill.com/blogs/pundits-blog/presidential-campaign/256159-a-look-back-at-trumps-first-run.

Staloff, Darren, *Hamilton, Adams, Jefferson: The Politics of Enlightenment and the American Founding.* New York: Hill and Wang, 2005.

"Statement of Principles and Positions." Republican Liberty Caucus. Accessed May 19, 2019. http://rlc.org/principles.

Stephens, Bret. "The Donald and the Demagogues." *Wall Street Journal,* August 31, 2015. https://www.wsj.com/articles/the-donald-and-the-demagogues-1441064072.

———. "Four Questions about American Greatness." *New York Times*, December 17, 2017. https://www.nytimes.com/2017/12/07/opinion/four-questions-american-greatness.html.

———. "Hands Up, Straussians! If All Values Are Relative, Then Cannibalism Is a Matter of Taste." *Jerusalem Post*, June 5, 2003. http://www.freerepublic.com/focus/f-news/9245 58/posts.

Stevenson, Seth. "The Many Faces of Ben Shapiro." Slate. January 24, 2018. https://slate.com/news-and-politics/2018/01/is-ben-shapiro-a-conservative-liberals-can-count-on.html.

Strauss, Leo. *Natural Right and History*. Chicago: University of Chicago Press, 1953.

———. *Persecution and the Art of Writing*. Chicago: University of Chicago Press, 1988.

———. "Progress or Return? The Contemporary Crisis in Western Civilization." In *Ten Essays by Leo Strauss: An Introduction to Political Philosophy*, edited with an introduction by Hilail Gildin, 249–310. Detroit: Wayne State University Press, 1989.

Szulc, Tad. *John Paul II: The Biography*. New York: Scribner's, 2007.

Tanenhaus, Sam. *The Death of Conservatism and Its Consequences*. New York: Random House, 2010.

Taylor, Jared. *Paved with Good Intentions: The Failure of Race Relations in Contemporary America*. New York: Carroll & Graf Publishers, 1992.

———. "The 'Tainted' Sources of The End of Racism." American Renaissance. November 1995. http://www.amren.com/archives/back-issues/november-1995/#article2.

———. *White Identity: Racial Consciousness in the 21st Century*. Oakton, VA: New Century Books, 2011.

Tell, David. "The Buchanan Accident." *Weekly Standard*, March 11, 1996.

Thomas Aquinas. *St. Thomas Aquinas: On Politics and Ethics*, trans. and ed. Paul E. Sigmund. New York: Norton, 1988.

Thompson, C. Bradley, with Yaron Brook. *Neoconservatism: An Obituary for an Idea*. Boulder, CO: Paradigm Books, 2010.

Thompson, E. P. *The Making of the English Working Class*. Harmondsworth: Penguin Books, 1991.

Timm, Trevor. "Is Hillary Clinton a Neocon?" *The Guardian*, June 27, 2016. https://www.theguardian.com/commentis free/2016/jun/27/hillary-clinton-necono-republican-endorsements-donald-trump-policy-issues.

"To John Adams from John C. Herbert, 10 June 1798." Founders Online, National Archives and Records Administration. June 10, 1798. https://founders.archives.gov/documents/Adams/99-02-02-2566.

"To Trump Disciples: You're Embarrassing Conservatism and Yourselves." TheBlaze. July 20, 2015. http://www.theblaze.com/contributions/to-trump-disciples-youre-embarrassing-conservatism-and-yourselves/.

Treier, Shawn, and D. Sunshine Hillygus. "The Nature of Political Ideology in the Contemporary Electorate." *Public Opinion Quarterly* 73 (2009): 679–703.

Trotsky, Leon. *The Permanent Revolution: Results and Prospects*. New York: Pathfinder Press, 1974.

Trump, Donald J. "President Donald J. Trump's State of the Union Address." The White House. January 30, 2018. https://www.whitehouse.gov/briefings-statements/president-donald-j-trumps-state-union-address/.

———. "Remarks at the South Florida Fair Expo Center in West Palm Beach, Florida." American Presidency Project. October 13, 2016. http://www.presidency.ucsb.edu/ws/index.php?pid=119180.

——. "Transcript: Donald Trump's Foreign Policy Speech." *New York Times*, April 27, 2016. https://www.nytimes.com/2016/04/28/us/politics/transcript-trump-foreign -policy.html.

——. "What I Saw at the Revolution." *New York Times*, February 19, 2000. https://www .nytimes.com/2000/02/19/opinion/what-i-saw-at-the-revolution.html.

U.N.E.F. Strasbourg. "On the Poverty of Student Life." Nothingness.org. Accessed May 19, 2019. http://library.nothingness.org/articles/SI/en/display/4.

United States Census Bureau. "1790 Census: Return of the Whole Number of Persons within the Several Districts of the United States." Accessed February 2, 2019. https://www.census.gov/library/publications/1793/dec/number-of-persons.html.

United States Conference of Catholic Bishops. *The Challenge of Peace: God's Promise and Our Response.* May 3, 1983. http://www.usccb.org/upload/challenge-peace-gods -promise-our-response-1983.pdf.

——. *Economic Justice for All: Pastoral Letter on Catholic Social Teaching and the U.S. Economy*, 1986. http://www.usccb.org/upload/economic_justice_for_all.pdf.

"Urban Progressive Hatred of the Local and Innocent (I)." YouTube. September 11, 2017. Video, 14:40. https://www.youtube.com/watch?v=WBYuGJkEvV0.

Utley, Jon. "Iraq, Syria, Iran . . . Are We to Destroy Iran Next?" *American Conservative*, December 14, 2017, http://www.theamericanconservative.com/articles/iraq-syria -iran-are-we-to-destroy-iran-next.

Vaisse, Justin. *Neoconservatism: The Biography of a Movement.* Cambridge, MA: Harvard University Press, 2011.

Van Tyne, Claude H. *The Loyalists in the American Revolution.* Safety Harbor, FL: Simon Publications, 2001.

Von Heyking, John, and Barry Cooper. "'A Cow Is Just a Cow': George Grant and Eric Voegelin on the United States." In *Athens and Jerusalem: George Grant's Theology, Philosophy, and Politics*, ed. Ian Angus, Ron Dart, and Peg Peters, 166–89. Toronto: University of Toronto Press, 2006.

Walsh, Matt. "To Trump Disciples: You're Embarrassing Conservatism and Yourselves." The Blaze. July 20, 2015. http://www.theblaze.com/contributions/to-trump-disciples -youre-embarrassing-conservatism-and-yourselves/.

Walt, Stephen M. "A Modest Proposal." *Foreign Policy*, November 20, 2009. http:// foreignpolicy.com/2009/11/20/a-modest-proposal/.

Waltz, Kenneth. "Structural Realism after the Cold War." *International Security* 25, no. 1 (2000): 5–41.

Wasserman, David. "Purple America Has All but Disappeared." FiveThirtyEight. March 8, 2017. https://fivethirtyeight.com/features/purple-america-has-all-but-disappeared.

Weaver, Al. "Glenn Beck: Trump Is 'Not a Conservative. He Is a Progressive.'" Daily Caller. June 17, 2016. http://dailycaller.com/2015/06/17/glenn-beck-trump-is-a -progressive-not-a-conservative-audio/.

Weaver, Glenn. "Benjamin Franklin and the Pennsylvania Germans." *William and Mary Quarterly*, 3rd ser., 14, no. 4 (October 1957): 536–59.

Weaver, Mary Jo, and R. Scott Appleby. *Being Right: Conservative Catholics in America.* Bloomington: Indiana University Press, 1995.

Weaver, Richard. *The Southern Tradition at Bay: A History of Post-Bellum Thought.* New Rochelle, NY: Arlington House, 1968.

——. "Two Types of American Individualism," reprinted in *The Southern Essays of Richard M. Weaver*, edited by George M. Curtis III and James J. Thompson Jr., 82–102. Indianapolis: Liberty Press, 1987.

Weigel, George. "Catholic 'Americanism.'" *National Review*, May 31, 2012. https://www .nationalreview.com/2012/05/catholic-americanism-george-weigel/.

——. *The Cube and the Cathedral: Europe, America, and Politics without God*. New York: Basic Books, 2005.

——. "Did the Pope Heal or Deepen a Catholic Schism?" *Newsweek*, January 25, 2009. http://www.newsweek.com/did-pope-heal-or-deepen-catholic-schism-78423.

——. *The End and the Beginning: Pope John Paul II: The Victory of Freedom, the Last Years, the Legacy*. New York: Image, 2010.

——. *Faith, Reason, and the War against Jihadism: A Call to Action*. New York: Image, 2007.

——. *The Final Revolution: The Resistance Church and the Collapse of Communism*. Oxford: Oxford University Press, 1992.

——. *God's Choice: Pope Benedict XVI and the Future of the Catholic Church*. New York: Harper, 2005.

——. *Lessons in Hope: My Unexpected Life with St. John Paul II*. New York: Basic Books, 2017.

——. "The Neoconservative Difference: A Proposal for Renewal of Church and Society." In *Being Right: Conservative Catholics in America*, edited by Mary Jo Weaver and R. Scott Appleby, 138–62. Bloomington: Indiana University Press, 1995.

——. *A New Worldly Order: John Paul II and Human Freedom*. Washington, DC: American Enterprise Institute, 1992.

——. *Tranquillitas Ordinis: The Present Failure and Future Promise of American Catholic Thought on War and Peace*. Oxford: Oxford University Press, 1987.

——. *Witness to Hope: The Biography of John Paul II*. New York: Harper Collins, 1999.

Weigel, George, and James Turner Johnson. *Just War and the Gulf War*. Washington, DC: Ethics and Public Policy Center, 1991.

Weiss, Bari. "Meet the Renegades of the Intellectual Dark Web." *New York Times*, May 8, 2018. https://www.nytimes.com/2018/05/08/opinion/intellectual-dark-web.html.

West, Thomas G. "Immigration: The Founders' View and Today's Challenge." In *The Founders on Citizenship and Immigration*, edited by Edward J. Erler, 75–113. Lanham, MD: Rowman & Littlefield, 2007.

——. "Jaffa versus Mansfield: Does America Have a Constitutional or a 'Declaration of Independence' Soul?" *Perspective on Political Science* 31, no. 4 (2002): 235–46.

——. *The Political Theory of the American Founding: Natural Rights, Public Policy, and the Moral Conditions of Freedom*. Cambridge: Cambridge University Press, 2017.

——. Review of *A New Birth of Freedom*, by Harry V. Jaffa, October 31, 2001, http://www.csub.edu/~mault/jaffa1.htm.

——. *Vindicating the Founders: Race, Sex, Class, and Justice in the Origins of America*. Lanham, MD: Rowman & Littlefield Publishers, 2000.

Westervelt, Eric. "ACT UP at 30: Reinvigorated for Trump Fight." NPR. April 17, 2017. https://www.npr.org/2017/04/17/522726303/act-up-at-30-reinvigorated-for-trump-fight.

"What Does Entryism Mean?" *New Statesman*, August 10, 2016, https://www.newstatesman.com/ politics/staggers/2016/08/what-does-entryism-mean.

"The White Nationalist Manifesto." Counter-Currents Publishing. Accessed May 19, 2019. https://www.counter-currents.com/the-white-nationalist-manifesto/.

Whyte, William H., Jr. *The Organization Man*. New York: Anchor Books, 1957.

Will, George. "Beyond the Reach of Majorities: Closed Questions in the Open Society." WorldCat. March 1, 2019. https://www.worldcat.org/title/beyond-the-reach-of-majorities-closed-questions-in-the-open-society/oclc/14643887.

——. "A Shrill Assault on Mr. Lincoln." *Washington Post*, December 29, 1981. https://www.washingtonpost.com/archive/opinions/1981/11/29/a-shrill-assault-on-mr-lincoln/453b1986-761e-4a86-9b71-759ce0729f87/?utm_term=.9913973997b4.

Williamson, Kevin D. "Witless Ape Rides Escalator." *National Review*, June 16, 2015. http://www.nationalreview.com/article/419853/witless-ape-rides-escalator-kevin-d-williamson.

Wilson. "Irish U2 Frontman Bono Perfectly Sums Up the American Ideal." Glenn Beck. May 7, 2018. https://www.glennbeck.com/2015/02/13/watch-irish-u2-frontman-bono-may-have-perfectly-summed-up-the-american-idea/.

YouTube Channel of Walt Bismarck. YouTube. https://www.youtube.com/channel/UCLziPZRfH3CZEozrVBo7BKw/videos.

Yukl, Gary A. *Leadership in Organizations*. Englewood Cliffs, NJ: Prentice Hall, 2009.

Zielonka, Jan. *Counter-Revolution: Liberal Europe in Retreat*. Oxford: Oxford University Press, 2018.

Zuckert, Catherine, and Michael Zuckert.. *The Truth about Leo Strauss: Political Philosophy and American Democracy*. Chicago: University of Chicago Press, 2008.

Contributors

Boyd D. Cathey, a native North Carolinian, holds an MA degree in American history (as a Thomas Jefferson Fellow) from the University of Virginia, and a PhD in European history (as a Richard M. Weaver Fellow) from the University of Navarra, Pamplona, Spain. He served as assistant to Dr. Russell Kirk from 1971–72, taught on the college level, and was State Registrar for the North Carolina State Archives until retirement. He has published widely and internationally on history, political philosophy, opera, and film. In 2018 his book *The Land We Love: The South and Its Heritage* was published by Scuppernong Press.

Joseph Cotto is chief editor of the *San Francisco Review of Books* and co-host of the interview program *Cotto/Gottfried*. He previously covered current events and style for *The Washington Times*'s "Communities" section.

Nicholas W. Drummond is an assistant professor of political science at Black Hills State University. He completed his PhD in political science at the University of North Texas. His publications have examined the American Founding, multiculturalism, and the impact of religion and human rights on American foreign policy.

Paul Gottfried is Raffensperger Professor of Humanities Emeritus at Elizabethtown College, a Guggenheim recipient, and the author of multiple reviews and articles and thirteen books, most recently *Fascism: The Career of a Concept* and *Revisions and Dissents*. He is currently editor in chief of *Chronicles: A Magazine of American Culture* and on the advisory board of *The American Conservative*.

Grant Havers is Chair of the Department of Philosophy (with a cross-appointment in the Department of Political Studies) at Trinity Western University. He is the author of *Leo Strauss and Anglo-American Democracy: A Conservative Critique* and *Lincoln and the Politics of Christian Love*.

George Hawley is an associate professor of political science at the University of Alabama. His books include *Making Sense of the Alt-Right*, *Right-Wing Critics of American Conservatism*, and *Demography, Culture, and the Decline of America's Christian Denominations*.

Marjorie L. Jeffrey is an independent scholar with a doctorate in Political Science from Baylor University. Her areas of interest include classical political philosophy, politics and literature, Catholic political thought, and the political thought of Sir Winston Churchill. She is currently working on a book dealing with international relations in Winston Churchill's war histories.

Jack Kerwick has his doctorate in philosophy from Temple University and specializes in ethics and political philosophy, with a particular interest in classical conservatism. His work has appeared in both scholarly journals and popular publications, and he is the author of four books. He teaches philosophy at Rowan College at Burlington County, New Jersey.

Richard T. Marcy is an Assistant Professor at the School of Public Administration, University of Victoria. His current research is focused on the strategic leadership and radical social innovation of nonviolent, sociopolitical vanguards. Some recent publications include *The European New Right as Radical Social Innovation* and *Breaking Mental Models as a Form of Creative Destruction: The Role of Leader Cognition in Radical Social Innovations*.

Keith Preston is chief editor of AttacktheSystem.com. He was awarded the 2008 Chris R. Tame Memorial Prize by the United Kingdom's Libertarian Alliance for his essay, "Free Enterprise: The Antidote to Corporate Plutocracy." His dissections of power structures in modern liberal democracies draw on traditions of thought going back to both leftist and rightist social critics of the past.

Jesse Russell is Assistant Professor of English at Georgia Southwestern State University. He has published in a number of academic journals, including *New Blackfriars*, *Texas Studies in Language and Literature*, and *Political Theology*.

Index

Lightning Source UK Ltd.
Milton Keynes UK
UKHW040702200521
383975UK00012B/194